WAR'S NOMADS

A Mobile Radar Unit in Pursuit of Rommel
during the Western Desert Campaign,
1942–43

Frederick Grice

Edited by
GILLIAN AND COLIN CLARKE

CASEMATE
uk
Oxford & Philadelphia

Published in Great Britain and
the United States of America in 2015 by
CASEMATE PUBLISHERS
10 Hythe Bridge Street, Oxford OX1 2EW, UK
and
908 Darby Road, Havertown, PA 19083, USA

© Gilllian and Colin Clarke 2015

Hardcover Edition: ISBN 978-1-61200-288-0
Digital Edition: ISBN 978-1-61200-289-7

A CIP record for this book is available from the British Library

All rights reserved. No part of this book may be reproduced or transmitted in any form or by any means, electronic or mechanical including photocopying, recording or by any information storage and retrieval system, without permission from the publisher in writing.

Printed in the United Kingdom by Short Run Press, Exeter

For a complete list of Casemate titles, please contact:

CASEMATE PUBLISHERS (UK)
Telephone (01865) 241249
Fax (01865) 794449
Email: casemate-uk@casematepublishers.co.uk
www.casematepublishers.co.uk

CASEMATE PUBLISHERS (US)
Telephone (610) 853-9131
Fax (610) 853-9146
Email: casemate@casematepublishing.com
www.casematepublishing.com

*To Oscar, Isobel and Inez:
grandchildren of Gillian and Colin Clarke,
the editors, and great-grandchildren of
Frederick Grice, the author*

Contents

List of Plates vi
List of Figures vii
List of Tables vii
Acknowledgements viii
Maps ix

Introduction by *Colin Clarke* 1

Part 1 On Draft

1 Embarkation 36
2 Crossing the Line 55
3 Cape Town, the Suez Canal and Cairo 78

Part 2 Erk in the Desert

4 El Alamein and the Western Desert 102
5 From the Green Mountain to the Gulf of Sirte 137
6 Out of the Libyan Desert 164
7 The Cities and Towns of Tripolitania: Reflections on Libya 179
8 Tunisian Finale 197

Epilogue 206
Appendices 209
Index 211

List of Plates

1. Fred at Ballasalla, Isle of Man, while on radar training, March 1942 15
2. Fred prior to embarkation, 24 April 1942 15
3. 'Winners of the Desert Line-shooting Trophy. A group of noble erks, 606, September 1942' 107
4. Unit 606 – the gharry with radar mast on top. Note petrol engine to rotate aerial beside truck 107
5. Fred in his dugout at Alam el Osmaili 110
6. 'Harry Allen (H. Cookie), 606, September 1942'. The figure on the right is Jack Scott (Cookie) 112
7. 'Five of us sitting on the roof and in the entrance of my dugout. It looks no great shakes here – but that was before the renovation.' H. Cookie is in front, and the others from the left are: Cpl Pryce, Jack Scott (Cookie), Fred and Jimmy 112
8. Sergeant Clark, Unit 606 (left) and Sergeant Budd, Unit 607 (right), Alam el Osmaili 113
9. 'Having my hair cut by an Indian,' Alam el Osmaili 113
10. Sunset in the desert, Unit 606, October 1942 116
11. Fred at Alam el Osmaili wearing his South African bush jacket and boots 119
12. Beyond El Alamein: the debris of war 125
13. Abandoned German tank with the palm-tree-and-swastika emblem of the *Afrikakorps* 125
14. A view from the tailgate of Unit 606's gharry: the pursuing convoy crosses the wire-line marking 'the entry into Libya, November 1942' 130
15. AMES Unit 606. Named by Fred as follows: Cpl Jack Pryce, Harry Allen (H. Cookie) back row; Alec, Bob, Fred and Jimmy next-to-back row; Jack Scott (Cookie), Roy, Sarge (Nobby Clark) next-to-front row; Norman and Sid front row. 'Taken at Gambut – one stage of the big offensive.' Fred holds the flit spray, while Jimmy and Sid have rifles. Between Norman's feet is the beautifully made German box for valves labelled *Mechaniker* 133
16. 'Italian colonists' farm near Barce'. The fascist inscription on the facade reads: *Il Duce ha sempre ragione* – 'The Duce is always right' 141
17. 'Breakfast in the "green belt" near De Martino' 143
18. Stopping for tiffin near Baracca: Alec (with mug), Cpl Pryce and Sid 144
19. Baracca: abandoned public building with marble floors. Members of Unit 606 in foreground 145
20. El Agheila: Cpl Pryce, on the left, and Fred foraging 150
21. The German dinghy in the surf at Sirte 157

List of Figures

1 The troopship *Highland Monarch* left Avonmouth and joined the convoy WS19 at Oversay, Islay, Inner Hebrides... x
2 The *Highland Monarch* visited Freetown, Sierra Leone and Cape Town, South Africa en route to the Suez Canal – Kabrit inset xi
3 Cape Town and neighbouring settlements xii
4 Cairo and neighbouring settlements xiii
5 The Western Desert Theatre of War, from Alexandria to Mareth xiv
6 Mediterranean settlements of Egypt and Libya from Alexandria to Tobruk xv
7 Cyrenaica: from Tobruk to Ghemines.. xvi
8 The Gulf of Sirte: from Ghemines to Misurata.. xvii
9 Tripolitania and Tunisia: from Misurata to Mareth.. xviii
10 'Home, 606. September 1942.' Fred's pen-and-ink sketch of his dugout at Alam El Osmaili 111

List of Tables

1 North-African Place Names and their Adjacent Landing Grounds (LGs) 3–4
2 AMES 606, Squadrons 260 and 213, and the Landing Grounds, 1942–1943 11–12

Acknowledgements

We are grateful to the staff of the following institutions for their help with the research for this book: The Public Record Office, The National Archives at Kew, London; the Air Defence Radar Museum at Neatishead, Norfolk – and especially to Roy Bullers, a radar specialist and former RAF Squadron Leader; the library of the RAF Museum, Hendon, London; and the Bodleian Library, Oxford University, especially to Sue Bird of the Radcliffe Science Library.

Additionally, we are indebted to the late Nigel James, cartographer in the Map Department of the Bodleian Library, Oxford, for drawing the maps of North Africa and the Mediterranean (Figs. 5 to 9). The remainder of the maps (Figs. 1 to 4) were prepared for us by Ailsa Allen, Cartography and Graphics Officer in the School of Geography and the Environment, Oxford University. We are grateful to her for her map-drawing and curatorial skills, and for preparing the black-and-white images for publication.

Gillian and Colin Clarke

Maps

FIGURE 1: The troopship *Highland Monarch* left Avonmouth and joined the convoy WS19 at Oversay, Islay, Inner Hebrides

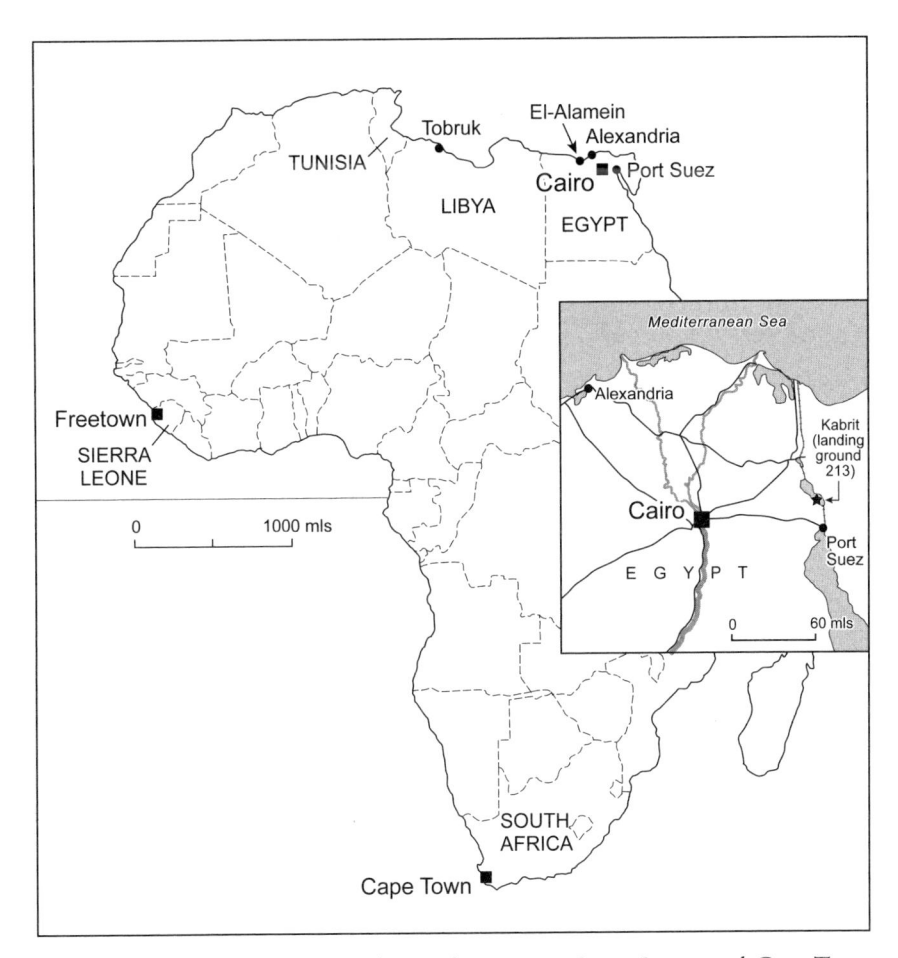

FIGURE 2: The *Highland Monarch* visited Freetown, Sierra Leone and Cape Town, South Africa en route to the Suez Canal – Kabrit inset

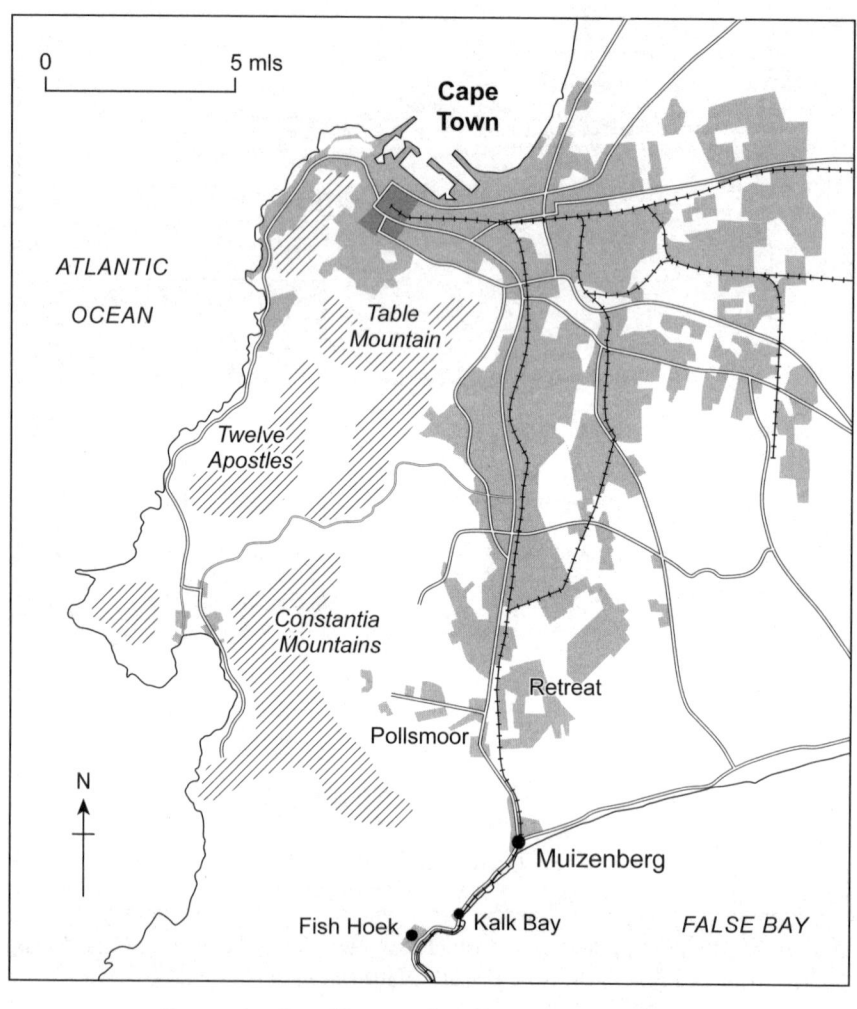

FIGURE 3: Cape Town and neighbouring settlements

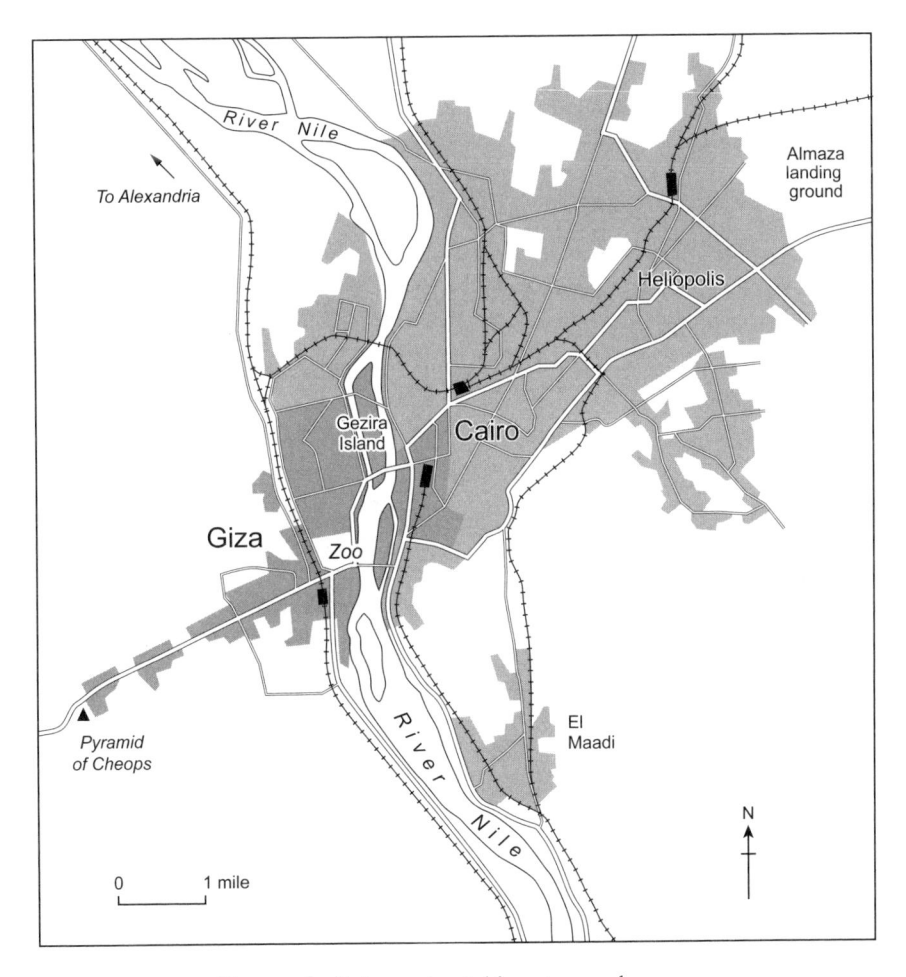

Figure 4: Cairo and neighbouring settlements

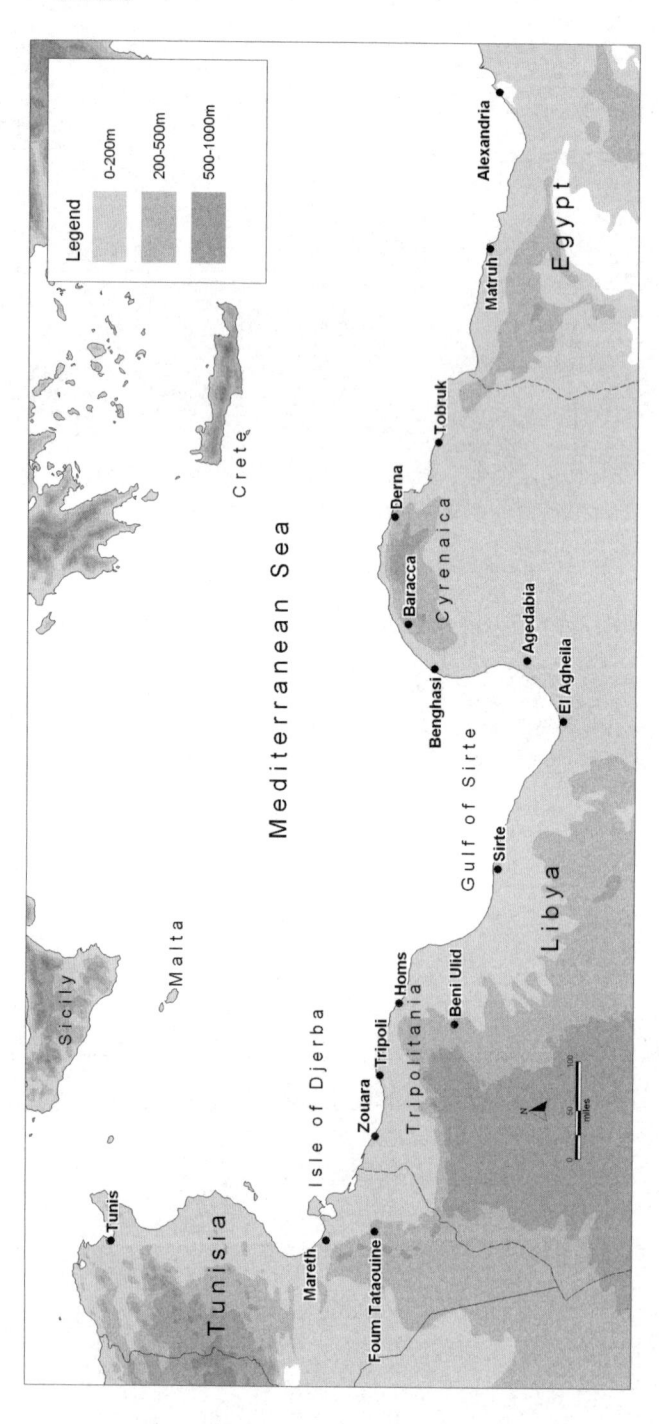

FIGURE 5: The Western Desert Theatre of War, from Alexandria to Mareth

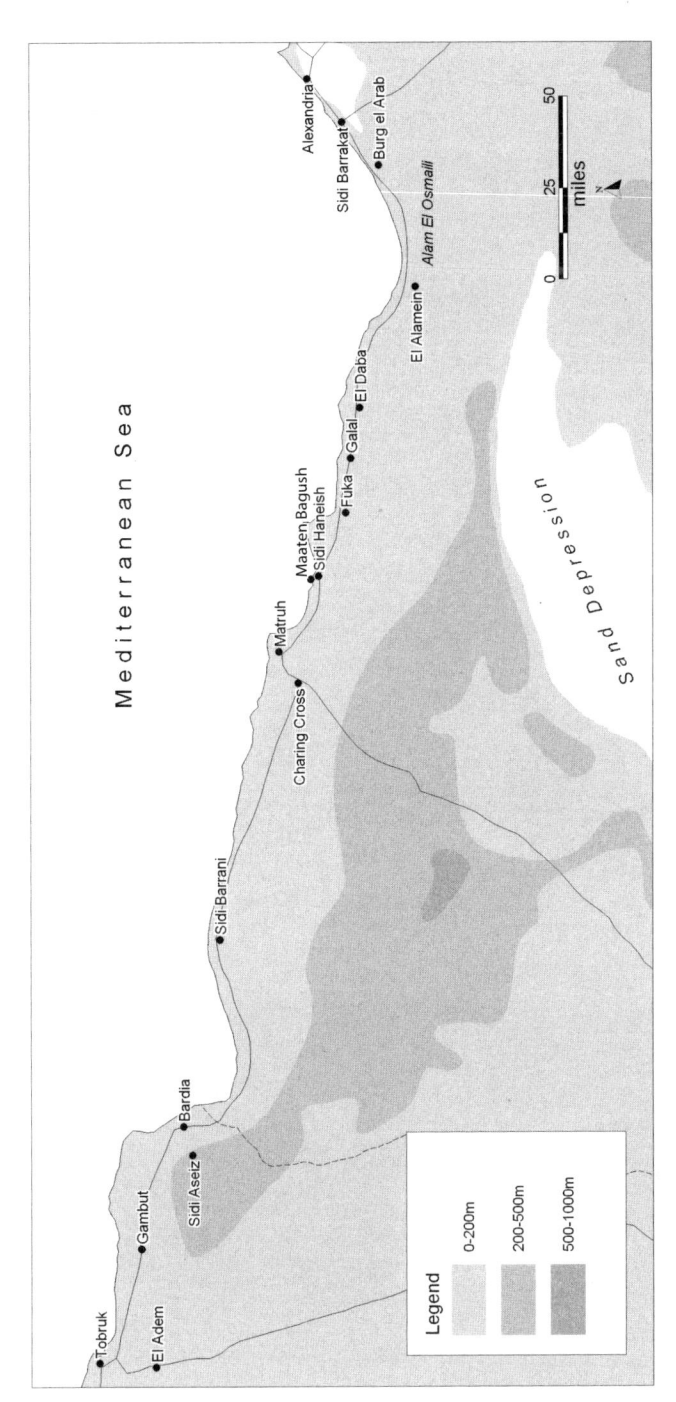

FIGURE 6: Mediterranean settlements of Egypt and Libya from Alexandria to Tobruk

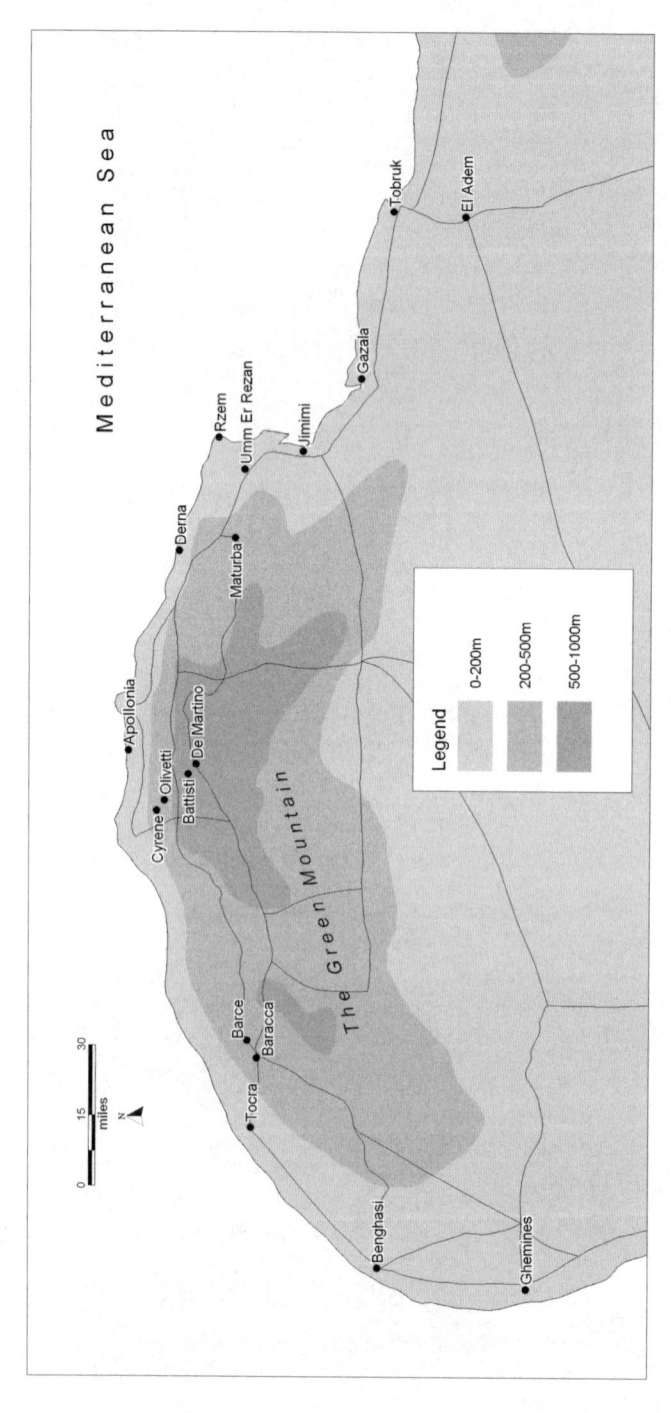

FIGURE 7: Cyrenaica: from Tobruk to Ghemines

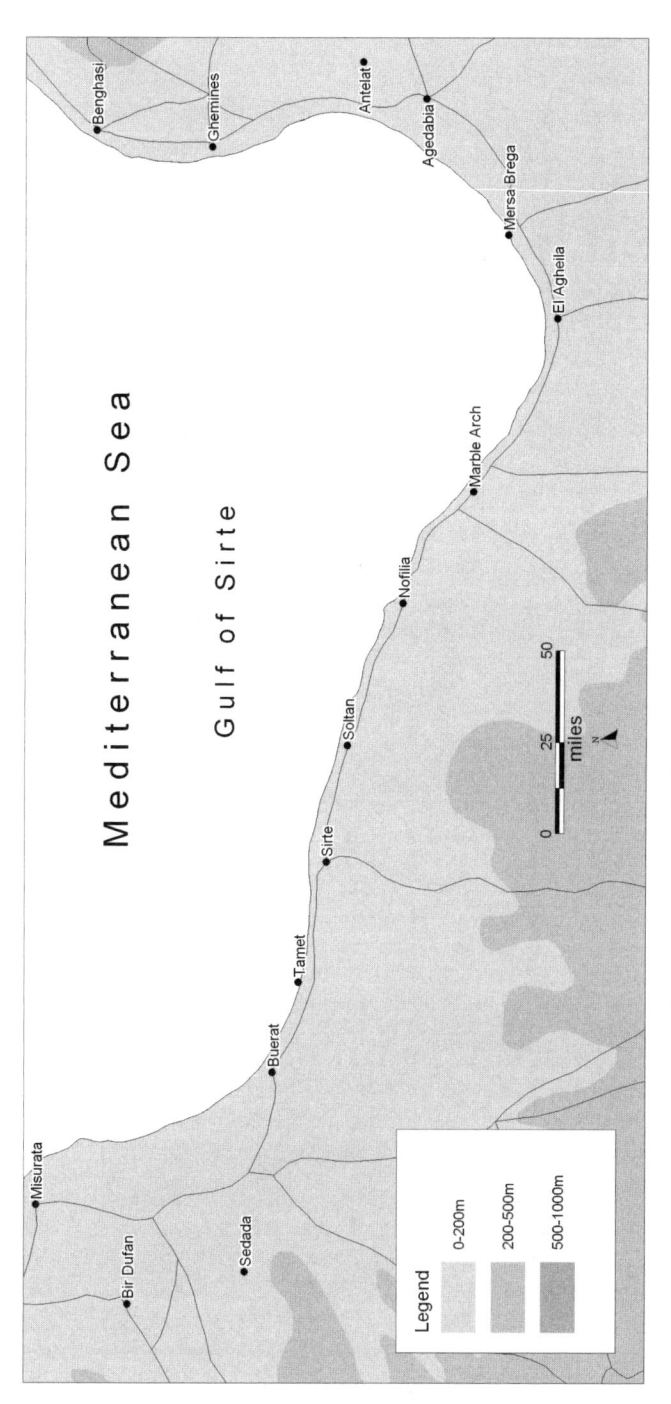

FIGURE 8: The Gulf of Sirte: from Ghemines to Misurata

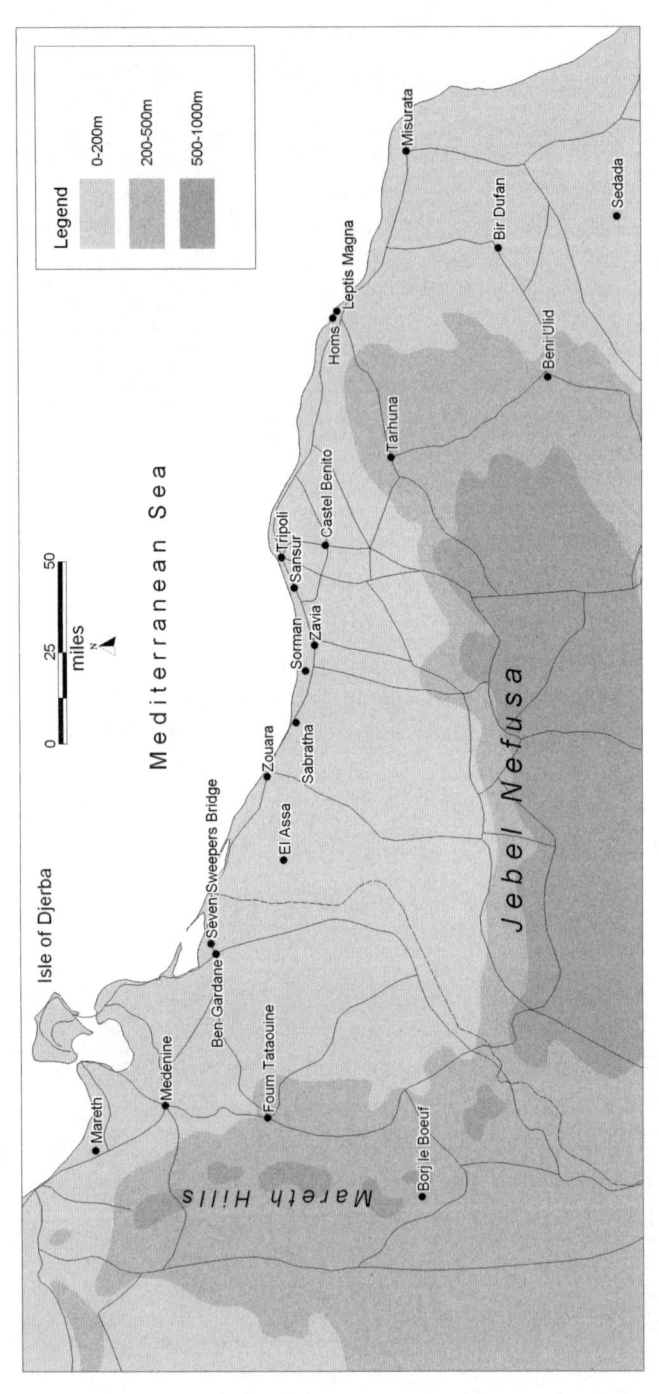

FIGURE 9: Tripolitania and Tunisia: from Misurata to Mareth

Introduction

Colin Clarke

The nature and scope of War's Nomads

Frederick (Fred) Grice's book, *War's Nomads*, provides a worm's-eye view of one of the key events of World War II, namely the military activity following the second battle of El Alamein in October-November 1942. Afterwards the British Eighth Army drove Rommel's *Afrikakorps* across Egypt and Libya into Tunisia, where it was finally defeated. Fred's account is unusual, not only because it was written from 'below', by an 'erk' or aircraftsman (AC), but because it deals with a tiny radar unit of rarely more than ten men, and links together the themes of air and land power. The Western Desert War was the first campaign in British military history, in which the Royal Air Force (RAF) and the army had collaborated so closely. The account is notable because of its quality – it was written by someone on the brink of becoming a professional author.

Fred Grice was an English graduate and grammar school master who, by the time he was called up in 1941, had already collected folk stories relating to the North of England. These stories, which he had told in his own words and had prepared for publication before he left England in May 1942, were proof-read by his wife in 1943, though the book, *Folk Tales of the North Country*[1] was not issued until November 1944. Moreover, from 1937 Fred had kept a regular journal, in which he recorded the varied activities of his literary and personal life and noted seasonal changes in the natural environment, witnessed on the rugged walks he took on the moors around Durham. In short, when he was drafted to Egypt in 1942, he was a budding professional writer with a keen eye for environmental detail and ear for language. He used these skills assiduously to produce the two handwritten journal volumes and typed memoir that cover the period 1942–43 and form the basis for this book.

However, this is not a history of derring-do, but a careful account of two phases in the early RAF career of a thoughtful and reflective young man. 'On Draft' deals with waiting to embark after initial training; describes Fred's journey to the battle zone; and records the privations of a low-ranking AC in barracks and on board a troopship. 'Erk in the Desert', a typed memoir written in first draft in East Africa a few months after the events, gives a detailed account of the activities of Unit 606, a radar crew that follows just behind the battlefront. Its task is to provide radio-detection cover for the advanced landing grounds being used, in this instance by RAF fighter-bomber squadrons, because these landing strips are the targets of attacks by the German Luftwaffe and the Italian Air Force.

As Fred himself records at the beginning of 'Erk in the Desert':

> I have no intention of dealing at length with the military events of this campaign. I have no right to do so, for the grim business of killing and being killed was, in the main, carried on out of our vision…It is rather for me to recall those less hazardous and sensational aspects of the desert campaigner's life – his working, eating, sleeping and relaxations, the businesses of his day-to-day life, the beauties and uglinesses of the land he campaigned in, the inconveniences it imposed and the pleasures it afforded.

Not only does he not deal, in a systematic way, with the military events of the Western Desert campaign, but, for security reasons, he singularly – and deliberately – fails to explain the purpose of his mission: to get to a targeted selection of the 240 landing grounds in the desert with all speed; and then to defend them against air attack by using a Light Warning Set (radar) developed to go operational within an hour (Table 1). Landing grounds – or a specific landing ground – are mentioned quite casually in the memoir; but the emphasis on speed and keeping up with front line of the army is never fully explained. Nor does he

TABLE 1: North-African Place Names and their Adjacent Landing Grounds (LGs)

Place names are spelled as they appear in the text and on the maps, but are also given in local, modern Arabic equivalents wherever possible. Adjacent early 1940s landing grounds (LGs) are given by name or number.

EGYPT

Alam el Osmaili		
Alexandria	*Al-Iskandarīya*	(LG 8)
Burg el Arab	*Burj al 'Arab*	(LGs 28 and 39)
Charing Cross		
El Alamein	*Al 'Alamein*	
El Daba	*Ad Dab'a*	(LG 105)
Fuka	*Fūka*	(LGs 16, 17, 18 and 19)
Galal	*Jalāl*	
Maaten Bagush		(LGs 14 and 15)
Matruh	*Marsā Matrūh*	(LG08)
Sidi Barrani	*Sīdī Barrānī*	(LG 02)
Sidi Barrakat	*Sīdī Barakāt*	
Sidi Haneish	*Sīdī Hunaish*	(LGs 12 and 13)

LIBYA

Agedabia	*Ajdābyā*	(Agedabia East and Agedabia West)
Antelat	*Antalāt*	(Antelat No 1 and 2)
Apollonia	*Sūsah*	(LG)
Barce	*Al Marj al Qadīm*	(LG)
Bardia	*Al Bardīya*	(2 LGs)
Baracca	*Al Marj al Jadīd*	
Battisti		
Benghasi	*Banghāzi*	(Benina and Benina North)
Beni Ulid	*Banī Walīd*	
Bir Dufan	*B'ir Dūfān*	(Bir Dufan 1, 2, 3, 4, 5 and 6)
Buerat	*Bu'ayrāt al Hasūn*	
Castel Benito (Tripoli)	*Bin Ghashīr*	(LG)
Cyrene	*Shahhat*	(LG)
De Martino	*Al Fa'idīyah*	
Derna	*Darnah*	(2 LGs)
El Adem	*Al 'Adam*	(LGs 144 and 157)
El Agheila	*Al 'Uqaylah*	(LG)
El Assa	*Al 'Assah*	(LG)
Gambut	*Kambūt*	(LGs 139, 142 aand 143)

4 • War's Nomads

Gazala	'Ayn Al Gazālah	(Gazala LG Nos 149, 150 and 152)
Ghemines	Qamīnis	
Homs	Al Khums	
Jimimi	At Tamīmī	(Tmimi 1and 2)
Leptis Magna	Labdah	
Marble Arch		(LG)
Maturba	Martūbah	(Nos 1, 2, 3, 4 and 5)
Mersa Brega	Marsá Burayqah	(LG)
Misurata	Misrātah	(LG)
Nofilia	An Nawfalīyah	(2 LGs)
Olivetti	Jaddaim	
Rzem	Ra's at Tīn	
Sabratha	Sabrātah	
Sansur	Janzūr	
Sedada	As Saddādah	(LG)
Sidi Aseiz,	Sīdī Uzayz	(LG 148)
Sirte	Surt	
Soltan	As Sultān	(LG)
Sorman	Surmān	(LG)
Tamet	Thamad Hassān	(LG)
Tarhuna	Tarhūnah	
The Green Mountain	Al Jabal al Akhdar	
Tobruk	Tubruq	(Tobruk Nos 1, 2, 3, and 4)
Tocra	Tūkrah	(LG)
Tripoli	Tarābulus	(Mellaha LG)
Umm Er Rezan	Umm ar Rizam	
Zavia	Az Zāwiyah	
Zouara	Zuwārah	(LG)

TUNISIA

Ben Gardane	Ben Guerdane	(2 LGs)
Borj le Boeuf	Borj Bourguiba	
Foum Tataouine	Tataouine	
Isle of Djerba	Ile de Jerba	
Jebel Nefusa	Jabal Nafūsah	
Mareth	Mareth	
Mareth Hills	Monts des Ksour	
Medenine	Medenine	(LG)
Seven Sweepers Bridge		

Source: C. G. Jefford, *RAF Squadrons*, 2001.

expand upon the importance of the Kittyhawks II and III (or Kitties) – American-built fighter-bombers that were crucial to the air superiority established by the RAF during the period 1942–43. Consequently, all these issues, and others relating to Fred's educational background and RAF training, are addressed in this introduction.

Part travel book – but travel, first, as a troopship experience, and, secondly, as military manoeuvres – part RAF memoir, this account merits publication because it records what has rarely, if ever, been described before, certainly by the participant of a radar unit under battlefield conditions. 'On Draft' deposits Fred back into the military version of the working class, while 'Erk in the Desert' recounts the daily experiences of Unit 606, which he must have equated subconsciously to the shared joys and sorrows of the working class in his colliery village. The experiences are raw, and the location of the author while in the desert is close to the key events. Moreover, Fred's clarity of expression, and his skill in organizing his material make this an accessible and coherent story – and an unsentimental one at that.

Fred's educational background and civilian career

Fred Grice spent the greater part of his adult life in Worcester, but the inspiration for much of his writing came from his childhood years in Brandon and Durham. He was born in 1910 in Brandon, where his father was a miner. At the age of eleven he won a scholarship to Durham Johnston School, where he developed a deep love of English Literature, that stayed with him for the rest of his life. After graduating in English with first-class honours from King's College, London in 1931, he returned home to the north and spent a happy year at Hatfield College, Durham University, where he obtained a teaching qualification and coxed one of the college boats.

By 1941 Fred, now married to Gwen, and with a daughter, Gillian, was teaching English at the A J Dawson Grammar School in Wingate, when he was called up into the Royal Air Force and subsequently posted to North Africa. When he was demobbed in 1946, Fred had spent almost three years in Africa, the latter part as a Flight Lieutenant in the Education Corps based at Eastleigh near Nairobi. 1946 marked a watershed in Fred's life, for he was appointed to a Lectureship in English at the newly-opened Emergency Training College in Worcester, and the family, plus a second daughter, Erica, moved to the West Midlands.

Before long, Fred became Head of Department at the now permanent college (today the University of Worcester) and devoted himself to the two things he loved most – teaching and writing. He was also active as a lecturer both within the city and at Welland, near Malvern. The first signs of a yearning for the life he had left behind in the North of England are evident in Fred's later journals. Here he began to record the world of his childhood, re-creating with great accuracy everyday conversation, but above all, paying homage to the unsung bravery of men like his father, who spent the greater part of their life underground in discomfort and danger. The journals published here may be thought of as precursors to his post-war preoccupations as a writer.

He recalled:

> I was born in the North East of England, in the far north, within hearing distance of the bells of Durham Cathedral. My father, who was a miner, worked in a small colliery a few miles out of Durham. I always think that I had the best of three worlds: the world of the pit village with its strikes, lock-outs, evictions and accidents, and the warm company of a close-knit neighbourly community; the world of the beautiful mediaeval city of Durham, where I went to school, a city of fine architecture and novel traditions of piety and erudition; and the world of the austerely beautiful and unspoilt countryside that encircled the colliery village, merging into the lonely dales to the west and the borderland moors of Northumberland to the north (Commire 1974, 96).

Fred's first book, *Folk Tales of the North Country* was a collection of legends and folk tales, many of them told by his father and other acquaintances, but all embodying something of the spirit of the land that was the mainspring of his inspiration. This was followed by further collections of folk tales from the West Midlands and Lancashire, but his first novel for children came in 1960 with the publication of *Aidan and the Strollers*, a story based on the life of strolling players in the early nineteenth century. Later that year *The Bonny Pit Laddie* was published.

The most popular of all his books, it is the one closest to his heart in that it is set in his native colliery village, incorporating much of the personal history of his own family, especially his mother and uncles, and drawing heavily on the vicissitudes of the mining community of Durham (shortlisted for the *Carnegie Medal* for children's fiction in 1960).

He wrote prolifically for children during the sixties and early seventies, taking inspiration from the North Country (*The Courage of Andy Robson*), historical themes such as the Civil War (*The Luckless Apple*), the lives of the navvies who built the British railways in the mid-nineteenth century (*Young Tom Sawbones*), and his own adventures during World War II in North Africa (*The Moving Finger*). Of his children's books he said, 'I do not write with children in the forefront of my mind. Rather I write about children, and the adult world as seen through the eyes of children' (Commire 1974, 97). Fred received *The Other Award* from the Children's Rights Workshop in 1977 in recognition of the body of his work and its social content.

After his retirement in 1972 Fred continued to give public lectures and to write poetry, but he increasingly turned his attention to the nineteenth-century diarist, the Revd Francis Kilvert. With the support of the Kilvert Society he spent the last ten years of his life writing articles and undertaking the research for his final book, *Francis Kilvert and his World*. Fred died suddenly, shortly after the publication of this significant contribution to Kilvert studies, but with every intention of turning his own journal manuscripts, covering much of his adult life, into a book (perhaps for publication) not unlike Kilvert's famous diary of country life.

Although he made his name as a children's author and biographer, there were many other sides to Fred. He was a keen walker and lover of the countryside. In later years the bracing, empty moorland of his youth was replaced by the gently undulating Worcestershire lanes. He was frequently to be seen tramping around the lanes of Wichenford and Broadheath, and he never lost his childlike love of paddling in brooks, catching minnows and flying kites – much to the delight of his grandchildren. He was a great raconteur with an impish sense of fun, a lover of football (he was a lifelong supporter of Newcastle United), the theatre and the arts. In addition to his children's books and biography of Francis Kilvert, there remains a substantial body of unpublished poetry, as well as his journals.

How *War's Nomads* came to be written and conserved

The book, which the editors have entitled *War's Nomads* following Fred's use of these words in 'Erk in the Desert', is based on three documents. Two of them are handwritten notebooks taken from Fred's journal series of more than 30 volumes: the first is called 'On Draft' by Fred, and the second the 'Black Book' by us. 'On Draft', recorded in an exercise book, deals with Fred's posting to the Middle East, the journey by troopship to Cape Town, South Africa, and his experiences of a military camp in its vicinity. The 'Black Book' is a small notebook, less than A5 in size, with a black cover, and was bought by Fred in Cape Town on 25 June 1942.

The 'Black Book' begins with a description of the area round the Suez Canal, where Fred disembarked in late July 1942, and Cairo. It then provides a detailed account of desert warfare, written as events unfold, running through until mid-December 1942, when the book ends. The text is, understandably, more hurried than 'On Draft', and much of the content is in note-form plus a few pen-and-ink sketches. The third document is 'Erk in the Desert', a considered memoir written by Fred while in East Africa, and completed in first draft in the autumn of 1943. This is based on the contents of the 'Black Book' from September to December 1942, but extended by Fred's recollections to cover the period January to March 1943.

Fred's 1943–44 journal, an additional source written in East Africa, contains some retrospective information about western Libya from which he draws, and he is able to supplement this when writing his memoir by using library resources in Nairobi. Fortunately, the material in the memoir for January to March 1943, though not covered by the 'Black Book', is also backed up by materials in an Air Ministry publication dated 1950, but dealing with the war in Tunisia in early 1943, in which Unit 606 played a small but noteworthy part (Air Ministry 1950).

It was originally Fred's intention, in retirement, so his journal tells us, to produce a text dealing with his wartime experiences. Accordingly, Gillian and I have combined 'On Draft' and 'Erk in the Desert' to form a single volume in two parts. The 'Black Book' has been used in two ways: to conclude the journey from Britain to South Africa recounted in 'On Draft' and to carry it through to Cairo; and, additionally, to provide immediate eye-witness accounts of military events by introducing small sections of it into the text of 'Erk', using a smaller size of typeface for the inserted material.

Fred's own use of the 'Black Book' material in his memoir 'Erk in the Desert' is skilful, but, in his zeal to conceal military secrets and to play down the violence he is witnessing and the danger he is in, he sometimes obscures or even omits what it is now important to reveal – for example, when and where his unit went operational, and the military circumstances under which they functioned. These are precisely the materials that the less inhibited 'Black Book' sets forth in an unvarnished manner, and that render the 'Black Book' eminently quotable . Unfortunately, we don't know whether or how Fred intended to explain the precise role of Unit 606, but I have attempted to provide an answer to this key question in the last section of this introduction.

The 'Black Book', written literally in the heat of battle, supplied a vital clue in our research into the activities of Air Ministry Experimental Station (AMES) Unit 606, to which Fred belonged. It specifically mentions Squadron Leader Young as the RAF officer who led Fred's unit westwards across Egypt and away from El Alamein in November 1942. It was only by speculatively googling Young's name in conjunction with the RAF in North Africa that we discovered that M. H. Young had been the Squadron Leader of 213 Squadron (Gumbridge 1968). From that single lead we were able to access 213's Operations Record Book (ORB),[2] only to discover that 213 Squadron's Hurricanes, though highly active at El Alamein, were of little use in bombing and strafing after the break-out – hence the detachment of Sqn Ldr Young from his unit and his deployment on the ground with AMES 606 and 607.

Even more relevant than 213 was 260 Squadron and its ORB,[3] which gives much detail that has been cited in the footnotes. 260, with its sister squadrons 112, 250, and 450 in 243 Wing, followed the same pattern of movement (at similar dates) to the advanced landing grounds as Fred's radar unit (Table 2) (Jefford 2001). It will be seen that AMES 606 and 260 Squadron (both associated with 211 Group) were closely linked, not only during the Egyptian and Libyan campaigns, but especially so during the attack on Tunisia. Table 2 brings land and air together in ways that the memoir, for reasons of secrecy, does not. Squadron Leader Young gave up leading AMES 606 on the ground after El Adem in late November 1942, at which point he said a final goodbye to 213 Squadron.[4] 260 Squadron remained at Maturba (also written Martuba) in Cyrenaica until mid-December, when it overtook 606 at Marble Arch on 18 December.

The editors were keen to discover whether an Operations Record Book (ORB) existed for AMES Unit 606 in The National Archives at Kew, but searches revealed no such document or any reference to it. Either it was never kept, or if it was, it was destroyed or lost during the war. However, we were able to access and copy ORBs for two of the other small Type 6 radar units that were operating in North Africa at the same time as 606 – namely, AMES 608[5] and 610[6]. They not only showed us what ORBs for Type 6 radar units looked like, but gave invaluable insights into the activities of the units and their methods of operation. However, these entries were essentially mundane and perfunctory in a military manner, and they give no flavour of the life of individuals posted to the units.

The ORBs for AMES 608 (12 pages) and 610 (4 pages) provide information about the operation of the equipment, and the unreliability of the Crossley lorries in which it was transported. Even if an ORB for 606 had existed, it is unlikely it would have added very much to Fred's record of events, other than in terms of radar procedures and dates

Introduction • 11

Table 2: AMES 606, Squadrons 260 and 213, and the Landing Grounds, 1942–1943

	260 Squadron 233 Wing/ 211 Group	AMES 606	213 Squadron 243 Wing/212 Group
1942			
June	**Kittyhawk IIA introd.**		
11 July	LG 97 (s. of Burg el Arab)		
21 Aug			LG 85 (s. of Burg el Arab)
9 Sept		Alam el Osmaili	
21 Oct			LG 172 (e. of El Alamein)
6 Nov	LG 75 30 miles s. Sidi Barrani)		
7 Nov		leave el Osmaili	LG 20 (w. of Daba)
9 Nov		Maaten Bagush LGs	
10 Nov	Sidi Aseiz		
12 Nov		Sidi Aseiz LG	LG101 (w. of Maaten Bag)
13 Nov		Gambut LGs	LG125 (e. of Tobruk)
14 Nov		Tobruk & Gazala LGs	
15 Nov	Gazala no2		
16 Nov		Maturba LGs	
18 Nov			
19 Nov	Maturba no4		
20 Nov			El Adem
25 Nov		El Adem LGs	Maturba
27 Nov			
28 Nov		Tobruk LGs	
29 Nov		Maturba LGs	
30 Nov		to Barce	
1 Dec		to Benghasi LGs	
2 Dec		Gemines	
3 Dec		Antelat LGs	
4 Dec		Agedabia	
4–19 Dec		El Agheila LG	
10 Dec	Belandah/Benghasi		
18 Dec	Marble Arch LG		

20 Dec		Marble Arch LG
25 Dec		Soltan LG
31 Dec	Gzina LG (s. of Soltan)	Tamet LG
Dec	**Kittyhawk III introd**	

1943

1 Jan	Hamraiet (s. of Sirte)		
4 Jan	Hamraiet (s. of Sirte)		
6 Jan			
12 Jan	Bir Durfan		
13 Jan			
18 Jan	Sedadah	Sedadah LG	
20 Jan			
21 Jan		Tarhuna	
23 Jan			Misurata West
24 Jan	Castel Benito	Castel Benito airport	
7 Feb	Sorman	Sorman LG	
14 Feb	El Assa	El Assa LG	
2 March	Ben Gardane	Ben Gardane LG	
8 March	Nefatia (w. of Ben Gardane)		
20 March	Medenine	Medenine LG	

Sources: C. G. Jefford, *RAF Squadrons*, 2001; *Operations Record Book*, 213 Squadron, RAF, 1942–43, AIR 27/1316; *Operations Record Book*, 260 Squadron, RAF, 1942–43, AIR 27/1537. Movements of AMES Unit 606 as recorded in this book.

of arrival at, and departure from, landing grounds – though all these pieces of information would have been helpful. So, with some certainty, we can claim that 'Erk in the Desert' is, in all probability, the only definitive account of a Type 6 radar unit's operations and of its men's lives over several months in the last phase of the Western Desert War.

Neither Gillian (Fred's daughter), nor Colin (his son-in-law) – the editors of this book – knew of the existence of 'On Draft, the 'Black Book' or 'Erk in the Desert' before Fred's death in 1983, when his widow, Gwen, gave us all his papers (journals and other documents). Fred had, from time to time, talked about life in the desert, telling us about the gharry in which the unit travelled, and explaining that this was one of the best and healthiest times in his life; but he made no specific reference to Unit 606, its military objectives or the equipment they used.

It was a complete surprise to us, in the early 2000s, to find the three key documents (and later the photographs, some collected together, but others scattered through his later journals), out of which this book has been constructed. The only member of Fred's unit of whom we had heard was Sid Rapperport, whose name cropped up from time when the desert was mentioned in the late 1950s and early 1960s. In 1979 Fred told us about Sid's plan to visit him in Worcester, but we have no record of the visit.

'On Draft' had a handwritten label 'Invaluable – not to be lost' attached to the cover of the exercise book in which it was written; and the handwriting of the text is minute and in black ink and pencil. Because of the movement of the boat, the parts written at sea were particularly hard to transcribe, and the passages written during storms were at times almost impossible to decipher. Frequently both editors had recourse to a magnifying glass. The 'Black Book' was also kept in a small hand and in black ink; some parts were comparatively easy to read, but the battlefield sections required constant consultation between the two of us prior to transcription. Fortunately, much of it could be checked against the typescript of 'Erk'.

There are, in Fred's papers, two versions of his memoir, 'Erk in the Desert'. The first, attributed to Flt Lt F. Grice, had been accurately typed on thin typewriting paper, though a new title page had been added in handwriting plus his new address – Training College, Henwick Road, Worcester. The rank F/Lt had been crossed out, and the final page was missing. We think that this document may have been professionally typed – possibly in East Africa – from Fred's version, finished, according to him, in Kenya on 23 October 1943. On that date he wrote:

> By an extraordinary coincidence, I have finished the last chapter of my book today, the anniversary of the great Alamein barrage! Of course it is not finished. Now to re-write and re-type – a long job. But the back of the work is broken. I can more easily revise than rebuild the whole book.

The second version of 'Erk in the Desert', also with a handwritten title page – and very similar in all respects to the first – is called 'Western Desert Diary' by Mr F. Grice, and the college address (with Henwick Grove instead of Henwick Road) is given accurately, but no date is provided. It may have been typed by Fred. It post-dates and corrects the first version, though it is typed on plain, torn-out sheets removed from an exercise book. Marked 'Badly typed copy' it turned out to be carefully corrected in ink and complete. The editors found this the more reliable typescript, because it contains occasional typed expansions of the first version, and corrections in Fred's own hand. Crucially, it includes the missing final page, and is the version used in this publication – only rarely did the editors resort to a few words peculiar to the first account, though they have opted for its name, 'Erk in the Desert', as the title for the second part of the book.

Background to 'On Draft'

Training as a radio operator/radar operator

World War II had been in progress for almost two years when Fred was called up from the A J Dawson Grammar School in Wingate, Co. Durham. His English post was not reserved (that is exempt from national service), but at the age of 31 he seemed rather old for active duty, even in the RAF, which he entered on 7 July 1941. The need to supply new and specially-trained units for the drawn-out Western Desert War in North Africa probably explains his posting, as his service record shows, as an Aircraftsman Second Class (AC2) to Number 18 Reserve Command of the RAF Recruits Centre on 12 July for 2 months of basic training at Padgate, Lancashire.

Fred was sent to the Number 2 Radio School at Yatesbury, Wiltshire on 19 September, and after a month passed his examination as a Radio Operator. A week later, on 26 October, he was posted for training to the Air Ministry Experimental Station (AMES) 77N at Scarlett Point, Castletown on the Isle of Man, and on the last day of December 1941

INTRODUCTION • 15

PLATE 1 Fred at Ballasalla, Isle of Man, while on radar training, March 1942

PLATE 2 Fred prior to embarkation, 24 April 1942

he passed out as an AC2 Radio Operator. Fred must have continued working in radar on the Isle of Man, because there is a photograph of him in uniform taken at Ballasalla, near Castletown, in March 1942 (Plate 1), though family records also show that he was in Poling, Sussex, that same month, where there was a radar station – part of the fixed chain facing the French coast.

On 11 April Fred was sent to Number 30 Maintenance Unit, but he was at home in late April, when another photograph of him was taken, presumably on pre-embarkation leave (Plate 2). He was promoted AC1 on 5 May, and after delays embarked on 7 May for the Middle East, which he reached via West and South Africa (with further hold-ups), disembarking at the Suez Canal on 26 July. After a month in Egypt, mostly in the vicinity of Cairo, on 31 August he was posted to his unit AMES 606.

After so many months at sea or time wasted waiting for troopships and minor relocations, Fred, and no doubt other radio and radar operatives, required additional training under desert conditions. This 606 got at or near Alam El Osmaili, while General Montgomery was preparing his breakout from El Alamein. On 6 October Fred was re-classified as a Leading Aircraftsman (LAC) with a 90 per cent pass in the examination that he took in the field; on 1 November, while waiting at El Alamein, he was promoted Leading Aircraftsman (LAC), and on 31 December, while on active service, became a LAC Radar Operator.

An aircraftsman en route from Britain to Egypt

Despite Fred's degree in English and his career as a grammar school master, he seems not to have been a candidate for a commission when he was called up to the RAF – perhaps because he didn't volunteer. He therefore entered military service as an Aircraftsman Second Class, and moved up to First Class only on the eve of his posting to the Middle East. This had financial and status implications for him and his family, none of them good.

Fred found himself below the vital social-class barrier that, in the military, divided the British middle and upper classes from the lower class – a distinction that roughly followed the line between the Commissioned Officers, on the one hand, and Non-Commissioned Officers (NCOs) and other ranks, on the other. While his RAF rank fitted his home background, since his father was a coalminer, whose whole life had been led in the mining community, Fred's education and employment had turned him into a member of the middle class.

This lack of a commission had an immediate and deleterious impact on Fred's wife, Gwen. There was a substantial gap between the wages of an AC2 and the salary of a grammar school master, and Durham was one of the few Local Education Authorities in England not to make up the difference between their former teachers' wages and the payments they received from the armed forces. Gwen, with no job (she, too, was a teacher but had had to give up her post as soon as she married in 1939) and a young child, suddenly found her finances spinning out of control, and it was only by selling the family home and moving to cheaper rented property that she was able to stabilize them. It is for this reason that Fred expressed his delight in the 'Black Book' on 26 August 1942 to know that their house had been sold.

Fred embarked on His Majesty's Transport J10, which involved a long and tortuous trip from Avonmouth, Bristol via South Wales and the Irish Sea to western Scotland, where on 10 May 1942, at Oversay in the Inner Hebrides (Fig. 1), it joined the convoy (WS 19) to Cape Town, South Africa, travelling via Freetown, Sierra Leone in West Africa (Fig. 2). Especially galling for Fred was that he and his fellow aircraftsmen were treated with scant consideration. His annoyance at their perfunctory-to-humiliating departure from England, with scarcely a word of goodwill from the officers or NCOs, was matched by what he saw as the degrading, indeed squalid, conditions under which the other ranks lived both prior to embarkation and on board the troopship, the *Highland Monarch*.

The *Highland Monarch* (62A in the convoy), had seen service before World War II as a meat transporter from Argentina to Britain, and Fred draws the obvious parallel between the hanging of animal carcasses and the pendant sleeping conditions of the aircraftsmen in their hammocks below decks (Winston Special Convoys in WW2 – 1942 Sailings). Fred was scandalized by the officer class's life high-on-the-hog, while the ratings received indifferent food and often suffered a shortage of water; and the casual greed of the officers in purloining the cramped space of the other ranks for their own luxury and entertainment. He was equally alienated by the swearing and general boorishness of many of his companions below decks (and in the barracks before embarkation), though he shows considerable skill in mimicking their expressions and turns of phrase.

It was only towards the end of the voyage to Cape Town via Freetown (Fig. 2), when he met the padre and medical officer, was invited onto public discussion groups and brains trusts, and asked to lecture on 'The Future of Education' that Fred's self-confidence re-asserted itself. Apart from his clarity of thought expressed in the text, this is the first glimpse we get of his positive personal qualities – accomplishments that are going to enable him to cope with the privations of a military campaign in the Western Desert, and to enjoy the camaraderie of his fellow men in Unit 606. The men of 606 seem to have shown a more positive interest in education than the erks on the *Highland Monarch*.

Fred's associates in South Africa were a liberal white family (the Eakins), who hosted him and other servicemen at Fish Hoek outside Cape Town (Fig. 3), and military men from Commonwealth countries, whose units made up the allied cause in North Africa. Contact with Africans was non-existent in Cape Town (which emerges as a white city), as had been the case in Freetown, where the *Highland Monarch*'s passengers were not even allowed on shore. The only comment relayed by Fred about South African blacks was the 'white man's failure to educate the native' – a view expressed by his host and almost certainly endorsed by Fred too. In Cairo, however, the 'Black Book' reveals that Fred and his companions were allowed to wander at will, and his account contains many sympathetic vignettes of Arab artisans, traders and businessmen, as well as descriptions of European suburbs, notably Heliopolis – and the Pyramids (Fig. 4).

The leitmotif of 'On Draft' is the boredom of waiting – for everything, according to Fred's account. With boredom went ignorance – of their precise destination, route and timetable for arrival. Much of this can be put down to the need for secrecy about the deployment of troops to the battlefields, and, in Fred's case, the absolute secrecy associated with the use of radar. The journey to Egypt was, of course, made much longer than was geographically necessary by the unacceptable risk of using the Strait of Gibraltar for convoys that the British could not afford to lose, and by the need to select routes that were free from German naval attention. Key to the journey to Africa was the port of Cape Town, from which convoys were despatched to the Middle East (including the Suez Canal) or beyond. But even as they waited to leave Britain, the malaise they were experiencing was already dispiriting, as Fred reveals in his poem:

Education

After years studying the beauties of Old English,
Melting over the plaintive Dream of the Rood,
And stirred at those heroic saints who made the dawn of our race glorious,
I complete my education in His Majesty's Forces,
Learning, after a thousand years of progress away from St Cuthbert and St Werburgh,
How to deceive an equipment clerk for a new pair of boots,
To steal a meat pie from two half-vigilant cooks,
And to lie my way out of any embarrassment
My criminality may land me in.

Fred's intense irritation over waiting, and his sense of outrage over mistreatment were to continue to Cape Town, after which, transferring temporarily to the comparatively luxurious *New Amsterdam,* camping in South Africa at Pollsmoor (Fig. 3), and socializing with other Commonwealth soldiers, many of whom Fred found very congenial, the quality of life improved – if not the waiting. Fred celebrated his 32nd birthday on 21 June near Muizenberg, Cape Town (Fig. 3), but had to endure more than another month, much of it at sea in the

Indian Ocean, before the *Highland Monarch* reached the Suez Canal. Then he had yet another month to wait before he was on active service as an erk in the Egyptian desert.

Background to 'Erk in the Desert'

Fred's Western Desert campaign

When Aircraftsman Fred Grice was arriving in the Egyptian desert immediately to the west of Alexandria in early September 1942, the battle between the newly-appointed British commander, General Montgomery, and his German adversary, Field Marshal Rommel, was taking place at Alam Halfa, a ridge immediately to the south of El Alamein (Fig. 2). It was the final eastward thrust of the *Afrikakorps* in its attempt to outflank the British forces and take Alexandria and the Suez Canal – and the turning point in the British Eighth Army's fortunes in North Africa (Hastings 2012) (Fig. 5).

Informed of German battle plans by Ultra decrypts at Bletchley Park, UK, Montgomery was able to deduce that Rommel's attack would come from the south, and his innovative use of army-air co-operation, his digging-in of his tanks, and the dominance of the Desert Air Force over the Luftwaffe ensured that the El Alamein box, sandwiched between the desert and the Mediterranean Sea, remained intact and accessible from Alexandria (Smith 2011). The British victory at Alam Halfa enabled Fred to get to his radar unit, 606, at Alam El Osmaili, a rocky outcrop looking towards El Alamein from the south-east. From there, while under additional radar and rifle training, probably in the company of other AMES personnel, he witnessed the second and final battle of El Alamein from 23 October to 4 November (Fig. 6).

Reinforcements had given the British a decisive advantage: the British Eighth Army (including its Commonwealth troops) deployed 195,000 men against 104,000 Germans and Italians; 1,029 tanks against 489; 750 aircraft against 675; and it had vastly superior artillery. Informed again by decrypts of Rommel's strategy, Montgomery proceeded to engage in a set-piece tactical battle, using camouflage deception, concentrated artillery barrages and constant air attack. Rommel, faced with a chronic shortage of fuel and armaments, exacerbated by the destruction of supply ships leaving Italy, and suffering from personal ill-health, withdrew after almost two weeks of bombardment (Hastings 2012).

There then began Rommel's long retreat along the desert coastal strip following the Mediterranean to Tunisia, crossing first western Egypt and then the whole of Libya. The British forces pursued Rommel all the way, and Unit 606 was just behind the Eighth Army front line for much of the chase, both before and after the occupation of Tripoli. An attempt by the Eighth Army to encircle the Axis forces at Mersah Matruh was frustrated by rain, and they escaped by 7 November; Tobruk was re-taken on 13 November, but again Rommel's forces escaped the trap; an opportunity to outflank Rommel at Agedabia in December was cautiously declined for fear of counter-attack (Fig. 5).

Montgomery has been criticized for his failure to finish off the *Afrikakorps* while it was in full flight, but he was afraid that Rommel, with his greater mobility, might turn the tables on Britain's 'citizen army' (Hastings 2012, 379); and so he erred on the side of caution, content to chase the enemy into Libya and Tunisia towards the British and American forces of *Operation Torch,* who had landed in Vichy French Algeria and Morocco on 8 November 1942. Although the US military unsympathetically dismissed the Mediterranean as tainted by British imperial ambitions, Prime Minister Churchill and President Roosevelt agreed there could be no Continental D-Day in 1942; and it was soon acknowledged that North Africa might form the base from which to attack Italy and southern France – hence the allied approval given for *Torch* (Hastings 2012) (Fig. 5).

As Fred's account shows from the Eighth Army side, amid winter rain and mud, the Germans were able to frustrate efforts to rush Tunisia, as *Operation Torch* tangled with the end of the Western Desert Campaign. However, the tide of war was with the Allies, and by the end of February 1943 Ultra revealed Rommel's intention to use all three of his weakened panzer divisions to attack Montgomery's troops as they approached the Mareth Line in southern Tunisia (Smith 2011). Fred witnessed the British victory at Medenine on 6 March, after which Rommel, a sick man, left Africa. But surprisingly, Fred too was not present at the failure of Montgomery's first assault on Mareth on 19 March, though he did witness the military build-up involving the New Zealanders beforehand, which he describes in some detail (Fig. 5).

At this juncture Fred was plucked from the military activities in southern Tunisia and flown from Medenine to Tripoli and then on to Cairo, seeing from the air, within one day, the entire route of Unit 606's journey in pursuit of Rommel. This erk, Fred, was now en route to a commission as Pilot Officer and a new career as an Education Officer in East Africa. Perhaps his promotion was part of the general re-appraisal of manpower and military strategy after the fall of Tunis in January 1943; perhaps his age (he was 32), his degree and his teaching qualification warranted a non-battlefield posting.

In addition to reflecting on the effacement of the traces of war by the incursions of the desert during his flight back to Egypt, it is likely, too, that Fred would have pondered the earlier phases of the Western Desert War in North Africa, and, in particular, the existence of the airstrips which were so frequently the destinations of the various legs of his own military journey from Egypt through Libya to Tunisia. It is to these landing grounds, and their construction during the battles of 1940–1942, that I now turn.

The see-saw war and the landing grounds

The British victory at the second Battle of El Alamein and the pursuit of Rommel into Libya and Tunisia was the last and decisive phase of a back-and-forth struggle that began in August 1940 with the invasion of neutral Egypt by Italian forces based in the Italian colony of Libya. The Italian offensive was halted by British and Commonwealth troops stationed in Egypt, and in December 1940 a counter-attack was launched, resulting in massive Italian losses and their retreat to El Agheila on the Gulf of Sirte. A total collapse of the Italian army was prevented by the arrival the German *Afrikakorps* and units of the Luftwaffe, and Germany – represented by General Rommel – became the dominant element in the Axis partnership in North Africa (Hastings 2012) (Fig. 5).

Axis forces launched two more large-scale assaults against the British, each time forcing them back to Egypt, but both times the British retaliated and recovered the lost ground. During the first Axis push in 1941, the front line stabilized at the Egyptian border, but Tobruk, with its Australian garrison, was isolated and besieged for 240 days. Later in 1941 Tobruk was relieved, the territory gained by Rommel was re-captured, and the front line again set at El Agheila. At this juncture the Eighth Army was formed out of British, Australian (soon to be re-deployed), Indian, South African and New Zealand units.

As a result of Rommel's second offensive from January to July 1942 the British and their allies were driven back into Egypt, defeated at the Battle of Gazala (Fig. 7), and Tobruk fell for the first time. The Eighth Army under Auchinleck halted the Axis powers at the Alamein Line on 1 July 1942, only 70 miles short of Alexandria, at the first battle of El Alamein (Hastings 2012) (Fig. 5).

> During July, gloom suffused the British in Cairo, matched by visible exultation among Egyptians. On the notorious 'Ash Wednesday', Middle East headquarters conducted bonfires of secret documents and many families fled to Palestine. (Hastings 2012, 365)

Fred's narrative in 'Erk in the Desert' opens at the beginning of September 1942, soon after Churchill replaced Auchinleck by Montgomery as the commander of the Eighth Army. Max Hastings's evaluation of the British position at that moment makes chilling reading:

> Britain's fortunes in the Middle East, and the global prestige of its army, had reached their lowest ebb. Churchill's attempt to exploit Africa as a battlefield against the Axis had thus far served only to make Rommel a hero, and grievously to injure the morale and self-respect of the British people at home (2012, 138).

In reality, however, Rommel's situation was less than favourable: the outnumbered Axis army facing El Alamein stood at the end of a tenuous 1500-mile supply chain; fuel and weapons from Germany were always inadequate; informed by Ultra decrypts, the Royal Navy and the RAF began to destroy fuel, tank and ammunition shipments to Rommel across the Mediterranean (Smith 2011). Furthermore, once the Eighth Army had broken out of El Alamein, there were few strong points that could be defended by the retreating Axis troops (though there were previously prepared defences running inland at El Agheila, Buerat and Homs – all in Libya), while a string of landing grounds (that could be used by the advancing RAF) ran along the Mediterranean coast road across Egypt and Libya into Tunisia, or followed the course of the Egyptian railway from Alexandria to Sollum (Jefford 2001).

These landing grounds had been constructed by the RAF from late 1940 onwards, and once checked out and cleared of debris, would be used by the pursuing Desert Air Force, made up of RAF, South African Air Force and Greek Air Force units, plus US reinforcements. There were 240 landing grounds in Egypt, Libya and Tunisia potentially at the disposal of the Advance Army and RAF Headquarters at Burg el Arab (Fig. 6), but only about 70 lay in the path followed by the Eighth Army (Table 1). Each had been constructed on flat land cleared of bush, and had a landing strip of about 1000 yards in length (Judge 2009). Dating from the earlier phases of the Western Desert Campaign, they were organized into a landing-ground (LG) numerical series in the Western Desert in Egypt, and given place names in Libya and Tunisia (Jefford 2001).

Almost all the destinations of Unit 606 were landing grounds (with 20 likely visits), and this applied both during its progress westwards in November and December 1942 along the Mediterranean coast and in 1943 when it turned inland as road conditions, fortifications and military strategy required, particularly in the approach to Tripoli and in Tunisia (Table 2). The conditions of the formerly-abandoned landing grounds needed to be verified, and repairs carried out; a rendezvous with a squadron might be made; in case of danger, protection might be found with the Bofors and Lewis gunners of the RAF Regiment, if they had already taken up defence of the air strip. Most important of all, Unit 606 might be expected to go operational and give early warning to the squadron on the ground of air attack by Axis fighters. In one of his few references to the flying and land operations of the RAF during this phase of the war, Fred noted:

> While the aircraft were leapfrogging forward their support came over the desert in a fleet of gharries, hour after hour churning through soft sand that blew up into the nostrils and eyes or bumping shockingly over rock and stone (Were Your Knees Brown? 1943, 4).

What was Unit 606 up to in the desert?
Why was Fred so guarded about what he wrote in his memoir, and why was the explicit purpose of Unit 606 in the desert so effectively concealed? Fred was engaged in the second most secret aspect of warfare after the Bletchley Park decrypts – namely, radar.[7] Radar, or Radio Detection and Direction Finding (RDF), had been developed by the British Air Ministry in the 1930s to provide a fixed chain of stations along the east and south coasts of Britain facing the Low Countries, France and the anticipated aggressor, Germany, to give efficient air-raid warnings (The Air Ministry 1952).

After the fall of France in 1940 it became imperative to protect British territories and interests in the Middle East from Vichy French and Italian colonies in North Africa, and 5 stations were identified for installation in the area of the Nile Delta and along the Suez Canal in Egypt. Because of the delay in delivering equipment, a mobile set of instruments was brought into operation during early 1941 in Alexandria at Ikingi Mariut, and mobile equipment in vehicles was supplied to Ikingi Mariut, Aboukir (adjacent to Alexandria), and El Daba, to the west of El Alamein (The Air Ministry 1950).

The Air Ministry acknowledged that 'with so few stations in such a vast territory it was inevitable that from the operational viewpoint the outlook was very parochial' (The Air Ministry 1950, 161). In the vast areas between stations radar coverage could be obtained only by the development of Mobile Radio Units (MRU), which took four hours to go operational and days to erect and dismantle. By December 1940, two MRUs were deployed in the Western Desert Campaign, often concentrating on the main ports of Tobruk and Benghasi, and reporting to 258 Fighter Wing – but 'it was practice never to deploy RDF units in very forward positions'(The Air Ministry 1950, 172) (Fig. 7).

> Although all Mobile Radio units were adequately briefed on the destruction of their equipment to prevent it from falling into enemy hands, unnecessary risks could not be taken. Security was not the only factor to consider in this respect; the marked insufficiency of RDF apparatus within the Middle East Command at that time precluded the adoption of any policy which would unnecessarily jeopardise the equipment (Air Ministry 1950, 172).

By the autumn of 1941 45 radar units were operational in the Middle East (23 of them in Egypt and one in Libya at Tobruk) and while 'the coastal chain was fairly satisfactory, ... the Suez Canal defences were still in an embryo state' (The Air Ministry 1950, 179). Some 50 Air Ministry Experimental Stations (AMES) were either already in operation or in transit from Britain, or waiting despatch to the region. Among them were more than 25 Mobile Radio Units (MRU), radar units of the Type 2 series with 'floodlight facilities', and 15 Type 5 series Chain Overseas Low (COL) units (some mobile), which could detect low-flying aircraft (The Air Ministry 1950, Appendix 14, 564). The COL units could engage in Ground Control Interception (GCI) by calling up a fighter and guiding it to attack the target plane.

In addition, five Type 6 series (604, 605, 606, 607 and 608) AMES units were listed on 30 November 1941 as 'in the course of manufacture'– Fred's unit was 606 (The Air Ministry 1950, Appendix no. 14, 564). Fred joined 606 in September 1942 (roughly 10 months later), which was a measure of the lead time required to get British kit and men operational in the Western-Desert theatre – given that the only acceptably safe supply route from Britain to Egypt was via South Africa. The Type 6 stations, with their Light Warning Sets (LWS), were capable of erecting their equipment within one hour, and of going operational within two. It was their mobility over the ground and the speed of 'going operational' that made Unit 606 (and its sister units) so crucial to the defence of the Advanced Landing Grounds.

> At all stages the Light Warning units were used as forward RDF screen for the longer-range COL/GCI equipment. Being smaller, more mobile, and taking far less time to become operational after arrival on site, the LWS's were better able to take advantage of rapid military gains which were occurring. In addition, being smaller and less valuable equipment, the permissible margin of security was less. The forward siting of Light Warning Sets on COL type sites thus provided the best possible low cover over the battle area at all stages (Air Ministry 1950, 297).

Lightweight portable radar units had originally been developed by the Radio Branch at Middle East Headquarters at Cairo, and were used successfully in Crete in early 1941. Technical plans were sent back to Britain for prototype production, and the kit was subsequently adapted in Egypt for operating at high temperatures. With these improvements, the Light Warning Sets were subsequently manufactured in the UK. Units 601 and 602, with pack-sets 'suitable for mule or camel transport in the absence of motor transport' (The Air Ministry 1950, 180), had been made up from Airborne Surface Vessel (ASV) sets – radar for maritime patrol aircraft. They were deployed for the first time in November 1941, when they provided radar cover for RAF advanced landing grounds on the Egyptian-Libyan border.

> As this was an innovation untried in previous desert operations, a wireless observer screen, also reporting back to Wing Operations, was thrown round the Advanced Landing Ground Area. The Air Officer Commanding, Air Headquarters Western Desert, was notified that the portable RDF sets provided might be of little use, and that it was clearly better to make all plans assuming no RDF cover in the forward area (Air Ministry 1950, 180).

Fears about the unreliability of the equipment belonging to Units 601 and 602 proved initially correct, since the range-finding they obtained for planes was inadequate for early warning, and the sets were returned to Cairo as 'useless' in December 1941, and categorized as 'undergoing special inspection' (The Air Ministry 1950, Appendix No. 14, 564). However, it was soon realized that the units had been operating on low-altitude sites, and tests subsequently carried out at Matruh (Fig. 6) showed that the equipment could produce ranges of 30 to 40 miles on aircraft of unknown height, and an aircraft flying at only 500 feet was observed up to 20 miles away (The Air Ministry 1950, 182).

While the problems with AMES 601 and 602 were being sorted out, No. 510 COL station, which had been made fully mobile, was moved forward in December 1941 to locate near El Agheila (Fig. 8). It quickly had two 'kills' to its credit in addition to the provision of satisfactory early warning. In January 1942 Wing Commander J. A. Tester, 'took command of the station personally with the intention of controlling fighter aircraft directly from the site of the COL station' (The Air Ministry 1950, 182 and 1952, iii-iv). But the next Axis military advance drove the British out of Libya and 510 COL with it.

By the time the fifth iteration of retreat and advance in the Western Desert War had brought Rommel to his siege of El Alamein in 1942 (Fig. 6), a great deal had been learned by the British about desert warfare: the necessity for co-ordinating army and air force operations at Burg el Arab (Montgomery, as soon as he took command, had brought the two headquarters close together); the need for mobility and the importance of speed of communications, largely by wireless, which required that signals and radar operators would become conversant with one another's procedure and practice (The Air Ministry 1950, 185). As a result of these attempts at co-ordination, the Ministry of Defence claimed, 'there could be little doubt that when the moment arrived for our ground forces to launch their counter-offensive, the experience and technical efficiency of the mobile RDF units would be adequate to meet all calls upon them' (The Air Ministry 1950, 189).

Montgomery's massive counter-attack of 23 October 1942 at El Alamein led to the breakout in early November, which involved the 5 mobile radar units that were already under Western Desert Command and were battle-hardened – 220 MRU, Numbers 510, 515, 522 and 526 COL, plus 5 MRUs, three mobile COL units for fighter control and two Type 8 Ground Controlled Interception (GCI) units specializing in night-fighter control (The Air Ministry 1950, 191). This was, of course, as the Air Ministry later commented, 'a ridiculously small number viewed by home standards but to the Western Desert Air Force it was a luxury' (1950, 191).

In addition, however, there were the Type 6 stations with their Light Warning Sets, essential to the defence of the landing grounds in a fast-moving desert war of the kind envisaged. It is possible that as many as ten 600 Units, each with the crew and kit carried in a three-ton Crossley waggon, were deployed in the advance from El Alamein, though I have seen concrete evidence for the use of only seven – Units 602, 606, 607, 608, 609, 610 and 629.[8] However, there were

> occasions when early warning by RDF equipment might be required before it was possible to reach an Advanced Landing Ground by motor transport. In keeping with the policy of manning such Advanced Landing Grounds by personnel and equipment flown in by air, two LWS and crew were prepared, suitable for air-lift in either Bombay or Hudson aircraft (The Air Ministry 1950, 190–91).

On 18 December, for example, one of the Type 6 stations was flown into the Marble Arch landing ground (Fig. 8) in the vicinity of Fred's 606, which was being delayed in its progress along the coast by landmines. The airborne unit's Bofors gunners were killed in an explosion soon after landing, and the radar operators had difficulty in getting clear of the field and escaping to safety (*War's Nomads,* 155; The Air Ministry 1950, 192).

The basic radar strategy after the breakout from El Alamein was to obtain early identification of the enemy from the Light Warning Sets belonging to radar units that could take advantage of rapid military gains, and use them to protect the advanced landing grounds; and then to bring in the RAF fighter-bombers using mobile COL stations with longer-range equipment. As the ground forces advanced westwards, some mobile radar units (not the Type 6s) would peel off the line of attack, and extend the defensive radar cover along the North African coast facing the Axis in Greece and Italy (The Air Ministry 1950, 191 and 297) (Fig. 6).

A similar strategy to that for radar was followed by the Desert Air Force, with RAF 211 Group combining with the Eighth Army in its attack on Tripoli (and later Tunisia), using Kittyhawk fighter-bombers (The Air Ministry 1950) (Fig. 9). At the same time 212 Group, with older Hurricanes – replaced by Spitfires only in New Year 1943 – were re-deployed after Christmas 1942 as a prelude to the Italian campaign which was being planned as the Western Desert War wound down (Jefford 2001). For example, some squadrons, such as 213, took up Mediterranean coastal duties, including convoy patrols, before falling back on Egypt in 1943.[9]

The experience of Unit 606 was unusual in that, after the fall of Tripoli, it proceeded to Tunisia with 211 Group and the Kittyhawks type III, as did Unit 609 – and Unit 629, which was held in reserve to assist the New Zealanders as they advanced north of Mareth[10] (The Air Ministry 1950, 295). This extended tour of duty in February and March 1943 adds greatly to the value of Fred's record. During this last phase of the war, 606 continued to work closely with the RAF squadrons of Kittyhawks – 260, 112, 250 and 450 (now 239 Wing), plus the Spitfire squadrons, 145, 601 and 92, and Hurricane squadron 73 (244 Wing), which were needed for the intense battles against Rommel around Mareth (Jefford 2001) (Fig. 9). In contrast, the ORBs for AMES Units 608 and 610 show that they were back in Egypt by February and March 1943 respectively.

One of the outstanding features of Fred's Type 6 unit was its smallness and lack of commissioned officers. The normal establishment was 13 men, with two non-commissioned officers (NCOs) – Unit 606 had a changing complement of 8 or 9 airmen, plus a corporal and a sergeant. In addition to 6 radar operators, there were usually 2 wireless operators to report to the Wing or Group filter room, which would direct air operations against the enemy. When the station was operational, the operators usually worked shifts throughout the 24 hours, though the work period was often reduced to daylight hours. The remainder of the crew were radar and wireless mechanics, a motor mechanic and a cook. We know from his RAF record that Fred was a radar operator, and the text reveals the names of the cooks, technicians, handymen and photographer, but the remainder of the crew who are named, are perhaps deliberately not associated with specific military tasks.

Fred's 'Black Book' refers to eating 'all meals in the gharry – one half is operations room, one half common room' (entry 8 or 9 September 1942), while his memoir explains that 'the three-ton Crossley...served as our operational room' (this book 106). Likewise, the evidence of Unit 610's ORB for 13 November 1942 observes that 'due to excessive heat in lorry from apparatus when operational attempted to improvise fans from windscreen wiper motors'.[11] AMES 675, admittedly working in Algeria as part of *Operation Torch*, noted similar circumstances on 27 November 1942: 'the equipment was installed in the front of the three ton lorry provided, and an Operations room and a Workshop was constructed in the rear'.[12] In all these cases for which we have evidence it seems that the intention was to cut out the hour nominally spent assembling the station in a tent – an adaptation perhaps made in North Africa to accommodate the fast-moving nature of desert warfare.[13]

The aerial for picking up the signals of incoming aircraft was power rotated, and Unit 606 carried two petrol-operated generators for this purpose, which was standard issue. Key elements in the station itself were the control panel or screen on which aircraft could be detected, and a plotting board, which would show the relative position of enemy aircraft over time in two dimensions. This information would be reported to 239 Wing or 211 Group filter rooms, which would activate the response. Using its radio beam, the Type 6 unit could detect aircraft up to a distance of 50 miles with a limited height-finding capability up to about 5000 feet. Information about planes at higher altitudes was (theoretically) provided by fixed stations with masts (The Air Ministry 1950).

The most extraordinary aspect of 'Erk in the Desert' is the dedicated, relentless way in which the crew of Unit 606 participated in the chase of Rommel across the Western Desert – often with only the haziest idea of what was likely to happen next. Although the unit had no commissioned officer (except Sqn Ldr M. H. Young, who relinquished his command of 213 Squadron to lead Units 606 and 607 on the ground for the first two weeks after the breakout from El Alamein),[14] their endeavours were so committed to the military action that there were apparently no disciplinary problems of any seriousness.

As the Air Ministry later reported, 'with only a Senior NCO in charge, these small stations had to fend mostly for themselves' (1950, 290). Fred himself comments at the end of his memoir that it was remarkable that Unit 606's crew got on so well for more than 6 months, essentially on their own, though they were, of course, in constant radio contact with 211 Group or 239 Wing. Unit 606 was a vital if small cog in the military machine, linking ground-to-air-forces and defending the various squadrons' landing grounds, in the last and victorious phase of the Western Desert campaign in Egypt and Libya, and in the defeat of the German forces in Tunisia.

Notes

1. Fred's major books are listed by date of publication in Appendix 1.
2. AIR 27 1316, The National Archives, Public Record Office (TNA, PRO).
3. AIR 27 1537, TNA, PRO.
4. Farewell of Sqn Ldr Young.
5. AIR 29 183, TNA, PRO.
6. AIR 29 183, TNA, PRO.
7. A third secret aspect of the Western Desert campaign should be mentioned, namely the operations of the British Long Range Desert Group, which carried out guerrilla operations behind the German lines (Goudie, *Wheels Across the Desert: Exploration of the Libyan Desert by motorcar, 1916–1942*, 2008).
8. Fred was in 606, and they were with 607 at Alam El Osmaili. We have ORBs for 608 and 610, and 608's ORB mentions 602, 607 and 609: 608 ORB, AIR 29 183, TNA, PRO. Unit 620 is mentioned only in Air Ministry, 1950, 295.
9. AIR 27 1316, TNA, PRO.
10. 239 Wing ORB 22 and 26 March, 1943, AIR 25/849, TNA, PRO.
11. AIR 29 183, TNA, PRO.
12. AIR 29 183, TNA, PRO.
13. These field-accounts of going operational in the lorry are consistent with one another, but at variance with the accounts and photographs preserved in the RAF Radar Museum at Neatishead, themselves corroborated by Ministry of Defence's 1950 volume *Radar in Raid Reporting*. The latter volume notes that Light Warning Sets were 'capable of erection in under one hour, housed in

a tent on a collapsible metal framework' (1950, 190). According to official sources, prior to going operational the Light Warning Set would be removed from the lorry to a tent, and the aerial removed from the roof of the lorry. Using the strength of the crew, the aerial system, consisting of two Yagi arrays, one mounted over the other, would be lifted on top of the tent. It seems likely that under the pressure to go operational in less than an hour in the Western Desert, not only was the radar equipment operated from inside the lorry, but the aerial was probably operated mechanically from the lorry roof. (See also Air Ministry 1950, 297 arguing why the equipment used in the tent could be transferred to 'a lorry to increase its mobility', though speed of going operational is not mentioned.)

14 ORB 213 Squadron, AIR 27 1316, TNA, PRO.

References

Commire, Anne (ed.) (1974) *Something About the Author: Facts and Pictures about Contemporary Authors and Illustrators of Books for Young People*, Vol. 6. Detroit, Michigan: Gale Research Book Tower.

Goudie, Andrew (2008) *Wheels Across the Desert: Exploration of the Libyan Desert by Motorcar, 1916–1942*. London: Silphium Books.

Grice, Frederick (1943) 'Were Your Knees Brown?', unpublished typescript.

Gumbridge, G. Q. (1968) *A Short History of No 213 Squadron*. 213squadronassociation.homestead.com/50anivbookletpages.html

Hastings, Max (2012) *All Hell Let Loose: The World at War, 1939–1945*. London: Harper Press.

Jefford, C. G. (2001 sec. ed.) *RAF Squadrons: A Comprehensive Record of the Movement and Equipment of all RAF Squadrons and their Antecedents since 1912*. Shrewsbury: Airlife Publishing.

Judge, J. W. B. (2009) *Airfield Creation for the Western Desert Campaign*. www.laetusinpraesens.org/guests/jwbj/jwb1.htm

Smith, Michael (2011) *The Secrets of Station X: How the Bletchley Park Codebreakers Helped Win the War*. London: Biteback Publishing.

The Air Ministry (1950) *Radar in Raid Reporting*. London (Confidential).

The Air Ministry (1952) *Fighter Control and Interception*. London (Confidential).

Winston Special Convoys in WW2 – 1942 Sailings. www.naval-history.net/xAH-WSConvoys05–1942A.htm

Part 1

On Draft

Chapter 1

Embarkation

Saturday 25 April 1942

The last formalities at Wing HQ were completed. We were paid – a month in advance – notified about promotions, equipped with the last missing items of our home kit, 'cleared' and then dispatched to the Embarkation Personnel Centre at West Kirby (Fig. 1).

Being the first of the draft to arrive, we had time to look around and inspect the camp. What infinite dreariness! In the middle of a flat featureless landscape, a little township of gaunt dusty barrack rooms, separated from each other by dried cracked earth and dusty barrack squares. Our hut was coal-tarred on the outside – every inch of wall, gable and roof, so that it looked black as a funeral. The black tar had spilt and splashed over onto the green grass around the hut, and even clung to the door handles and left them sticky. At each end of the hut stood a broken, rusted stove, battered, empty, and down each side a row of scratched and marked double-decker beds, looking more like the furniture of a stable or byre than of a human home. Each bed had three square greasy little 'biscuits' (as we called the sections of mattress), four blankets, out of which the dust flew in clouds, as they were shaken, and one incredibly filthy pillow. No civilized man can imagine the filthiness of those pillows. They were layered over with grease – black – the blackness had begun to shine, as though someone had polished floors with them. At night-time, we had to spread a pullover or vest or spare cloth over them to keep them from contact with our heads.

So much for this cold sordid barn with its whitewashed walls peeling off, and its dangling lines of bulb-less electric fuse wires. Nothing could have been more cheerless. But the ablutions surpassed it in dirt. There were a score of handbasins, but not one had a plug. Apparently the plugs had vanished long ago, and the men had made a practice of stopping up the holes with paper. Bits of sodden newspaper clung to the sides of the basins; more lay on the floor; more had worked its way down the pipes, and had blocked the drains so that the dirty water stood smelling and stagnant in the gutter. More paper, torn in patches of all sizes, littered the lavatory floors, or was trampled into the pools of water and urine. And more urine stood and stank in the gutter of the urinal.

It was a repulsive place. One had always to fight against a shock of nausea at the first sight and smell. Yet, as more and more of the draft arrived, spirits rose. By supper time the hut was full of a noisy crowd arguing backwards and forwards about everything. By bedtime the talk had become a babel of complaint, jollity, and scurrility.

We were the perfect breeding ground for rumours. Not one of us knew where we were bound, what chances there were of being exempted from the draft, when we were to be kitted, how many days we would spend at the embarkation centre, and what we should have to do here. Anyone who had any experience of embarkation, anyone who had been on a draft before, anyone who had or claimed to have the least shred of inside information – the minutest suggestion of 'gen' – was listened to eagerly.

'You'll get another leave. Of course you will! We'll be waiting about here for bloody weeks yet, man. You see, they'll send us home again.' said one man, and our hopes soared. But five minutes later another could be heard discoursing to a knot of eager listeners,
'Christ, no! You'll get no bloody leave! One of these nights, you'll be confined to camp, and before morning you'll be off, and nobody'll know where.'

So we went from hope to despair, from anxious foreboding to almost pleasant anticipation. I remember listening to one young chap at tea, saying;

'I've just had a letter from one of my pals, and believe me, it's bloody terrible. He says you spend every damned day spewing here and spewing there, and running from the bucket to the side of the ship. Not for me! Not for me! You see, tomorrow I'll be out of this bloody racket.'

He made me laugh, as we all laughed, to hide my concern (I'm of a timorous nature). But half an hour later, a corporal was holding forth and I caught him saying,

'I've just met those fellows that are back from overseas – and England – they spit on it! This bloody place, they say. Let them get back to Palestine. One of them says he'll do all his 21 years there – if they'll let him go back once he has seen his folks.'

And so we see-sawed in our opinions. We were all the more ready to catch at straws because we were cut off from reliable information – and left idle. We paraded at 8.45 every morning – to troop back into the huts, to wait. Once we were called out and told to prepare for an FFI (Free from Infection) inspection. We stripped to the waist and stood in a long line along one side of the barrack room. As the doctor passed we dropped slacks and raised arms. He went past like a whirlwind. Almost 40 men were inspected in 30 seconds.

Monday 27 April 1942

For lack of anything better to do, I'll describe the scene in this hut this afternoon. We were supposed to parade at 1.45 pm after dinner, but no NCO has called us out, and we have drifted into our own little activities. Half a dozen are asleep, lying on their backs in the bunks. I can see their chests rising – very little and soundlessly – as they lie. They look peaceful against the background of flapping window curtains. Four or five others are writing letters – and the rest are split into two card parties. In the corner in front of me eight are playing on the bottom deck of a bunk – all bent inwards to the cards, and talking fairly quietly. There are three noises – the intermittent wooshing of the wind, buffeting the corner of the room; the voices of the men – 'Twist me one of them' – 'I'm happy' – 'You wouldn't think it was bloody possible, would you?' – 'Bust' – 'Jesus wept!' – and the clinking of the money as the pennies and small silver are thrown into the kitty. Every now and then someone will walk in and throw a loud remark among the players. 'You aren't bloody players! They've got four pound in the kitty next door!'

But he provokes few answers, and the busy half-silence descends again. Then someone calls out loudly 'On Parade'. A few, taken in by the joker, roll out of bed, or look up from their cards, or put down their letters. But the joke has been played so often, he is like the boy who cried 'Wolf!' No one heeds him now.

So the afternoon wears on and on. The sun moves perceptibly round. Soon another day of 'bugger-all', as the men call it, will be finished.

Fear

Some men are not easily frightened.
You should see the good spirits of all these fellows
Leaving their wives and children, perhaps for ever
To run the gauntlets of submarines, sharks, drowning and
God knows what.
But, as for me, I'm a perfect coward.
I'm damned if I can face all these things with equanimity.
All my days are apprehensive,
And I want nothing more than to play with my child in
the wood,
And to read to my wife out of some rich book in the
peaceful evenings
– And let who will have the power and the glory.

Snatches of conversation:

'Poor tack, isn't it?'
'It's worse on the boat, they say.'
'Hell!'
'Yes – they give you a couple of slices of bread and you have to catch your own fish.'

Procedure when being posted overseas

1. Embarkation leave
2. Back to Wing – cleared – paid – inoculated – medically examined – given pay & service book
3. Sent to PDC (Personnel Dispatch Centre)
4. FFI and dental inspection
5. Hand in certain clothing – be issued with overseas kit
6. Waste most of day in barrack huts – occasionally doing fatigues or PT
7. Lectures – medical, on tropical diseases, and general, on how to behave on draft
8. Code number issued and put on kit bags
9. Inspection of kit bags by CO
10. Inspection in full kit and webbing, gas clothing
11. Confined to camp
12. Night journey in train
13. Embarkation

Monday 4 May

Went to Chester, which I liked very much (Fig. 1). Mean to write account of afternoon for Gwen.

Language

Synge has a most valuable preface to the *Playboy of the Western World* on language. What a contrast between the language of the Irish peasantry

and the men here. A writer ought to be realistic above everything and true to what he hears. Here is a perfectly uncensored selection of conversation from this barrack room:
'What the bloody hell's that there?'
'You'll fucking get it, I know.'
'Fuck me! One two three four five six.'
'Where the bloody hell is that bastard tenner?'
'Oh fucking hell! It's in the fucking cards.'
'A lot of fucking coppers and no bloody silver!'
'Shove it up your fucking arse. Fuck me, look at this prick here.'

'Coming to the boxing match?'
'Oh, no! There's only one man I know who's a good boxer.'
'Who's that?'
'The undertaker!'

When I come home

On that great day, being home again at last,
I'll find you sitting, dearest, in your chair,
In that still corner where the sunbeams cast
Slanting magnificence across the air,
And on your rounded cheek and smooth brushed hair,
Then shall I see
Your neat hands turning easily
The pages of some book laid on your knee.
And then, being come again to that sweet place,
Seeing again the beauty of your face,
I'll take that big red book where you and I
Have written all the lovely history
Of our most dear companionship, and there
Put down this prayer:
'Tonight let nothing in this world take hurt
In all the land, let no child wake with fright

>   To hear its parents quarrelling in the night;
>   Let no bird mourn,
>   Its blue eggs broken, its nest all torn;
>   No tempest smash
>   The good boughs of the oak or of the ash.
>   In all the families
>   Of flowers and birds and beasts and men and trees,
>   Be armistice,
>   Because the feast day of my life has come
>   And – I am home.'

Scene: The barrack room of a Personnel Dispatch Centre: almost all in bed. One light still shining. Coffey comes in, talkative with beer. He begins to make his bed noisily.

'I'm telling ye. There's only one man going to win this war, and that's Joe Stalin. Up with the USSR.'
'Oh man, whisht.'
'I'm telling ye. It's the only damned country left that's any good. Communism! That's what we want in this country.'
'And who's going to bring it here?'
'Aye – is McGovern and Jimmy Maxton[1] – that lot?'
'Wherefore not?'
'McGovern's a prick!'
'I'm telling ye. They've got their ideals, them men.'
'Och man, pipe doon. Once we get home we'll be that pleased, we'll stand anything after this bloody thing is over.'
'It doesnae matter. I'm telling ye.'
'For God's sake, shut up and let a fellow get to sleep.'
'Shut up! Put a sock in it!'

(Short silence; uneasy rollings and creakings of the frame of the double-decker)

'I'm telling ye. It's the working man that'll have to win this war.'

'We all agree – but for Christ's sake give it a rest for tonight.'
'I'll shut him up.'

(Someone leaps out of bed and puts out the light)
(Darkness, and another silence…)

'Up wi Joe Stalin! I'm telling ye. The USSR is the only…)
'Shut him up, somebody. Hit him with a boot!'

(Silence at last. A few minutes' pause, then heavy breathing becomes a snore. We all fall asleep.)

All this interminable waiting! We wait in long queues for breakfast, dinner and tea: we wait in the NAAFI for tea and the YMCA for chocolate; at the post office for mail; on the stations for trains; in the canteens at evening; on parades to be inspected; at the ice cream van for blocks. Everywhere we wait, wait, wait.

Someone has scribbled on the wall of the dining hall these pathetic words, 'Died waiting'.

Continuing

We were ordered to parade at 8 pm for supper, then at 8.30 pm for final roll call. An interminable wait, all strapped, laden and weary with our equipment – and all for little purpose. Then a move. We marched with kit bags to a big drill shed, where we again lined up and waited. While we waited officers sauntered up and down the ranks – tantalizing, neat, free, elegant, leisured, unconcerned – blandly ignorant of our wretched frame of mind and distressed bodies. The men could barely stand it. Restless, they barked back at an insolent NCO – imitated his voice – booed, and began to sing over and over again, 'Why are we waiting? Oh why are we waiting?'

Why indeed – but to wait is second nature now to us. We wait all day, for so little, so pitifully little a blessing. By and by, when more senseless rigmarole had been gone through and we were waiting again,

one cheeky voice broke out with,
'When this wretched war is over
O how happy I shall be
When…..
No more soldiering for me,
No more church parades on Sunday.'

His song was loudly applauded. But, oh my God the weariness!

And so it went on all the time. We waited again at the station, until the light had gone out of the sky, until a train arrived, departed and arrived again – and the Service Police were walking around with hurricane lamps, and we were sitting on the ground and in the gutters for weariness.

But *en train, enfin*![2] A long journey with snatches of sleep – waking to hear the train racing hard and metallic; then to realize it had stopped somewhere; then to hear it chuffing slowly – finally to find it gliding slowly, with a leisurely slipping movement through between warehouses and cranes – an unfamiliar landscape.

We had reached the port (Fig. 1).[3]

The troopship

Here are a few notes about the troopship written in the fine new fountain pen I have managed to buy for myself at the barber's. I have never lived in conditions so primitive as those that exist on a troopship. In a space as big as a small ballroom, 16 yards by 16, about 250 men live, eat, sleep, work and store 250 kitbags, 250 rucksacks, 250 water containers, 250 gas masks. When we are seated at table, with our apparatus neatly stacked to right and left, the effect is admirable. But set these 250 men in motion, some finding towels, some looking for a stray overcoat, some washing up, sweeping up, changing shoes – and the effect is indescribable – hell is let loose. In these poorly ventilated quarters the heat is serious when 250 men are in motion. And the obstacles in the way of washing, finding kit, eating and cleaning up are so great that a day is spent on those simple activities which at home are over in a few minutes.

But do you know, I've just had a beer. I was typing for Pilot Officer or Flying Officer Drummond – God bless him – and he bought me my first ship's beer – and I think it has gone to my head. I'll go on with this later.

What a miserable send-off we had from our native land! As we paraded in the vast drilling sheds of our last land station, dejected with long waiting and the certainty of leaving home perhaps for good, no officer or NCO spoke a kind or encouraging word to us. Our last homeland meal was an unsavoury dish of stew and thick cocoa, eaten in a cookhouse evil and repellent with its odours of unemptied garbage tins; and when we mildly complained, we were told by a cock bantam of a flight sergeant to eat it, or leave it and get out. And when, later, we were standing in the sheds, the officers took no more notice of us than if we had been cattle. It would have been a generous gesture if one of them had said to us, 'Now we know that you are about to undergo great hardship and discomfort. But we who are left alone at home with our wives and children and acquaintances and comforts, we think highly of you and beg you to endure all inconveniences patiently. Good fortune go with you.'

But instead, our only valedictions were the neutral chirping of the sparrows among the high rafters of the sheds and the bullying voices of the NCOs. At this never-to-be-forgotten embarkation centre, we were housed like criminals, fed like criminals, detained like criminals and sent off like criminals.

On the boat we were fortunately in the care of a competent and kindly officer – a Scot with a broad black-jowled face, a bald head and an extremely energetic disposition; but his friendliness could do little to mitigate the wretchedness of our living conditions. I have mentioned conditions on the mess deck during the day. The evenings were just as chaotic. After we had slung our hammocks or laid out our mattresses, there was scarcely an inch of space left; and at times the atmosphere was suffocating. I must say that when we had all settled to bed, and the lights had gone out, the atmosphere grew remarkably clear and cool, and we slept well. And a hammock is certainly a delightful bed.

It is most easy to sling and to pack, and the slight swinging movement is more soothing than otherwise. Yet, day or night, the satisfaction of every little need, the finding of a towel, or cigarette or handkerchief, involved so complicated a train of actions such as removing baggage, replacing or restacking the disturbed pile of rucksacks and haversacks – that it was weary and burdensome.

And the lavatories and ablutions! The lavatories were open pens, wide and deep enough to contain a lavatory pan only. We sat in rows and conversed together along the row. And the only available washing water was cold sea water. You picked up one of the loose bowls lying about, filled it from the showers, and emptied it into your particular bowl. The usual procedure, and the most economical, was to clean the teeth first, then wash in the same water, then use it a third time for shaving. And of course, the best of shaving soap and toilet soap only was of any use in the salty water.

We were driven to various shifts and subterfuges to keep clean. I volunteered to be batman to two padres. I was up at 6.30 in the mornings to take their cup of tea, clean their shoes, polish their buttons – and to seize a wash in soft water in an adjoining room. After breakfast, I was there again to tidy up the cabin – and to seize if possible another wash and clean my teeth. Meniality and guttersnipe cunning! But it was urgent to seize privacy wherever it could be seized, and to keep clean at all cost.

I ought to add that this was written at the end of the second day on the *Highland Monarch* – before we had set sail.

A dream

During my first night on board ship, I had a most wonderful dream. I dreamt that I was much older, a middle-aged man, driving a horse and trap home. It was peacetime, and the evening was lovely with the spring. There were three children with me, all mine – wilful, with exuberant spirits, and running disobediently into the bushes and through the orchards. I did not mind their wilfulness, but was content to drive slowly and let them take their pleasure in the woods. It was wonderful, quietly glorying in the good spirits of my three children. Gwen I did not see, but her presence was in my dream. I knew she was somewhere near, and pleased. It was so happy a dream that I woke with a feeling of quiet delight and contentment that has lasted all day.

Last night, all the night long, I was anguished with homesickness. That's what you get for reading *Cymbeline* – the story of parted lovers. All night long I was maddened by the thought of Gwen, far away and with others. I have never felt jealousy so profoundly.

Getting a newspaper on board ship

While we were in port, we sat on the open decks, like prisoners calling from our prison to the dockers who walked backwards and forwards along the quay. We let down long ropes from the deck and the kind-hearted dockers tied their newspapers to the end of the lines. We pulled them up and greedily read the news. It was amusing to see sailors and airmen alike dangling their long cables and appealing for anything to read.

I write this in the forward lounge, a beautifully furnished and panelled room, where scores of us come to get away from the cold windy decks, to read, write, play cards and listen to the piano-playing.

> When many years after this,
> I sit at home, looking fondly through my books,
> Watching my wife, prettily busy, as I know she will be,

And telling my children how I came by this volume,
How I chanced to write that and that passage,
And pausing to read them a line here and there,
Or tell them when first I thrilled to some splendid stanza,
Then I will recall this time,
How I lay in my hammock in the hot between decks,
Listening to the hearty bawdiness of my mess mates,
How I knelt in a cabin cleaning a padre's boots,
Sat lonely on a cold deck among the bored card-playing sergeants
Or struggled to souse my dirty face in cold sea water
All this I will recall, but only as a saint
Who, having reached his paradise at last,
Remembers his purgatory.

This war has made me nothing but a dreamer!

There are at least 3 Wellfield[4] people on the boat –
1 Dennis Wood – a Wingate Co-op boy and a relation of Bob Poole's
2 Forster or Foster – a tallish slim boy, whom I used to teach in the sixth form – now a sergeant observer
3 Me

The whirligig of time brings in its revenge. I'm thankful I was kind to Foster (or Forster).

Underway

Quite without warning, today we left the dock.[5] The men were lying sunning themselves on the decks, or card playing, or dozing, when three tugs came alongside and tied up to us. Immediately there was a great stir; sleepers woke, players packed in their cards and made for the side. But leaving port is always a slow and unspectacular affair. Very slowly we moved, and frequently we stopped. Out of tedium at watching the snail-slow operations most of the men went back to their snoozing or playing. And so – most unceremoniously, we left dock.

Five women on a steamer at a quayside waved us goodbye, and some of the men answered them with silent gestures. But there was no cheering, no rousing demonstration at our departure. Two or three final letters were flung overboard at the last moment; one man leaned over and slapped his hand on the last piece of English ground he could reach. But as only the sparrows gave us goodbye at our last land station, so now the only sounds that bid us farewell from England were the hoarse, sharp clamourings of the gulls, and the cheerless clanking of a bell buoy out in the open channel. Clank – clank – clank – the funeral knell of many great friendships, companionships and affections. Clank. Clank. Clank them dead, for many a promise made in this country will be broken in the next land; many a woman that prays to be remembered will fade from remembrance from this day on; many a good man and boy will not come back from this voyage – or if he does, never the same fellow.

I can barely describe how I feel. I dare not think too deeply of Gwen, left at home alone and with a baby. I dare not contemplate squarely the long, long loneliness before me. For I shall have no friend or companion like Gwen – so in some way I seem to have anaesthetized myself. Grief would be too serious to entertain. I dismiss it – I leave it to invade me when I am asleep, and haunt my dreaming. What else can I do?

Listening at night to foul and ulcerous talk in the mess, I shudder at the wretchedness I have been brought to. At times, looking at my dirty nails and hearing myself talk, I wonder what Gwen would think if she were to come upon me. But I am inconstant. Clean, looking over the calm water, talking to a pleasant-mannered friend, I thrill to the adventures that are in front of me, and look with anticipatory pride at the successful conclusion of them all.

I am reading about Innogen hurrying to Milford Haven to see a husband she did not expect so soon home – I find myself sailing past it – an attractive rocky islanded coastline (Fig. 1).

Little white seagull with the black back,
Dipping in the glass green valleys of the water,
Wheeling where the boat's prow throws
Its gorgeous ravelled lacery to right and to left.
Fly, little seagull, fly as quick as my thoughts,
Fly to the little house where my darling is.
And tell her by night and day,
Asleep or awake, in blue weather or grey,
Beats my heart always to the pulse of hers
And my thoughts always return to her,
Tender little pigeons of thoughts that home always
To where she is.

Class distinctions

Class is far too clearly distinguished from class on board a troopship. The officers live in great comfort and want for nothing. Flight sergeants, sergeants, too, are extremely well fed and cabined. Their meals are luxurious and daintily served, and they have many privileges such as use of the library and special lounges. Even corporals are kept separate from the ACs. The smallness of the distinction between a sergeant and an AC does not warrant so drastic a difference in treatment. I wonder how much better dealt with by their senior NCOs of the Red Army are their privates. Surely the differences there are not so wide.

Two strong impressions of today remain in my memory. Rising early this morning, and running up on to the cool deck, I was momentarily charmed by the sight of a new coastline.[6] Along the grey of the water lay a line of darker grey, the tumbled and uneven line of the Welsh coast: and above it, like a golden bird in a bush, the sun. My second is of the wind pure and pouring like water on to the upper decks, where I strode backwards and forwards for an hour or more. We had to lean into the wind and turn our faces away from it. But it was masterful and invigorating. That springing up on the toes, striding up and down in the wind was tonic.

Spirits are now improving on the boat. I suppose we are adjusting ourselves to the conditions. I must admit I like the boat better, and get up each morning fresh and eager to see where the new day has brought us. For the last five nights I have dreamt of Gwen.

Courtship

Before I met Gwen I had often gone walking with another girl, Emily.* She was the daughter of a high-living, junketing publican, and a quiet, industrious, stern mother. She was unhappy at home, and had left to become a nurse. In disposition she was all kindness, but her kindness was not the spontaneous giving of a heart that could give and take with equal grace. Emily was a hurt personality. The vulgarity of her home and an unfortunate love affair had brought her to hate herself. She looked upon herself as a sinner, and expiated her sins by giving her life to nursing other hurt people, and by a martyred self-sacrificing charity.

Poor Emily! I understood her very well, and helped her to overcome her self-contempt. Having a thread of that colour in the cloth of my own temperament, I sympathized with her. I took her home on occasions, and she became a great favourite with mother; and such was my loneliness that, in spite of the disasters which I could foresee from the mating of neurosis and neurosis, I, at times, contemplated asking Emily to marry me.

But meeting Gwen put an end to my faltering. Gwen was afraid of me, and found it difficult to behave spontaneously. She was stiff, shy and unconfident. I, on my part, was rude to her and deliberately hurt her. Yet within a few weeks of our first evening, I knew that I should have to tell Emily that I could not now marry her. What anxiety I went through before I brought myself to perform that unpleasant act! How important I considered myself – the tragic man on the horns of this dreadful dilemma! With what care and seriousness I penned that letter to Emily, and another to John and Gertrude,[7] and with what

---
* A pseudonym.

pompousness did I announce my decision to Mr and Mrs Danby! Oh dear – I was certainly consumed with my own self-importance and imagined that all this epistle-writing – which John, Gertrude and Emily will laugh at, now that I remind them of it – was indispensible. So earnestly bent was I on doing nothing underhand – on being heroic, above board and candid. What a prig!

Those letters, declaring so uneloquently that I had fallen in love with Gwen and meant to marry her, and that there would be no swerving – were gross misrepresentations of my mood. My feelings towards Gwen in those early weeks and months of our courtship were far more complex. I found her beautiful. And she was always sweet to kiss and to caress. The spring was in her cheeks, the flowers in her complexion, the May morning in her breath, and she looked so neat and charming-o! She was independent and adventurous. But across her lay the shadow of a sadness that made her hesitant and quiet. Accustomed as I had grown to the vivacity of the Danbys and the Currys,[8] I found her stillness disconcerting. A coldness, a lack of enthusiasm, a want of positive mental energy – this estranged me. Charming, lovely, attractive as she was, the gay spark did not fly from her to me. Many things remained unspoken between us. The invisible barrier was there. I said 'I love you' – and looked across a distance at her. She said 'And I love you' – the sound came, as if it had been spoken far away – thin and weak.

Annoyed at this wretched lack of understanding, this cross-purpose wooing, I often grew moody and surly. Once when Gwen and I were alone in the kitchen at Ardenlee, a friend called Beryl*, paid a visit. Beryl was not an entertaining girl. I found her most undistinguished, and as the conversation went from triviality to triviality I grew more and more restless. At last, under pretence of wanting a drink, I went out and drove to Merrington where I spent a comfortless but at least solitary half-hour in the pub.

---

* A pseudonym.

That was a rude act, and both Beryl and Gwen were sensitive enough to realize how offensive my conduct was. But I could be no more than apologetic and explain to a distressed Gwen the motive for my rudeness.

On other occasions I was unreasonably surly and taciturn. In a fit of self-reproach for having behaved boorishly, I bought one day a driving licence for Gwen and offered to teach her to drive. But though in those days I was probably the best of teachers in the classroom, for Gwen I was the worst driving instructor in the world. I tried to be patient, but my vexation at her lack of confidence made me testy, and our driving lessons ended in a glum and tearful silence.

Scenes like those, in which I was forced by a wretched and tearful Gwen to confess my disappointment in her, and my poor opinion of this or that action of hers, occurred with distressing frequency. Over and over again she desired to break our agreement and see no more of me. I would remain silent, and I think there was a part of me that even liked these scenes – so contrary was my nature at that time. They were tragic, dramatic: to blame Gwen and to hear her blaming herself for this or that inanity was to move the blame for this unsuccessful union from my own shoulders – yet, sullen and unhappy though I was, I could not bear to let Gwen go. In the depth of the quarrel, some small voice made me remember that only an act of positive love would do. Recriminations, partings – these would not do. Sympathise. Forgive. Be loving. Your silly, silly pride – your brains and intelligence! These gaudy silly defences around yourself – break them down and be kind. Then a great wave of tenderness would come over both of us. I would kiss her passionately, wet cheek to wet cheek, passionate lip to passionate lip. And we were reconciled.

Notes

1. Jimmy Maxton (1885-1946) Scottish socialist politician and leader of the Independent Labour Party. A proponent of Home Rule for Scotland.
2. Getting going, at last!
3. Avonmouth, outport for Bristol.
4. Wellfield, in Wingate, Co. Durham, where Fred's school was located.
5. The *Highland Monarch* (code number 62A) was joining Convoy WS (Winston Special) 19 which assembled off Oversay, Islay in the Inner Hebrides. The convoy, made up of two sections sailing mainly from Liverpool and Glasgow, often split into fast and slow groups, before making for Freetown, Sierra Leone and then going on to the Cape. At the Cape, Fred's section stopped in Cape Town, before sailing for the Suez Canal. Although shorter by far, it was not safe in 1942 to send British troops through the Strait of Gibraltar into the Mediterranean and from there join the North African theatre of war.
6. The *Highland Monarch* must have entered St George's Channel at this point in the narrative, with the Welsh coast visible to the east.
7. John and Gertrude Danby. John Danby had been at the Durham Johnston School with Fred as a schoolboy, and they were close friends. John eventually became Professor of English at University College, Bangor, in North Wales.
8. Luke Curry was a master at the A. J. Dawson School in Wingate, and a colleague of Fred's.

Chapter 2

Crossing the Line

Today has been bitterly, bitterly cold. A grey thin mist hangs over the dim coastlines, and a grey white combed sea goes slapping and slipping past the ship. The wind beats down blow after blow upon us like a fighter. Standing at our boat stations with the water swirling round our plimsolls, we feel wretchedly cold. Every face is whitened gooseflesh, and screwed up to resist the wind. Tonight I'll describe the scene down here on the mess deck.

I couldn't describe the mess deck. We were all at the concert – B Flight concert in the forward lounge. And very good it was, too. The lounge was crowded, and volunteers stepped up thick and fast. Some were painfully awkward. The sight of an ineffectual personality failing, in spite of all his efforts, to hold the attention of a crowd makes me feel nothing but commiseration. That poor little bald-headed toothless man who began to sing 'All the nice girls love a sailor' and got nothing but cold contempt for his pains! But most of our volunteers were talented. A sailor did an excellent piece of miming – a lady sewing on a button. We had a brazen-faced, brazen-minded comedian of the George Formby school. One of the nurses sang. There was general fun and games, and the evening went merrily.

The mess deck at 2 in the afternoon

I am sitting on my lifebelt with my back against a rack of kit-bags. On my right and laid out one by the other are eight mess tables, each with room enough for 16 men, although the floor area is about half that of the average cricket square.

Dinner is over, the washers-up have left their pots, pans and cloths on the end of each table, like a tributary offering to the God of Food, and have vanished. The more energetic of the feeders are on deck, sitting in the weak sunshine, walking up and down in the breeze, or playing housey-housey. The less energetic are still here below. Some are playing cards on the mess tables, some writing letters which they hope to post at the first port, and many asleep. On mattresses on the floor, on the floors they sleep – out of pure boredom – inert as the corky lifebelts that lie beside them.

X

I have grown to detest X – as I have never detested any man in my life. In appearance he is not objectionable – except for little eyes, muddy and protruding. No, it isn't his appearance I dislike. But every day affords more evidence of the meanness of his nature – a meanness disgusting in its greed and essential littleness. At first you would find him a pliable companion. Quite unassertive, he is in the habit of agreeing with whoever he happens to be conversing with. He will draw out your opinions and views, and lead you on to enlarge on them, seeming to agree all the while – in a simple-minded kind of way. But behind that facile acquiescence, he is looking out on you and on the world with his own peculiar eyes, the eyes of a malicious seagull, looking always for its own advantage. Rouse him, you will be appalled at the virulence of opinion that lies below his seeming acquiescence. It is when his comfort – for comfort is all his god – when his ease, wants, filling of his belly, pocket, leisure are threatened – that the hatred and odious anger in him shows. Once I was travelling in a train with him, when an old lady from our compartment left without closing the door – and through the open door came a little draught. I shall not forget the hatred in his face and the vulgar, abusive note in his voice when he spoke about that absent-minded old lady. Nor the malignity of every sentence in the quarrel which took place at the end of that journey.

I happened, by no contriving of my own, to spend a lot of time as X's only companion. I could watch him at meals, picking among the food, like a seagull picking among scraps, greedy but concerned to have only the good. I could see his little eyes turning like a seagull's from right to left, and left to right, watching how much others were getting, watching what was happening to the spare piece of butter left on the plate. I watched him manoeuvring to be out of sight when any unpleasant duty was to be performed – slying pieces of chocolate and sweets from his pockets, and never asking anyone to share. I once saw him volunteer to be a batman – to escape from other more onerous duties – and then curse at the work he had to do, when he found that his manoeuvre had not turned out to his advantage. How I grew to dislike every motion of those lips, those thick stubby fingers, those little seagull eyes.

Two more things about him. His interests never went beyond his creature comfort. Where he was going, would the food be good, would the climate be congenial, would there be little to do – those were all the thoughts that exercised his brain. Beyond that nothing. He never read – but dosed away his leisure in the sunshine – eyes closed, but ready to open, whenever there was anything to be seen. He had fallen into the annoying habit of saying 'Eh?' to every sentence spoken to him, although he had heard perfectly – and often when someone near him spoke, to a third person, not to him at all, apropos of nothing at all that was his concern, then would break in his harsh 'Eh? Eh?' – all ears he was to pick up any scrap of gossip. I noticed by the way that he never said 'I beg your pardon' or 'I'm sorry, I didn't catch you' – always 'Eh?' 'Eh?' I grew – and I wasn't the only one – to hate the sound of that Eh? Eh? Eh? Ah dislikeable X – never have I seen anyone less capable of a generous thought and a disinterested action than you! You hypocrite!

A few days ago, a young fellow here lost his wallet containing five pounds and ten shillings, and someone kind started a fund for him – threepence or fourpence each. Wasn't that a generous thought!

Diary of a day on board ship

- 6.30   Wakened, jumped out of hammock to wash and shave
- 7.00   Rolled up hammock, stowed it
- 7.10   Went on deck to eat an orange and smell the morning air
- 7.20   Took the padres their morning cup of tea, cleaned buttons, boots for them
- 7.45   Breakfast. After breakfast snatched 2 minutes for a smoke on deck, then returned to wash up
- 10.30 All ready for inspection. The Admiral and all his gang around to see the state of things
  (If I had not been mess orderly I'd have been at boat drill from 10.20 – 11.00)
- 11.00 Up on deck to walk up and down taking the air, noting disposition of convoy
- 11.50 Waited impatiently for dinner
- 12.00 Dinner arrived and was eaten with relish
- 12.30 Set about washing up again
- 13.30 All cleared away, set about making my notes, writing and reading – then dozed
- 15.00 Woke, roused myself, went to wash. Sea water only available – unsatisfactory. Then walked up and down deck again, talking or thinking or reading
- 17.30 Had tea and set about washing up for the last time. Ate orange I bought this afternoon
- 18.30 Washing up completed. Washed again. Went up on deck again to watch the sea, to take exercise and play darts
- 21.30 Down below to sling hammock
- 21.45 In bed, listened to the scurrilous conversations around me. Great noise and fooling
- 22.00 Lights out. Went to sleep

Thursday 14 May 1942

Entered Ship's Essay Competition yesterday. Weather – still not warm. Nothing at all to indicate where we are. Nothing at all – as cold as crossing to Isle of Man.[1]

Nostalgia

Washing-up was a long business, with hot water to fetch from far aft, along draughty corridors and down steep steps slippery with vomit, and sixteen mugs and thirty-two plates to wash and dry, and then the mess space to sweep up; and when it was over I lay down with my lifebelt under my head to rest for a few minutes. Up above on deck the weather was wet and harsh, and few had courage or inclination to stay on the cold, slippery decks. As soon as I had washed down the table, it was invaded by the housey-housey school. So I settled down to muse and listen to the school leader's fascinating incantation. When he had sent out his nark to canvass players, and was satisfied that the school was big enough, he began –
'All in? All paid and all weighed?'
'All in' called back his nark, with his fist full of coppers.
'All right then, lads! What are we having? Top line only? Top line it is then! Here we go – all in and eyes down for a top line!'

The deck became very quiet. All I could hear was the rattling of the wooden counters in the dirty bag, and the even-voiced incantation of the schoolmaster.
'Three and one, 31; four and seven, 47; Kelly's Eye, number 1; by itself, number 3; key of the door, 21; doctor's favourite, number 9; all the fours, 44; blind, 80; half a crown, 26, and another dip in the bag.... Off we go again – seven and six, 76; three and five, 35' until suddenly some one cried 'House!'

'House here!' came the reply from the high priest of the game, and still in his unnatural monotone, like a tribal witch doctor chanting out some ritual, 'House here! Eyes in everybody! Eyes in for a check.' Then the check was called, and the copper clattered on the table, then on went the voice again. 'Full house this time, boys? Pyramid? All in for a full house! All in, all paid, all weighed, off we go! First number – by itself, number 3; dinky doo, 22; four and one, 41; unlucky, 13.'

I lay on my back, listening desultorily, and sniffing the faint whiff of old vomit that came from the lifebelt under my head, growing hotter and hotter. As the game went on, the school grew bigger and bigger, and the air became hotter and heavier, and the sweat was glistening on the face of the housey-housey leader. Breaking the spell of his rhythmic chant, I jumped up and went above.

The well decks were uninhabitable. Although a weak sun was shining through the cloud in the west, the wind beat down on the hatchways with violence, the tarpaulins lifted and bellied and smacked back sharply with every gust. A heavy rain, mixed with the spray from the bows whirled round the corners and flung itself down in sharp showers. But, further up, the promenade deck was more sheltered. I strapped my lifebelt over my shoulders and began to pace up and down the slippery wooden floors.

It was a violent night. The ship pitched like a rocking horse; and as its bows fell smack in the water, the gorgeous ravelled spindrift was flung out and out. As the waves rose, their heads gleamed a pure pale jade, then crashed furiously into the whitest of whiteness, that spread, dillied and dallied for one moment, then dissolved its glimmering lacery into heavy leaden waves.

> The chidden billow seems to pelt the clouds
> The wind-shak'd surge, with high and monstrous mane,
> Seems to cast water on the burning bear
> And quench the guards of th'ever-fixed pole.
>
> (Shakespeare, *Othello* 2, i)

Through such a sea, I thought, Othello sailed to meet his Desdemona

– but we all, alas, were sailing away from home, away from our Desdemonas.

Nevertheless it was invigorating to walk the decks in such a sea – to feel the wind wrapping the trousers round the legs and blowing the feet pitter patter down the deck – and then to turn and force the way strenuously up against it. The rain sneaked under the roofing of the deck and splashed now and then in the face. But the air was pure with the purity of a million million acres of unpeopled water – and a joy to breathe. Up and down I went, enjoying the buffets of the wind until I was tired.

When my lifebelt was too wet, remembering that it was my only pillow, I looked around for shelter and went under an awning, well forward. There were a few others there, listening through the open windows to a concert in the lounge; and I could hear sounds of raucous laughter coming from inside. Some comedian was just finishing his act. I could not see, but I heard the ovation his bawdiness won him. And then another entertainer went up to the stage. What was it? A piano solo. A piano solo – the word was passed back from those nearest the window to us behind. The information had just reached me, when the pianist began to play the first few chords of *Wien! Wien! Nur du allein*.

Wien! Wien! – Oh God, why did he play that? As he played, my heart stood still. Like a subtle scent caught in the woods, transporting one back to a glorious boyhood minute, the music opened the floodgates of my memory and cast me back, back, back to the years before the war, to the opening of the year and the spring of our married life. I was coming downstairs, fresh after sleep and was pausing on the stairs to listen. Gwen was dusting. She had come now to the piano – Gwen, lovely as the morning itself, whose face was lovely as the moon as she bent over me while I was waking. She had come to the piano, stopped, and was playing the tune she so often played before breakfast in those cool mornings, *Wien! Wien! Nur du allein*.... Ah Gwen – so far away now!

When the music stopped, I did not care to walk any more. Down again into Hell's Kitchen to lie and grow cold-hearted and unfeeling, to stupefy myself with the foul atmosphere and the scurrilous talk – to forget.

The housey-housey game was over and nearly all the hammocks were slung. Before the war this deck had been a storage room for carcasses of Argentine beef. How little the change! All trussed up close to the roof in their hammocks, or lying stretched out inert on the floor – the men looked like more sides of beef. Probably considered less profitable. No profiteer could have looked less kindly after his sides of beef and shoulders of mutton than 'they' looked after us.

In this little place, no bigger than a village cricket square, and so low that the tall among us hit their head against the rafters –two hundred men slept, fed, played and were sick. Many of them were laid out now with not enough energy to sling a hammock. Prostrate on the floor, they lay and retched, while others stepped clumsily over and on them.

The heat was almost insufferable. It was so great that we could not bear a blanket to touch us, but lay and sweated uncovered in the hammocks. As the boat rolled the hammocks all swung over together, paused, shook, then swung back again violently; and as it pitched, a wave seemed to pass from the ankles to the calves, then up the back and into the head. But not even all these sickly motions could completely silence the men. The old familiar catcalls still rent the room.
'Put those bloody lights out, you!'
'Leave the buggers on!'
'Go and get stuffed, you stupid cunt!'

But there was less tumult than usual; and when the boat pitched badly, a noise that was half a groan, half a cry ran through the deck.

Misery, misery! As I settled in my hammock and began to read, two of the sick men crawled on their hands and knees and began to spew into the pail that stood at the end of the table, and which we used for washing up. Shockingly they retched, and I put my fingers in my ears and closed my eyes, impatient for the lights to go out, and for sleep to come. Ah *Wien! Wien!* Ah – so far away now – so far away.

What a wonderful bird – the guillemot! Weather most beautiful. On upper deck I read *No Man's Wit* by Rose Macaulay – a book about the aftermath of the Spanish Civil War. And the sea – a magnificent blue, true ultramarine, a true Reckitt's blue. An idle day – all reading, conversation and no thinking.

Weather muggy and warm, drizzling, wet and a heavy overcast sky. The corporals are all talking this morning of a shocking orgy by the officers in their lounge – caterwauling and yahooing, indescribable hooliganism and smashing of glasses, howling and struggling and singing of filthy songs. The adjutant very drunk and abusive to the orderly sergeant. Our opinion of the officers sinks low after beer-house scenes like this. But romanticism – no glorifying of the common folk and vilipending of the upper classes. Last night our mess deck all uproarious for hours with the filthiest of filthy talk – the lowest depths of licentious abuse. *Canaille!*[2] – the people of both orders who wallow in dirt like this.
– *Canaille!*
– And to think of the fine, sensible fellows, commissioned and non-commissioned, who could rule a ship with sobriety and intelligence and good humour.

Flying fish, porpoises seen. And I had a marvellous view just half an hour ago of two dolphins – sharp fins, backs brown as horses, up in an upward dive and then down again under the water.

Slept on deck last night and this poem's the result. Washing day yesterday – less room than ever in the Inferno with the lines of washing.

Before Sleep
Softly the ship steals into the arms of the night,
And softly, softly close the doors of the dark;
The doors of the dark all studded with gems of stars;
Softly swings the moon in her silver hammock.

Crocus and campion, one big star in the south,
Stirs in the paradisal draughts of the night,
Glittering down on the heads of the sleepers here.

And now come the little stars, crowding together,
The inquisitive eyebright stars, listening together,
Listening down through the silent skies towards me.

O open the jewel-crusted doors of the dark!
Turn, oaken portals, turn on your azure hinges!
And let your dreams, little stars, come down to me now,
Visions to smooth the brow of my lonely slumbering,
Visions of her who is far – so far – away.

Flying fish

Saw hundreds of flying fish today – they rise out of water and fly – not leap – really fly for yards, waving wings and stretching out back fins for rudders. I saw some fly 50 yards – little toy aeroplanes whirring off – coloured like swallows – white shining bellies. They land awkwardly with a splash. Lovely to watch.

Lost and found

Next to the intense, scarce-sufferable heat, our greatest inconvenience was lost kit. At no given moment, during the whole of the journey, was every man in possession of all his kit. The only near-solution of our problem was the packing and repacking of each separate item of equipment as it was needed or finished with – to open the kitbag for a towel, wash, then put it away again; open the rucksack for socks and stow away the old pair; to stand over your washing until it was dry; never to part company with your life jacket or hat, your raincape, your 'irons'; – your every article in constant use and need, to keep them all within sight and reach, even in bed. But those conditions were insupportable as the heat. Lifebelts were whipped from beneath your nose. Rucksacks were unstacked, scattered and restacked while you were at the ablutions. Caps were absentmindedly moved from hand to hand until they were untraceable. Hammocks were shifted as constantly as pebbles in a stream. Even the most conscientious constantly lost equipment. Even the most cautious had to put aside half an hour every day for finding missing articles.

As for the more careless, like myself, people used to abundant space and an uncrowded life, 20 per cent of our day was spent in chronically futile searching. Hour after hour we spent in the Inferno, looking up at hammock labels, turning over disorderly piles of webbing, unpegging and repegging arrays of overcoats. The longer the voyage lasted, the longer the hours of searching – and the shorter the tempers. At any time of the day men could be seen moving moodily and irresolutely from mess to mess, the sweat of tropical heat and indignation rolling down their faces, uttering the most bloodthirsty threats.

Wrangling, counter-wrangling, pushing, shoving and purpled bawling, with every altercation the air grew hotter – until the heat stifled. No solution but to say goodbye to your undiscoverables – and wait till some mysterious reshuffle deposited it – as a wave will throw up a bottle or a spar – before your eyes again.

New mood

A new mood is animating the ship today. We are wearing tropical kit for the first time, and feel all new and smart. The bathing pool has been opened, and we used it today for the first time. The weather is wonderfully clear and fine. Hundreds of flying fish can be seen skimming over the waves. Sleeping on the upper deck is a success – no more sweltering in the suffocating heat between decks. The VADs[3] are in print dresses – the padres in civvies – the sailors in white. There was a concert this afternoon in the Warrant Officers' lounge for us – a Beethoven quartet. And we are only two days from Freetown.

Gaiety, relief, expectancy – all mingle here today.

Boat drill

Every morning, at 10.20 hours, all troops assembled at various boat stations for some obscure purpose. I cannot write 'at their proper boat stations' for no one ever knew his proper boat station; and what's more, there seemed no one on board who was competent to say authoritatively 'This is Port 3 Raft. This is Starboard Boat 6' etc. After a few days of being bewildered, most people attached themselves to some station, much as a cat will take to a particular corner – and with admirable patience and constancy turned up there at 10.20 every morning.

We stood by these stations every single day of the journey for half an hour a day. Occasionally an officer came to watch us at this rather boring pastime, but he said little. Often we wondered why we had to stand there – which raft we would have to cling to if the boat was torpedoed – what we would do with it – what we would do with ourselves. But no one knew. No one imparted any information at all. Eventually at 10.45 or so, the little groups disintegrated and we all considered ourselves dismissed.

But towards the middle of the second week, a new officer appeared. It was difficult to know just what he looked like, because most of his face was hidden behind a pair of sun goggles and a straggly moustache. However, he appeared brisk and business-like. Action at last? Alas, no. Standing on a gangway stair, the begoggled officer did no more than count us – this way and that way – and write the total or totals in his book. Heaven only knows what purpose these entries served – there must have been a different total every day. Nevertheless, he seemed content to count and write. We let him count and write, then as usual disintegrated when the mass-soul in us felt that it was time to disintegrate.

But this morning our paragon arrived brisk with energy. He stood on the stair, looked liverishly over us. 'Attention!' he bawled. 'What the hell are you doing?' – this to Ivor, who was resting innocent and indolent against the raft. 'Attention! Some of you will fall in in future on this side, some on that. And…'

Surely, we thought, advice at last. At last, we are going to learn how to move these rafts expeditiously, how to fix lifebelts correctly, how to jump correctly overboard. And – the oracle went on, with great dignity and impressive spleen, 'The correct dress is white shirt, topee, shorts and stockings! Where are your stockings, man?' (to a happy, cool AC2 in the front line). 'Get below and get them, and put them on! Tunics are not necessary, but stockings are! Remember that!'

We stood silent and incredulous. But the officer, feeling that these instructions fully covered the occasion, spoke one more fatuous speech. 'I am going to dismiss you, but no one must move from this place till 11.15 am. To the right, dismiss!' and disappeared along the officers' deck.

The correct dress! Poor AC2s. We couldn't dream of telling you what to do if you get into a tight corner to save yourselves and get back alive to your wives, sweethearts and children, but we can tell you this – and we insist on it. Remember, if you are to drown, you must drown in your stockings. The King demands it, the prestige of the Empire demands it. We officers of the RAF demand it. You must not drown without your stockings.

Oh imbecility!

Austerity

The officers on this ship live far too luxuriously. They rest, sleep and dress in great comfort, and have servants to do everything for them. The other day, they had turkey for dinner. That in itself is nothing, but for most of the turkeys to be thrown away, since the officers could eat the delicate parts only, is a wilful waste. I suspect too that every lunch and dinner a printed menu card is on the table. This is difficult to defend in the face of the acuteness of the paper shortage at home. All in all, the officers are enjoying a first-class peacetime crossing, with few restrictions. Their food, accommodation and service is at peacetime standard. More than that, not content with monopolizing most of the best living space on the ship and having their own private promenade deck (and of course access to the decks we use) today half of our main deck has been declared out of bounds, so that the officers may use it for outdoor meals. We take our meals in Hell's Kitchen, which has not one window or porthole. We rely on being able to use the C deck for fresh air and shade. But the officers, not content with possessing already a dining room with abundant windows, have seen fit to rob us of half our space.

This is austerity of living. Certainly we live austerely. We poor AC2s. But the officers still live in luxury and abundance. This boat is a little England – English society in microcosm!

SS

A Short Sunderland saw us away from England. We were sorry to see the last of it. But today a new one appeared to see us in.

> As if it had been a Christian soul
> We hailed it in God's name!
> (Coleridge, *The Rime of the Ancient Mariner*)

Later a Lockheed H flew over.

Gwen

I have a photograph of Gwen, taken when she was very young, which shows one little peculiarity of feature, which I noticed when I first met her. The right half of her upper lip had fallen a little, so that the mouth was not symmetrical. This little droop was not permanent, for when Gwen was happy, the relaxed muscles that had caused the droop seemed to come into play again and her mouth resumed its fine symmetrical shape.

In the first year of our married life, the droop of the lip was very marked. How strange that although it appeared and disappeared, this unconscious manifestation of malaise should have remained from childhood. But after the change came over us (the change I have already partly described) it vanished, almost for ever. One day, when I was parting with Gwen to rejoin my unit after one of those short, precious leaves, seeing that little lip quiver downwards again, I realized that for months and months I had never noticed it. It had gone entirely, and with it, the faint overtones of sadness and imperfect happiness that went with it.

The disappearance of that sad droop was one of the signs of our happiness. The banishment of it was more than symbolic. It was a real triumph over sadness and the shades of sadness.

A swallow

Today a swallow, a real English swallow, flew over the ship! To think that it is probably on its way home – that it may be flying over the white cliffs in a few days' time! Happy swallow! I wonder if it will nest anywhere near Gwen.

Raffles

Recently we have had a spate of raffles. It is about a week ago since someone with an eye to exploiting the troops began promoting sixpenny raffles. Two sergeants initiated a daily sweepstake on the 'ship's mileage', and within a few days they were paying £13 in prizes. And presumably this was not a great fraction of the total; for, from morning to night they hawked their sweepstake with such assiduity that it was difficult to believe them disinterested. Emulating their obvious success, a loud-voiced huckster of a fellow began a daily practice of raffling a 7lb tin of ship's tobacco at threepence a time, the raffle being restricted each day to one Flight. After him came another stranger raffling a fountain pen; and the latest promoter has been offering – to be drawn at sixpence a time – a Ronson lighter – 'A simple model Ronson lighter. Any one for it, gents? I have a customer here who will give 35 shillings to the man that wins it. Now, who's for it, lads? Who's for it? Anybody else?'

At first the raffles were popular. But *'tant va la cruche à l'eau qu'à la fin elle se casse.'*[4] The raffle masters are finding it harder and harder to find customers now.

Temperature on Mess Deck today about eleven in the morning – 87 degrees.

Freetown

I can describe it as I sit here, because we are riding at anchor now and the town lies before me, across the bay. But the approach first. This morning, at long last, we saw land – a bold blue sierra against the skyline – a lofty landscape of flat-topped mountains and deep cut valleys, with a massive web of cloud caught on it. Very slowly we approached – and snail slow came through the boom into the harbour.

Freetown lies in a bay, at the foot of those hills that, blue in the distance, show now a heavy green, clothed with trees and shrubs from the water's edge to the summit (Fig. 2). This vegetation gives them a woolly 'clothed' appearance strange to English eyes. And just as foreign is the soil. On the banks close to the water, and where the scrub has been burnt away, the soil is a hot raw red. And against the red and the heavy green shine the white and grey houses, spreading disorderly along the low places and up the hillside. A small, straggling, new-looking, hot township – rather smaller, from what I can see, than Redcar.

No bum-boats or native boys to entertain us yet. I can see a few little canoes bobbing up and down on the water around some of the other boats in the bay. Just now the boys are paddling for their lives as if they were being driven away by an officious launch crew. Probably they are. And so my first view of Africa!

24 May 1942
Tropical storm

We had no shore leave at Freetown, but discipline was relaxed a little. We were allowed to smoke after dark on the superstructure deck where we slept – this in itself was a thrilling concession to men who had endured a three-year-long blackout. It was a lovely evening. To be in port, to feel safe, to show a light here and there without fear of penalty, and to look at the shining portholes and the lights from the town – all winking and gleaming like fairyland again! The evening too was warm and very still. Perhaps if we had known more about this climate, the stillness and the warmth might have made us uneasy. But, innocent, we spent the evening gaily enjoying the privileges, watching the black fellows on an oil tanker which lay alongside scrambling for pennies and cigarettes thrown from our decks down to theirs. Yet, in spite of the excitement, tiredness came early, and by ten we were all asleep.

It was about five in the morning when I woke – sharply. Something enormous was in the air. Looking up, I saw my neighbour stirring and the edge of a big black cloud very low on the horizon. I felt two drops fall – then the storm burst. The lightning – very white thunderless lightning flashed all round the bay, and the rain was a deluge, spattering on the awning and making it bulge like a hammock – running in rivers along the deck. Immediately there was confusion everywhere – a hasty packing of all clothes and tack instantly into the hammocks and mattresses and a precipitate flight down below. But in the confusion everyone seemed to pick up what came first to hand and run with it. After a minute's search I had to abandon my slacks, belt, life jacket, matches, cup and run through the rain in my pyjamas. To make things worse the corridors were awash with six inches of water – the only way to get through was to walk ankle-deep in it, falling on ropes in the dark, clutching a bundle of wet blankets, trousers, shorts.

When B Flight collected itself together on the mess deck, it was a sorry bedraggled crew – half swiftly turning over piles of wet kit, prying for their lost goods, half lying disconsolate where they had sat down, too discouraged to do anything. It was two hours before any kind of order was restored. And by that time, miraculously enough, most people had recovered their own.

Now after three nights in Freetown conditions almost insufferable. Intense, damp heat – feeling of imprisonment, being in sight of land, but not able to leave the ship – intolerable conditions on mess deck – quarrels, thieving, short tempers, bickering all day long – thirst – no proper sleep. I've been rained out of bed twice out of three nights – kept awake the third by the hooliganism of the officers. Every night electrical storms – violent, fantastic. I call the lightning 'God's morse'.

Walking up and down the promenade deck last night with nowhere to go – watching the officers drinking and laughing – in their spacious lounge – we felt like serfs. Not a working class but SERFS. This ought not to be. Never.

All grumbles

Conditions grow worse and worse. It becomes more and more difficult to perform the simplest necessities. The diet is bad and appetites are failing. The weather is close and sultry all day – so moving out up on deck away from the stifling heat is so slow that exercise is almost impossible. The open decks are crowded like the exercise yard of a full prison. To be sure of having a shave before breakfast, we must rise at 5.30 in the morning and wait, first in a long queue, for the fresh water to be turned on. To do our laundry we must scheme to catch a moment when the water is still running, to make our own clothes line and sit over the washing until it is dry. Beer is short. Fruit – incredibly – is non-existent. Drinking water is rationed; in the hot afternoons and the long sultry evenings, the supply is cut off.

At night, the deck where the authorities planned that we should sleep, is so hot and foul that three parts of the troops are forced up on to the open decks, and since there is no organized allocation of sleeping space, the principle is first come, first served, and the consequence an unscrupulous scrambling for a few yards of hard deck area. Only with the help of great patience and a certain guttersnipe craftiness in stealing a march on neighbours, can we keep moderately comfortable. But, of course, this day-long scheming, particularly in so trying a climate as this, imposes a strain on all. Tempers are very short. There is on all sides a lack of trust and cooperation. Sauve qui peut! And the man who comes between you and your drinking water, you and your clothes, you and your sleep – is your enemy. Rows and quarrels are pandemic. The smallest incident makes tempers flare. The smallest altercation releases the suppressed irritation of weeks. Lately some of the men have come to blows.

These conditions, shocking though they are, would be more patiently endured if it were not for the obvious contrast between the provision made for the ranks and that for officers. We lack all the comforts of a home. They lack none, indeed many of them are living in far greater luxury than on their home stations. And worst of all, they have the bad taste and imprudence to flaunt their privileges and to remain disgracefully indifferent to the distresses of the troops. The last few nights I have slept in the winter garden, which adjoins the forward lounge and the officers' lounge. The officers dine late and after dinner they come to their lounge to drink and make merry.

To all intents and purposes we have no lounge. The time between tea and bed we must spend on the deck – and, since most of us must stay near our beds to watch them, we winter garden sleepers see the evening out within sight and sound of the officers. We have nothing to drink. We have no chairs. We have no light. But on the other side of the window, there is everything in plenty – beer, water, spirits, fruit, light, comfort – and the officers make the most of them. It is galling to sit like a serf outside the windows and watch them. One would accept the situation more calmly if they were obviously our betters in manners, dignity and intelligence. But they are often noisy, bawdy, rude and inconsiderate. We must be in our beds at 10.45 – must lie down, stop smoking, keep quiet. The adjutant becomes abusive and sneering if the rule is broken. Yet, on the other side of the wall, within sight and sound, the officers keep up their inconsiderate revels. What humiliation.

Not good enough! Not good enough!

This was written in the morning. Now we're under way again. Surprising how much better things seem. At 13.39 hours today we crossed the line, and never knew it. No ceremony so far. But I certainly must buy one of the Neptune certificates – two, if possible. Not so much grumbling now. Weather much drier and most pleasant. Glorious sky all day. Clear burning heat.

King Neptune

'Hear ye. Hear ye. Give heed all ye land-lice and dwellers on terra firma – ye land lubbers and sand crabs – and know that King Neptune has graciously consented to come on board this ship and will hold his court at 9.30 hours in the forenoon watch tomorrow. And to all that attend his ceremony, he will grant a safe prosperous journey over his dominion, and make them at last come safely to Davy Jones's locker. Hear ye!'

We were having a film show on the mess deck – a delightful Charlie Chaplin – when a knocking was heard and a bosun's whistle – the film stopped, lights switched on – and we saw King Neptune! First a naval officer with a bosun's whistle, then the Clerk of the Court, who spoke that speech above – all disguised and patched, with blue chin, very red nose, clothes patched, coloured, spectacles, strange hat, walking stick with bottle for handle, hieroglyphics chalked on his coat – then King Neptune himself, powdered, painted with long straw hair, bare legs etc. and others of the retinue. This was the delightful prologue to the Neptune ceremony which takes place now – today. Must hurry to get there.

DIPLOMA

To all whom it may concern   ATLANTIC OCEAN
AD 1942

Know all men by these presents that 28 May 1942 in Lat. 0 on board the good ship 'HMT J10' in accordance with Ancient Maritime Usage and Customs, Frederick Grice was tried before a Special Court of His Majesty King Neptune, and was found Guilty of attempting to invade His Majesty's Territories, without pacifying His Oceanic Majesty in the customary manner, and was sentenced to the full penalties of travelling by Troopship, and that the said Land-lubber underwent these ordeals with such Conspicuous Bravery that His Oceanic Majesty has been graciously pleased to grant this Diploma to enable the said Frederick Grice to voyage peacefully on the Mighty Deep and pass without further molestations as a Loyal and Faithful Subject of His Majesty. Given under our Hand and Seal on the day and year above written.
R. H. Robinson
Nautical Assessor to His Oceanic Majesty

Geography

Thank God for my geography! I prophesied we would run into fair dry weather a few days out of Freetown, and we have – lovely windy, cloudless weather. Grand!

Saturday 30 May 1942

Getting good at dhobie work – washed a towel today magnificently
Mother's birthday today
Many people sleep on the top deck now. Montaigne was wakened by soft music in the morning. We are wakened by the swabbers. 'Wakey! Wakey! Up you get boys. Turn on the water!' Then follows a hiss from the hose pipe – our cue to get up and clear out quickly. 'Turn on the water' is our latest catchword.

Today's debate

Met today a delightful person – a young padre. He spoke on 'The Church and the Peace'. He shows us the other side of the picture. Some of the officers inspire no confidence or respect, but this padre, Squadron Leader Redmore and a medical officer, they are thoughtful, intelligent and good natured. Had an excellent time and made my voice heard for once.

Napoleon

Last night, about ten, we passed within sight of St Helena – and I never saw it! What a pity! I'd have given a lot for a view of the island, even in the dark. But I was lying down in the dark and no one roused me.

Have lost count of days. Last few days too busy and too interesting. I lectured on the 'Future of Education' yesterday with resounding success – now invited to go on Brains Trust – to speak again on Saturday – what fame!

Friday 5 June 1942 or so

Had a tremendously busy time – too busy to write – but exciting Two or three days ago – made a smashing speech on Education – been receiving congratulations right and left. Most flattering consequence – invitation to sit on the Brains Trust

Just think – to be selected as one of the seven brainiest persons on the boat. Nor was I outfaced. I take enormous joy in speaking – and have spoken with ease and eloquence that astonished myself – spoke on astrology – then initiative in Forces – then low moral tone during war and finally jumped in and made a beautiful speech on Basic English – wallop! An AC as prominent as anyone else – NCOs, officers, all in!

More congratulations! Recognition by all the officers – and a commendation from the CO. Tomorrow I have to speak in another debate, and the next day I am invited to sit on the Religious Brains Trust!

So the voyage ends with recognition.

Notes

1 Fred had done much of his basic training in radar on the Isle of Man.
2 Rabble.
3 Women in the Voluntary Aid Detachment – usually nurses.
4 'The pitcher is taken to the water so many times that in the end it breaks.'

Chapter 3

Cape Town, the Suez Canal and Cairo

Saturday 6 June 1942

First views of South Africa – up early in morning – just before dawn – up above the sky a deep deep blue – fading to azure – forget-me-not, lemon – gold and beautiful dusky red – silhouetted against the sky – a bold fine outline with Table Mountain as plain and level as in my imagination (Figs. 2 and 3). Far above it – that enormous glittering star we see at early morning – all the breath of the morning, the colour, the glittering star – magnificent.

Later in the morning we saw the coastline more clearly – a tumultuous, majestic range – high, shadowy, cliffed, precipiced – steep the slopes, soft the foothills – hard and craggy the upper mountains – patched here and there in mysterious white. Then the city – very white and attractive – white- and cream-walled houses, with dark red roofs – the red suddenly sprang into view. More seagulls than for months, and seals basking in the bay – and so we came into harbour and docked.

My greatest excitement was in the morning hours, up on the forecastle deck – drawing closer and closer to the coast – seeing the outlines changing – revealing more cliffs and houses built around foot of hills – above them – grassy slopes with a duller verdure than we see in England and then pine trees or trees resembling conifers – then hard rocky hill tops – it looks to us a mountain-ringed bay.

Saturday evening – in Cape Town
Sunday – spent with Mr and Mrs J. H. Eakin, Fish Hoek, Cape Province (Fig. 3)

Monday – deplorably wet – museums, opera

Impressions of Cape Town

Extremely fine city – new in appearance, most of the houses or buildings in town centre are imposing, clean and modern – white or cream dressed so that they shine in the sun – streets well kept, fairly wide – well lit – shops modern in design – whole gives impression of up-to-date cleanliness which cannot be matched in England. Perhaps in USA – the town has an American rather than an English appearance – trolley buses – clean and comfortable, well equipped – most of cars on streets are American. Plan of town etc. seen from the postcards I have. Black population and Cape Coloureds, Malayans, Indians – far more Cape Coloureds than pure natives. Mr Eakin had lots to say about the white man's failure to educate the native.

Monday 8 June 1942

Airgraph sent home

What a bind – 10 days before my birthday

A few days ago – told to move from B Flight accommodation on J10 to berths aft – immense confusion – no mess tables available, no sleeping spaces, no cups or plates – no hammocks. We had to do as best we could for two nights and days. Then at last orders to move. Up at 5 o'clock, on parade on fo'c'sle deck shortly after eight. Then a long long wait of over FOUR HOURS in full kit! Four hours on an open deck with all that harness and clothing! We lay down, slept, talked, nodded – anything to pass the weary, weary time.

At 12.30 pm began to move. But it took us an hour to get 200 yards – on to our new boat. From now onwards the officers deserted us. I'm afraid they often do in crises like this. We were directed to a foul spot deep in the boat's hold where hundreds of hammocks were slung in compartments where bugs and insects ran – the ex-home of Italian prisoners from Libya. And *sauve qui peut!* Half of us had no hammock. No one had blankets. We shirked the problem of finding places to sleep and wash, and went ashore.

That night I was fortunate. I fell in with soldiers who had a spare bunk in their cabin – soldiers on their way home from the desert. I was home by 8.30 in the evening – enjoyed the wonderful luxury of a semi-bath – teeth cleaning, underwear changing, clean hankie finding, nail scrubbing, talcuming, hair brushing, boot blacking – an orgy of cleaning. Then a cigarette, a book and bed!

But the others – poor others. They slept in the open air – without blankets – froze by 2 in the morning – were up by 3 – and slept on the floor below decks in that awful atmosphere till morning.

What misery – and now, five weeks from home, we are still waiting, waiting.
Where do we come from? Where do we go?

Very hasty notes on Cape Town

1. People in Cape Town seem extremely prosperous – cars are large and in good condition – suburbs extend for many miles around the coast. Holiday resort in the summer for people from all over the hinterland. Yet amusements etc. not outstanding or on large scale. Prevented from developing into a kind of Blackpool by the puritanical activity of Dutch element. Afrikaaners do not like the least suggestion of dissipation – dancing, card playing, Sunday cinemas etc.

2. Cape Town matches and cigarettes are poor. Beer tenpence a quart, matches a halfpenny, cigarettes 20 for tenpence or less. Brandies and wines cheap and excellent.

Cape Town, the Suez Canal and Cairo • 81

3. The silver leaf tree on Table Mountain – the silver leaf is a Cape Town souvenir – tree grows on Table Mountain only – is in danger of dying out.

4. Old tree – now stump only – in a square where slaves were bought and sold

5. Museums – wonderful furniture in Koopmans–de Wet[1] – importance of stinkwood as a furniture wood – excellent stuff. Ought to get some (Write to Woolworths, Plein Street, Cape Town for it)

6. Interesting things in South African Museum
Native weapons, utensils
Display of glorious savannah animals
Those stones that early travellers used to cut to put over their letters
The Conquest pillars made in Portugal and carried specially on board ship to erect in Africa
Bush paintings and rock etchings (chipped out of rock)
Remember physical qualities of Bushmen

7. Area 6[2] – but have never seen it!

8. Winter climate in Cape Town – I did see that. Rain every day of our stay.

9. Books are very dear, watches, jewellery extremely cheap – food in abundance – Woolworths there

10. A most wonderful Post Office – with a personal collection service I haven't seen anywhere else

11. The unusual vegetation seen on the mountain slopes at Muizenberg – all new, foreign and bushy – gay-coloured flowers even in winter – thick stunted tough vegetation.

The New Amsterdam

I must describe something – and this cabin on the *New Amsterdam* will do. This is how it must have been in peacetime. The cabin is the size of an average sitting room – two very wide and spacious bed bunks – made like beds, equipped with excellent mattresses etc. – middle of cabin wide and spacious. Dressing table cum writing table fitted in wall – two excellent cupboards – big central light – a heater, a fan, two devices for blowing air into room – hot, mixed or cold as desired – an excellent hat and coat stand – plug for electric heaters etc. – sprinkler valves (a fire bursts the valve and sets water spraying on wherever the fire is) – two large portholes – and a little bathroom attached, with excellent handbasin, lavatory and shower. A little radiator fixed beneath towel rail for drying towels, clothes etc. Fitted up for wartime work – now carries 6 not 2 in a cabin like this. I've now had experience of two boats – this and the *Highland Monarch*. This is certainly a superb boat.

Getting mobile

This is a history of the changing and chopping we have gone through in the last few days.

1. Evacuated B Flight on J/10 and moved to A Mess Deck – chaos and confusion – no allocation of sleeping places or mess tables – officers missing – sleep where you can, eat where you can.

2. Two days later – reveille at 5 am – parade 8.30 am – wait on fo'c'sle deck for four and a half hours. Evacuated J/10 and moved to *New Amsterdam* – more chaos – again sleep where you can etc.

3. Two days later – evacuated *New Amsterdam* – entrained to Retreat (Fig. 3) – marched to camp – IFTC (Imperial Forces Transit Camp) – tented down – dug trenches, tidied site, built drying lines etc.

4. Two days later – evacuated tents and moved to others 50 yards away. Some soldiers who were in our convoy left J/10, went to a camp, were washed out the same night, returned to J/10, were moved to *New*

Amsterdam then out to the camp again. Poor buggers! All this futile beating up and down from pillar to post is terribly disheartening. Still this camp is enjoyable.

Sunday 14 June 1942
The transit camp

On a wide acreage of sandy flats, flanked on the south by high craggy hills where the sunshine strikes in the early mornings, and on the north by a low coniferous wood. We wash in long sheds, letting the water run from the taps on to slanting sheets of corrugated iron – and the lavatories are long rows of oriental-looking pots, flanking long chests with holes and covers. We mess in a big wall-less shed, hastily constructed with pine logs and boards – and sleep in brown tents. The accommodation is primitive enough – yet living here is in the main enjoyable. It is fine to smell the fresh air in the morning, the lovely fragrant freshness of a countryside, to see the morning mountains wreathed in cloud – then see the far splendour on the distant evening hills – beauty melting tenderly down the sky. It is fine to sit in the tent after dark, in the light of the hurricane lamp, lying warm on the blankets, laughing and talking – to lie and smoke and speak our minds by the hour.

Eight is an excellent number for a group – not too big, not too small. Big enough for life to be always bubbling somewhere, but small enough for the shyest to make his voice heard. There's Strawbridge, who talks about his wife in a charming way for so poorly bred a boy. 'Look 'ee, I love my wife that much that I'd give anything for'n. I'd give my life for'n, I love her that much' – and Ken Smith, a fine earnest fellow whom I like very much, and Charlie Stapleton, irrepressible and a great raconteur, Rupert from Montreal, Tony Harrington, quiet, girlish, youthful, George Buchan from Brechin, a mine of inaccurate information about everything, Ivor Harding (now replaced by another Canadian) and myself.

What do we do, and what do we talk about? Dig trenches, titivate the tent, organize oil lamps, dustbins – cookhouse fatigues – and the conversation runs from wives and marriage to being frightened, to exciting experiences – to the ways of animals and insects. I enjoy it all – most of all because at last I have fallen among friendly men, with whom I can go walking, drinking, talking.

Rain

Day after day passes and we are still in this dreadful camp. For the last three days, it has rained more or less steadily, and we are waging a losing battle against the damp. The floor of the tent is fairly dry, because the canvas is strong and of good quality. But the dampness from the ground outside is slowly seeping down and under and up again beneath our beds. My palliasse is wet, my blankets are damp – and nearly all my clothes wet. I am writing this dressed in khaki shorts, blue woollen sweater (the one that Gwen made me). My overcoat is wet, my trousers are lying to dry between the sheets of a newspaper, my shoes are sodden.

We are all in the same miserable boat – wet, idle, dispirited, sneezing and coughing. Every day the weather grows more and more inclement – the warm rain douches down unendingly on the canvas. Some mornings we have to work out in the wet – taradiddle jobs, putting up tents which blow down the next morning, route marching – work that serves merely to make us more sodden and wretched than ever. For the rest of the time we doze in the tents, play cards, talk inertly, or go out to sit in cool cinemas in wet clothes.

Like weather, like accommodation. Eight to a tent is room enough in dry weather, but no go on a wet day. The rain falls in on my bed which lies near the door. Like accommodation, like food. Twice a day, we have burnt stew and bread and butter. Like food, like spirits. I do not think I have ever felt duller and more dejected – more in need of artificial stimulation – never less eloquent and alert – never so benumbed – 'bewitched, buggered and bewildered!'

We left for our overseas station in the last week in April – April 26 or 27. Now it is June 17 and stalemate in Cape Town! Nearly eight weeks of snail-slow progress! At this moment General Ritchie is in need of reinforcements in Libya,[3] and British soldiers are here, picking up paper on a camp site.

Saturday 20 June 1942

After a week of calamitous rain, a fairly dry day – walked over the hills from Retreat to Kalk Bay (Fig. 3) – disconcertingly unfamiliar landscape – first a walk along shady lanes, joining farm to farm, by vineyards with little vines all neatly planted in rows – by willow-like trees and conifers – to lower slopes of hillside – clothed with shrubs and ready-made rockeries with little leathery-leaved bushes – heathery-like shrubs – not the soft turfy slopes we enjoy in England. The hillside strewn with boulders big and small. Higher, the shrubs grew less closely, giving way to patches of heather, mostly burnt so that only blackened stalks showed – sparse rough trees – thick-leaved plants – in sheltered places dwarfed but tough-barked thickset trees – the path sandy with white rough sand, eroded from the bare rock which showed everywhere. Flowers in plenty, but strange to English eyes, and nameless to me.

I had a good walk (and certainly a good meal at the end of it at Muizenberg) (Fig. 3) – at times it was like walking over our own moors at home. But the main feeling was one of walking in a dream atmosphere, where everything was unfamiliar and unreal.

The meadow at Philhope

When Gwen was evacuated to Makendon,[4] I stayed with mother[5] until the end of term; and these four weeks before the summer holiday were very lonely weeks for me. I had never been parted from Gwen for any length of time since our marriage, and I did not realize how I should miss her presence. No bridegroom waited more impatiently for his wedding day than I for the day of our reunion: and every evening before sleep, I would lie and yearn to hear and touch her, and fall asleep with the faint sickness of longing.

The first day after the end of term, I packed and went to meet her; and by teatime I was waiting in Harbottle for the car that would take me to Blindburn. McDougal, who owned the car, was pleasurably prompt, and there was still an hour or two of daylight left when he set me down at Blindburn to walk the last three miles over the moors to Makendon. On any ordinary workaday evening, that was a lovely walk – along the left bank of the Coquet to the dipping pens, over the shaky footbridge, by the right bank with the water splashing and the trout darting, to Philhope Farm – and then a twisting climb by Philhope House and through the meadow. But that evening it was memorable. I walked easily, lingering out the pleasure of being near to Gwen, watching a heron and two cuckoos on the knoll behind Blindburn, letting my eyes rest on the gracefully-moulded flowerless hill slopes. I did not expect Gwen to meet me. She would be busy attending to Gillian, smoothing her hair for me, tying her ribbon for me, waiting before the fire for me...

So I came to Philhope meadow and began to climb through it up to the brow of Philhope Edge. It was a small, uneven field, irregular in shape and surface. Here a straight stone fence ran along it, there it curved outward and in again making bays and corners; and here and there were knolls and hollows where neither reaper nor scythe could get. Little hay came from it, but the scant pikes[6] that were won there were dear to the Philhope shepherd. No heather or fern or thistle was allowed to stray into it from the moor around – it shone like a minature green island in the waste of brown heath – a tiny acreage of greenery in a world of brownness, sown with the fragile and scarce moor flowers. By the side of the track nodded the harebells, wet, tenuous, quaking with every breeze: deep in the greenness of the grass, the little mountain strawberry, daffodil yellow – best of all, fields of the tiny heartsease, the wild pansy, yellow and purple, lifting their human-like faces above the bents.[7] From the hills, lowering now in the wet close of the day, all sweetness came flocking and gathered in the meadow.

I stopped in the meadow to catch the fugitive scent of the thyme and look at the heartsease, when I heard the gate above me knock back against its post. Gwen was running down through the meadow to me, running with her hair blowing in the wind and her grey cloak streaming behind her. The magic of that moment! Down from the sky's edge she came, like an angel descending, with an angel's grace, an angel's beauty, an angel's gospel presence. In the little meadow where all the tender things sought refuge from the bleakness of the hills – in that meadow of heartsease, I met her again.

Written on my 32nd birthday, 21 June 1942, in a tent at Pollsmoor (Fig. 3), fifteen miles from Cape Town, with the sun shining at last outside, and Jack Putnam lying asleep at my side.

There is no record of Fred's journey from Cape Town to the Suez Canal, though we know that his boat, the *Highland Monarch*, docked at Suez, presumably Port Suez (Fig. 2), on 26 July 1942.[8] The narrative of his journey continues in the 'Black Book', as follows. *Editors*

Friday 7 August 1942
Suez Canal zone

Scenery round the canal – bare grassless stretches with higher hills on right and left – here and there oases, settled by Arabs – living in shockingly slum-like native brick buildings, flat roofed, little ventilation – fields of maize and vegetables, maize in all stages of growth – date palms – ploughing still done by wooden plough and oxen – patches of tough prickly vegetation, browsing grounds for sheep, cattle of fine hide, but un-English shape – deep chested – donkeys – motley sheep herds – brown, black, grey and pied brown, white, black and white – and goats. Women and children herd the flocks. Women voluminously dressed in full black robes – lake water very bitter and buoyant. This is where they feed the hens on ice cream to prevent them from laying hard-boiled eggs.

Saturday 8 August 1942

This account is meant to tell the story of our life from Kabrit[9] onwards. But I must mention, before beginning the story of how we arrived at our station, the adventure of the last night at Kabrit (Fig. 2). Harding had been ill all day – but no worse than a hundred others. Diarrhoea was endemic at Kabrit. Early in the evening he lay down and the rest of us, forgetting him, began a discussion on 'reading'. The discussion was long, heated, absorbing and did not finish till nearly midnight. But when it was over and we were ready to sleep, we remembered with concern that Harding had left the tent about eleven, apparently to go to the lavatory, and had not yet returned. Concerned, we scoured the neighbourhood of the tent for him, but, not finding him, began to fear that he had fallen into one of the deep pits that had recently been dug all over the camp. But he could not be found, and when after a long search we made sure that he had not reported sick and been taken into the hospital, we had no option but to ask the sergeant of the guard to call out a search party. A dozen guards searched with torches and lamps for over an hour, but still no trace of Harding. We disbanded and went to sleep, satisfied that we could do no more, but no nearer the explanation of his disappearance.

Morning came, but Harding had not yet returned. We anticipated extensive enquiries and sensational discoveries, but to our amazement, five minutes before breakfast time – in pyjamas and slippers – the missing man came walking home. Nothing more sensational than this had happened. In the darkness he had completely lost his way and wandered into the neighbouring aerodrome. There he was sheltered by the crew of a gun pit,[10] and put on the right track home as soon as daylight broke!

This morning we abandoned our tent on the ridge. It was overrun with mice. A few hours later we said goodbye to our new home. Farewell to Kabrit for good and all – and no regrets. It was a plague spot. Nowhere did we have so much illness. Every day a dozen men went down with a mysterious ailment that looked suspiciously like food poisoning. The flies were pests, the rats and mice everywhere, the dirt smells nauseating. Phew!

Tomorrow for new country, Egypt.

Sunday 9 August 1942
Almaza and Heliopolis

Yesterday, by lorry from Kanforest (107 Maintenance Unit) to AMES Middle East Pool at Almaza, near Heliopolis – a fairly pleasant ride, but through country which was in the main very arid – here and there a prickly half-bare thorn tree and patches of dry vegetation – but little else (Fig 4).

Last night – walked into Heliopolis. Heliopolis apparently a kind of residential suburb of Cairo – and a little township of extremely fine modern buildings (Fig. 4). Architecture in places really superb – a Lycée des Garçons (1937), an excellent building – one main shopping street – shops withdrawn from street in a kind of arcade. Stopped at a little drinking garden with tables set in open air – and certainly had money's worth of entertainment – visited by musicians, mango sellers, peanut sellers, beggars, hawkers of razor blades and toothbrushes, balloons, carpet slippers and underwear. As good as a picture show. Later sat in cool of evening at a boulevard shop – French spoken here. I had one conversation in French.

Prevented from enjoying everything to full by feeling of great weariness and sense of strain – heart not too good. Very amusing to see the laundry men ironing away in open-fronted shops – the sidewalk sellers of knick-knacks.

Monday 10 August 1942

Today I saw Cairo, and I think that seeing Cairo has been for me the most significant event of my travels. I cannot generalize with any accuracy about it – I've been in the city no more than a few hours – but it seems at first sight a sprawling disordered place, teeming with people, busy and baffling. I was fortunate enough to get a lift by lorry to the city and found myself dumped there, as it were without warning. And to be pitchforked into the middle of Cairo was bewildering and amusing. Up the not-too-wide streets went bumping the trams, three yoked together and lurching against each other, with a red-fez'd conductor who blew on a horn that sounded for all the world like a child's trumpet. Up and down outside the arcading where we found ourselves, five or six men walked. They had large glass cisterns of cool drink strapped to them, and as they walked they clacked two little metal plates together, making a sound like a muffin man's bell.

Selling is an extraordinary business in Cairo. Anyone can take a couple of cucumbers in a basket, sit on the pavement with them and be in business. Under the arcading were a score of little pedlars selling mangoes, knick-knacks, melons, grapes – and a score of things – some voluble, some silent. These – perhaps they were the genuine Egyptians catering only for Egyptians – did not bother with us. But we soon ran into the soldiers' pest, the shoeshine boys. What irrepressible cheek! What utterly dislikeable impudence! They followed us for yards crying 'Shoe shine! Shoe shine!' Only a show of force could turn them off – even then, one of the more persistent of these guttersnipes out of spite dabbed Rupert's and Jack's boots with heavy smears of blacking. Vexed beyond endurance, Jack took the gamin by the scruff of the neck and cleaned his shoe on the boy's long nightshirt affair. The young rogues!

Our purpose was not to see Cairo at all, but to go to the Pyramids – so that all I can mention is the various shops, all deeply recessed into the street, with no attempt at window dressing (in fact, often no windows at all) – but piled high to the ceiling with stuffs – the beggars sitting in the sun – the native men in their long night shirts, blue, green, grey, striped, pyjama-patterned, and the women in heavy black, dressed like Hindus (here apparently the men make a display of their dress, not the women) – the sellers, the women suckling children on the pavement, and the thousand and one foul smells in every street. Cairo, city of smells – and few pleasant ones. There was one street of cabarets we went along – it stank to high heaven.

Meeting Rigby and a few others at a corner, we found a guide and went in a party of about ten or twelve, off to see the Pyramids. The guide contracted to take us to the Pyramids, pay our tram fare there and back, give us the low-down on their history, and arrange for us to see everything for two shillings and a penny. And to all intents and purposes he kept his word.

We boarded a tram and had a really interesting ride – over the Boulac Bridge, across an arm of the Nile to Gezira Island, through the island, the favourite residential area for rich English, over the second arm of the Nile and out into the country (Fig. 4). The Nile does not look half so important as I thought it would – but the countryside around Cairo is everything the geography text book says – flat, irrigated, green, one big market garden, thousands of square miles of it – growing everything. Quite a pleasant looking countryside – broken here and there by a new French villa or indescribably filthy native village. These native villages must be photographed, or sketched and done in water colours, to be realized. They seem to have the minimum of doors and windows – flat roofs where all the manure, rubbish and old hay and maize straws are piled. Dung at your feet, dung at your threshold, a dung heap over your head!

Still, to my story. Less than an hour's ride and we were at the tram terminus, almost at the foot of the Pyramids. After five minutes' walk up a little bank we were at the foot of the great Pyramid of Cheops (Fig. 4). We looked at the Great Pyramid, over the valley to the hills where the limestone was quarried, the Second Pyramid with the smooth outer covering still partly left on it, and the Third Pyramid, the pit where the cement was mixed, three smaller pyramids, quite close by – then went down the hill (all on foot, except Jack who went on a camel) to see the Sphinx, and the temple of the Sphinx – then back to go inside the Pyramid to see the burial chambers.

If I stay to write everything in detail, I shall be writing all day. I'll make a list of all the things that impressed me – the accessibility of the Pyramids, their excellent site overlooking Cairo, the Nile valley, not the immensity of them (until I learnt the facts), the size of the separate blocks, the beauty and shapeliness of the Sphinx (though it was rather smaller than I expected) – and its secluded site: the wonderful basalt and granite – red granite pillars in the temple of the Sphinx and the priests' tombs there – wonderful stone cutting: the smell of urine as we entered the Pyramid by the robbers' entrance: the eerie climb – up steps, up the ramp, pause, up again, through the little low tunnel into the burial chamber – then into the queen's burial room – the magnificently cut granite slabs in the king's room – the flaring of magnesium ribbon there – the feeling of faintness that almost overcame me inside the Pyramid – the pipe player at the entrance – the delightful glass of lemonade after it was all over. Only one regret – I did not climb to the top of the Great Pyramid. I did not feel equal to it. But I'll go again if I get the chance, and do it.

I packed a lot into yesterday. If I'd been better, I'd have packed more. Speaking of smells, last night the streets of Cairo were filled with a lovely smell – a little sickly and exotic, but sweet. Where did it come from? The perfume shops, or those collars of little white flowers that some of the women were wearing?

Tuesday 11 August 1942
A walk through the streets of Heliopolis

Leaving the Services Club, we follow the tram lines that will take us home. The night is beautifully cool and dark. Three brown trams, all linked together, come to a stop suddenly near where we are. They are all full, the middle tram, which has no sides, with men in European lounge suits and fine dull red fezzes. A spark suddenly flashes from the cables overhead, the conductor blows his little toy trumpet, and the trams jerk away with a shock and a bump.

We let the trams go and walk on under the arcades of these fantastic dream-like Heliopolis buildings. A lady walks past, with a little necklace of small white flowers, and the air becomes sweet with a fine perfume. Is it the flowers or this little recessed shop with its shelves piled high with perfumes? We walk on. From a by-street comes now a foul smell, making us forget the sweetness of the flowers. In this lane it is dark and forbidding.

Now we come to more shops. Laundrymen are standing at tables piled with clean clothes, folding and ironing tirelessly. They are all dressed in long white gowns that reach below the ankles. One is chanting very quietly as he irons. Then a shoemaker's shop. It is late but he is still cobbling, stitching a sole to a shoe. Nearly all the shops are still open. In one, the barber is sitting on the doorstep before his empty shaving chairs. In another, a tiny triangular recess, not big enough for a bed, a basket weaver is working,

Now we leave the shops again. At the other side of the road, a big awning has been made. Its sides are hung with enormous tapestries, patterned like carpets, and it is filled with Egyptian gentlemen in smart

European suits and fezzes.[11] They are being served with cool drinks under the strong light of electric lamps. Why are they there? Is it a wedding, a christening, or a funeral? No one can tell us. While we are watching, we hear a pattering of feet and look round in time to stand out of the way of a shepherd driving three brown sheep down the street. More shops, and then we come to the last row. Outside the little cafés small tables are laid out. Men are drinking there, and in and out of the tables go the sellers of mangoes and small stuffs and underwear. Outside one big hotel, set in an enclosure above the road, wealthier folk are drinking in the lovely evening air, quiet and undisturbed. We walk on, beyond the city, on to the desert road, where the night arches blue-black over us and the Scorpion trails its jewels over the heavens.

These fantastic Heliopolis buildings – many-storeyed, quaint shaped, flat-roofed, and pinnacled, with strange platforms, spiral stairways, sun platforms, tall perpendicular windows, lovely bizarre sweeps and curves – surfaces, white and cream – the colour of the desert sand (Fig. 4). Heliopolis is like a city of a dream, or a fairy tale, diverse and bizarre, and many mosqued. From the top of the roof stick slanting aerial poles, looking as though some lazy fishers had gone to sleep there, and left their fishing rods, their lines dangling in the air for stars.

Meals – new style

7.30 am Breakfast   porridge, egg, marmalade, tea
12.30 pm Tiffin   salad, corn beef, sort of high tea
5.30 pm Dinner   normal lunch and tea
Tea with every meal – and how we love it!

Wednesday 12 August 1942
Love and longing

All last night, and the night before, and the night before that, I lay and dreamt of Gwen and home – all night long, at home under English trees in an English summer. Every night, it seems, as soon as I fall asleep, my spirit goes back to Gwen and England.

Thursday 13 August 1942

I am just beginning to emerge from a period of dreadful depression, in which I could do nothing but lie and ache for Gwen, home, Gillian, English scenes – my head ached, throat ached, back ached, heart ached. Oh, anything to be home again! I think I must have been ill, almost delirious. I haven't mentioned this to Gwen. Have I done rightly?

Monday 17 August 1942
Makendon days: account of an early marital tiff

The pleasure I had from walking on the hills around the farm was always doubled when Gwen came with me.

My greatest regret in my walks on the hills around the farm was that Gwen could not come often with me. It was difficult for her to leave Gillian for any time and she did not care to leave her baby even for a short while in the hands of Florrie, who was too irritable and worried to be handy with children. Most of my long walks therefore were done alone, but on three or four occasions we experimented carrying Gillian in her Moses basket and had good outings. Once we carried her to the old camps and picnicked in the caravan that stood there. Another day we pushed her in her pram to Blindburn and from there carried her in a clothes basket to see Mistress Lowes at Yearning Hall. A third lovely day, we went by the 'postie's road' to Buckhams, to old Mrs Little's great delight. A fourth expedition was to the top of the Dod, near the peat bogs. It is about that outing that I want to write.

It was a fine warm day and we ought to have been in good spirits, but I was in a surly, vexacious mood, sick in myself and ready to pick angrily on anyone's mistakes, hurt by my own troubled body and ready to hurt others. When we reached the summit of the Dod, we saw the

last range of the Cheviots rising before us with Buckham Wells like a little toy house on a green expanse, and beyond that ridge league upon league of fertile Scottish lowland. Gwen and I sat down on a tuft of heather and I opened my map.
'Would you like to pick out the names of all these landmarks, dear?' I said.
'Oh yes,' said Gwen.
'Good. Let's begin then.' And I began to look this way and that, identifying this and that point. Gwen said little, so I chivvied her a little.
'What would you say that is then, dear?' I asked, pointing to a prominent landmark to the north.
'I've no idea,' said Gwen colouring.
'But you can find out, can't you, from the map.'
Gwen looked at the map and said, 'I don't know where to look.'
'Well!' I cried. 'You mean you can't use a map.' In my mood I was easily huffed.
'We might as well pack up then,' I said 'if the map's no use to you.'
Gwen said little but looked at me with hostility, with justifiable hostility. But my love for her was dead that afternoon, and there was something in her that made me hurt her. After a few moments' heavy brooding silence, we picked Gillian up and went back down the hill.

At the tea-table and all that quiet evening I sulked and Gwen was hostile. I went out and splashed up and down the burn, throwing stones at boulders, and slashing the heads off thistles with my walking stick. After supper I waited moodily for her to feed Gillian and followed her sullenly upstairs.

In bed, I turned from Gwen and said goodnight to her. But she insisted on talking.
'It's no good saying goodnight like that. Here we are as bad as ever. What are we going to do?'
'Oh I don't know,' I said wearily. 'When you speak like that I wish I'd never married you.'
'Well, it's you who makes me like this.'

'But it's always the same story. I come to you enthusiastic and anxious to show you something which delights me, which is a discovery to any sensible sensitive person, and you pour cold water on all my enthusiasm.'

'You go about it the wrong way. You may be a good schoolmaster in school but with me you're the worst in the world. Oh!' suddenly bursting out, 'Damn you!' And twisting the ring from her finger, Gwen threw it across the room. I heard it hit the wardrobe and roll over the floor.

'I've never been really married to you so I'll throw it away.'

There was another silence. Our bodies lay together like two effigies, two bodies of lead.

'What are we going to do, Fred?' said Gwen a few minutes later. 'We cannot go on like this.'

'We'd better separate, Gwen. We cannot live with each other.' Yet I thought even while I am saying this, I do not believe it, we can, we can. But I still said, 'We'd better part somehow.'

There was another silence, then, 'Fred', said Gwen, 'Fred, even if we do part I shall always be proud to have known you.'

Then I could not speak for a while. It was the word of love that she was speaking, the spring to release all that dammed affection, dammed so high I could scarce speak. It was the word of love that made all the misunderstandings of the day clear. Turning to Gwen, weeping with relief and the anguish of outpouring love, I embraced her and would not let her go.

Gwen was up before me the next morning. When she came to wake me to have breakfast with her, she was looking beautiful and fair. And she was wearing her wedding ring.

More notes on Cairo

Drunken soldiers arguing at midday with natives and curious crowds surrounding some foolish blustering New Zealander threatening an

Egyptian
A man walking along with a basket of dazed diminutive ducks and chickens on his head
Sullen dragomen,[12] customerless at street corners
Bearded Sikhs on leave from the Blue[13]
Opulent Egyptians in red fezzes, white well-pressed jackets, neatly-creased slacks, handsome, neat and prosperous
Lovely flower shops, tier on tier of beautiful carnations, marigolds, lilies, roses, fragrant at night time
Big wheeled carts, with strong bodies, drawn by mules, and drays pulled by slow brown oxen
River boats hung with white awnings, shading little cabins and balustraded verandahs
A drunken soldier punching at the heads of the horses that draw the Victorian hansom cabs that come out at evening
A man washing down his donkey from a trough in the middle of a square
In the suburbs, squalid flat-roofed slums, with walls of petrol tins filled with mud stacked together: rooms with walls of flattened tins, piled with old iron and visited by hens, goats and sheep
A native with a travelling restaurant, a little glass encased box with plates of food: he draws one and serves it to his customer, sitting on his haunches beside him
Another with a score of pieces of melon, standing over them, swishing away the flies
A barber shaving his customer on the sidewalk
A woman lying full length on the pavement, asleep with her head in an open window

Saturday 22 August 1942

After sickness

Have been wretched the last few days, unable to eat, apathetic and suffering from a heavy dose of catarrh – unable to feel any joy or to write. Now I'm reawakening to the wonder of things, the burdensome heat, the lunatic flies, the lemonade men who came down the lines of the tents in the afternoon, crying like babies who want something they are denied. 'Limon-ade! O limonade-oh! Icy cold! Icy-cold limonade-oh! Lim-oon! Nicy limm-on!'

These angry lunatic flies! They are inescapable. They crawl everywhere – run viciously, jump into the air – buzz with spite and vexation – then settle again to probe, itch and suck. They crawl everywhere, even down the stem of this moving pen, right to the tip of the nib. I have never known them so multitudinous or vicious.

I must be recovering – to have resumed my journal. Yesterday at the Zoo, then to hear Schubert's Symphony in C Major.

Wednesday 26 August 1942

Glorious, glorious day – received two cards from Gwen! Wonderful. The house is sold.[14] They are both well. It means everything to me!

Notes

1. Koopmans-de Wet was a furniture store in Cape Town.
2. Before the post-World War II apartheid era, Area 6 in Cape Town was famous as a racially mixed neighbourhood.
3. Tobruk was about to fall to Rommel, the German commander, on 20 June, 1942. Ritchie was dismissed, and Rommel was rewarded with the rank of Field Marshal (Dimbleby, *Destiny in the Desert*, 2012).
4. Gwen and Gillian were evacuated to Makendon in the Cheviot Hills on the English border with Scotland. They lived with a shepherd and his wife, and thus avoided the bombing focused on Newcastle. When it became clear that the war was going to last longer than predicted, they moved back home.
5. In Brandon, Co. Durham. Fred was teaching at the A. J. Dawson Grammar School, Wingate, in the summer of 1940
6. A narrow pointed piece of land at the side of a field of irregular shape.
7. A name given to grass of a reedy habitat.
8. One of Virginia Nicholson's women, Helen Vlasto, a nurse VAD, travelled on

the same ship, and had better experiences than Fred (Nicholson, *Millions Like Us*, 2011, 205).
9 RAF Station Kabrit was a major RAF facility, located 20 miles north of Suez and 78 miles east of Cairo.
10 To protect the landing ground from German or Italian air attack.
11 A truncated-cone skullcap of a dull crimson colour.
12 Guides or interpreters.
13 The desert.
14 Gwen, who was totally dependent on Fred's income, had to sell her house and rent somewhere to live to raise the money to compensate for the difference in pay between a Durham grammar school master and an RAF Aircraftsman.

Part 2

Erk in the Desert

CHAPTER 4

El Alamein and the Western Desert

Introduction to sand

On 20 June 1942, Tobruk, which had been in British hands since it was taken by General Wavell in the first Libyan campaign, fell unexpectedly to the Germans (Fig. 5). The unlooked for and unwelcome fall of this port compelled the Eighth Army to retreat even further to the east than the original positions from which General Wavell had launched his offensive, and on 1 July they took up their stand on the now famous Alamein line, only sixty miles west of Alexandria (Fig. 6). On the same day, the Germans, anxious to reach the delta without delay, attacked in strength but by 4 July they were decisively checked by an army that had recovered its resilience, and by the end of the month there was stalemate on the Alamein front. The Axis forces, however, still eager to make a decisive advance on Alexandria, resumed their offensive on the night of 30 August and succeeded in pushing forward until the fortified position of El Alamein was enclosed in a 'box', with an escape way open only to the east. But again the thrusts were held, the Alamein positions were relieved, and the attack which Rommel had meant to be the last and crowning operation in the desert, had failed.

During those historic last four days of Rommel's attempt to reach the Nile, I was in the desert, but I took part in no heroic action. I did not even know that the Eighth Army, at the nadir of its fortunes, was being called upon to meet this new attack. Somewhere near Burg el Arab (Fig. 6), about twenty-five miles behind the bomb-line, and ignorant of the greatness of the issue that was being fought out in front of me, I was wandering, lost like a child in a wood.

At the time when Rommel's offensive was at its peak, I was posted from Cairo to Alexandria by rail (Fig. 2), and was met there by a lorry driver, who took me on the evening of the same day to an RAF station at Sidi Barrakat (Fig. 6), about twenty miles west of Alex. There I was given a substantial meal and a comfortable bed, and after a sound sleep, I reported to the orderly room corporal the next morning in fair spirits.
'Well,' I asked him, 'are we pushing on today?'
'What do you mean – we?' he replied.
'Aren't you taking me on to my unit – 606?'
'What!' he exclaimed, 'Us take you? You wouldn't nob it!'
I didn't nob it. I am afraid I was still too green to know what nobbing it meant.
'But…' I asked anxiously, 'how do I get there, if you aren't taking me?'
'You'll have to use your loaf,[1] chum.'
'But I don't even know where this 606 place is!'
'So what? Neither do we. You'll have to get on the main road again, catch any gharry that is going your way, and get to the DID[2] at Burg el Arab. You should find someone there who knows your place. Anyhow, you'll have to shufti[3] round for yourself. Sorry, chum, but that's the best we can do for you.'

I could scarcely believe that a greenhorn, who had been in Egypt for little more than a fortnight, and knew nothing of it outside the main streets of Cairo, should be expected to find his own way about the desert, and that he should be expected not only to make his way from unit to unit, but also to find, without the help of any information bureau, where those units were. But that was the undeniable truth of the matter, and in a few moments I found myself sitting by the side of the coast road, in the last depths of despair. I was without friends, without even acquaintances. I was burdened with two heavy kitbags, a steel helmet, respirator, webbing, mess tin, water bottle and topee. I was hungry and thirsty and surrounded by flies. And I was bound for a unit of which I knew nothing but the name.

As I found out later, that unit was less than thirty miles west of Sidi Barrakat, but it took me three days (and might easily have taken as many weeks) to cover those thirty miles. It took me half a day to find the DID from which 606 was supposed to draw its rations. It took me a few minutes to find out that the DID knew less of the unit's whereabouts than I did. At the end of the first day I had to sleep in a transit camp at Burg el Arab, further than ever, since the DID could give me no information, from reaching 606.

> *Black Book:1 September 1942*[4]
>
> I've left Almaza. I've left all my friends. I've left Cairo, Alexandria all behind me. And here I am all on my own almost stranded, in a transit camp nearer our front line than Alexandria.
>
> I came by rail to Alexandria – a good, interesting ride. I think I saw all the Egypt that – for the geography-book writers – is Egypt. The flat delta land, ditched and channelled everywhere, the little runnels, the deep high-banked canals, the broad reaches of the Nile itself, brown as tea, richly milked tea. And every square inch of land was cultivated – first with maize and palms – later with big fields of cotton, wheat, fruit orchards – and nearer Alex – banana trees. So into Alex.
>
> And from then on – a nightmare growing more and more unreal – a warm troubled night in an AMES station – a ride in an ambulance – an almost hopeless search for a ration dump where I was to be picked up – finally coming to a stop in another blessed transit camp, to begin my journeying again tomorrow.
>
> This is a sorry country – an arid countryside covered with finest of fine sand – continually stirred and blown up by the lorries that thunder past. There is a powdering of sand over everything, even over the barrel of my pen as I write. God help me! I've come to a strange and horrible countryside. If you were to see me now, my dear, you would weep tears of grief. God be merciful, deliver me soon from the desert!

Written in this wretched tent, with six other lost souls, lost and forgotten men here, on the first day of September.

The second day, feeling after further enquiries, as surely stalemated as the armies in front of me, I slept again in the transit camp. On the third day, weary with sitting and waiting for information which never came, I was reduced to contemplating returning to Cairo as best I could, beaten and disgraced, when a lucky meeting with an officer enlightened me. Thanks to him, I was at last put on my way. By that time, as I know now, the last German attack was petering out, and the Alamein box where 606 was sited, was relieved. While the fate of Alexandria and the Nile was being fought out, I had been sitting like a tramp on the roadside, concerned, not with the destiny of nations, but with my next meal, my next drink, my next cigarette and my next bed.

It was late in the afternoon of 4 September, when, after a long ride along the coast road, past innumerable alarming signs – those wayside pulpits of the desert – ('Do you know what to do if you are ambushed?') and over two famous tracks, the Bombay and the Sidney Roads, that I at last reached my station.

The nature of the countryside west of Alex had by no means charmed me. The first view of my station filled me with foreboding, and had I not been dulled by a long sea journey and sordid weeks in transit camps, and more au fait with the seriousness of the Alamein position, I should have been even more alarmed. Before me, as I jumped off the last friendly gharry,[5] rose a low ridge of bare rocky land (Fig. 6),[6] drifted over in places with soft glittering sand, and littered with sharp-sided grey and white stones. From this backbone of rock the ground fell away into shallow wadis,[7] their sides sparsely covered with twisted camel thorn; and prominent on its flattish top and very lonely against the waste of sand, stood a big drab Crossley waggon, with a flight of thick steps leading from the tail-board and dirty fly netting hanging loosely from the roof. Nearby was an array of disused petrol tins built into a three-sided open-air cookhouse, and beyond it, on a drift of soft sand, were four bivouac tents, irregularly dispersed. As I walked over to the lorry, a cloud of flies rose from a dirty porridge stick that lay on the ground. Another swarm buzzed assiduously over a stain in the sand where dirty water had been thrown. The loneliness, poverty and squalor made my heart sink.

A steel-helmeted sergeant came down the steps to meet me.
'I'm a new operator for you, Sarge,' I said.
'Well, that's the first I've heard of you,' he replied, 'but make yourself at home.'
'Where should I put my kit?' I asked.
'Just where it is, mate, on the deck. That's about the only place for it at the moment. Got a bivvy?'
'No.'
'My God – but don't worry. We'll fix something up. Come and have some dinner.'

I was hungry and ate with relish. When I was done it was nearly dark. I stretched out my blankets in a roomy dugout that I discovered just a little way from the gharry, and lay down to sleep, thankful to have ended my journey at last and to be done with the exhausting business of dragging two kitbags across the sand in the heat of the day. And about twelve miles away, Rommel's armies were nursing their new wounds and waiting for the next move.

Settling in

The next morning I met the men on the unit and learnt about the work and the life I was to share. 606 was a very small station, one of the smallest in the Western Desert. Its establishment consisted of one sergeant, one corporal, and eight 'erks' (Plate 3).[8] We possessed only one waggon, the three-ton Crossley, which served as our operational room, stores, dining room and transport (Plate 4). When we were called upon to move to a new site, all our equipment went on board beside us. The sergeant rode in the cab with the driver and the rest of us found

EL ALAMEIN AND THE WESTERN DESERT • 107

PLATE 3 'Winners of the Desert Line-shooting Trophy. A group of noble erks, 606, September 1942'

seats on top of our miscellaneous luggage. It would have added greatly to our comfort if we had possessed two lorries; but one was adequate, for our belongings were disconcertingly few – an assortment of cooking utensils, five bivvies, kitbags, two petrol engines[9] and our bed rolls.

The station had been formed for little more than a month, and very little provision was made for the welfare and convenience of the men. We worked and ate by day in the gharry, smoked the grey unlighted twilight away there and slept in the tiny bivvies.

PLATE 4 Unit 606 – the gharry with radar mast on top. Note petrol engine to rotate aerial beside truck

I ought to have been relieved that by the time I reached the unit the German offensive had failed, and that we were left more or less unmolested; but no one knows less about the course of a campaign than those who are in it. I did not know that a great defensive victory had just been won.[10] My mind was occupied with more trivial but more immediate problems. And my first few days there were wretched and unhappy, for the more I saw of the living conditions the more dissatisfied I grew. When I was working I had no time to repine, but the leisure hours were tedious. The presence of minefields and the great heat made walking difficult, and the only retreats were the gharry and the bivvies. As for the gharry, it was difficult to sit undisturbed there, for the flies were a constant distraction, swarming on the roof, crawling over hands and face and even walking down the nib of the pen as the fingers held it. The bivvies were fly-proof, but were low, uncomfortable and hot, and scorpions lodged under the walls. We passed the day reading desultorily and waiting for the evening and respite from the flies. But when evening came we possessed only one light and the imperfect blackout left us with no possible occupation except casual conversation.

> *Black Book: Tuesday 8 or Wednesday 9 September 1942*
>
> I have been at 606 for a few days now – how many I do not know – and hardly care to write about my life here. But here are some notes – picked up by Bert at the DID – rode on his waggon up to his station, had tiffin there – saw a Spitty shot down – came up to 606 – spent first night in a good dugout – the next night on guard in the gharry – the next two nights in the special dugout the sergeant and I dug with our own hands – saw two Hurricanes shot down within a mile of me – experienced two or three raids of a kind – with my heart in my mouth at the first – not so unquiet during the others – have worked like a stoker ever since I came – making our home, digging, filling sandbags, building the walls, roofing, designing – all for protection against these damned strafing MEs and Stukas – made an excellent latrine. What a line to shoot when I get away from here!
>
> Routine. All meals in the gharry – one half is operations room,[11] one half common room – food good – rations supplemented with bought

provisions foraged from any canteens within 50 miles of here – nearly every meal disturbed with some panic.

Five hours watch per day: 6 to 11; 11 to 3.30; 3.30 to 8 or 8.30. Three-hour guard every third night. Rest of time filled in with general duty operations.

Scorpions, little sand snakes, most venomous and spindly, a kind of centipede, lizards in abundance – pretty palpitating little things that move over the sand with surprising speed – and flies! God, the flies.

This was an empty and unprofitable state of affairs and after a few days I began to cast around for a home of my own where I could read and write in comfort. The dugout where I had slept the first night was a model dwelling, but since it was likely to be requisitioned at any moment for the use of any officers who might come to the neighbourhood I could not rely upon it as a permanent home. I decided therefore to make my own house. Being new to the Blue I imagined that even active service would leave me time for study. A veteran would probably not have gone to so much trouble, but being a novice I prepared to live as near as I could to home conditions and reaped benefit from my ignorance.

First I dug myself a pit in the sand, about eight feet by five feet and about four feet deep. I would have gone deeper, but after four feet the sand gave way to rock, and digging became too arduous and slow to be profitable. The walls were very insecure but I strengthened them with sandbags and petrol tins filled with sand. This area had once been fortified and bags and tins could be found everywhere. When the walls had been built up to about five feet, I laid three sheets of corrugated iron across them, weighted the roof down with more sandbags and covered it with a few inches of sand and soil and stones (Plate 5). I soon found that although the desert looked at first sight so empty and barren, it was a treasure house of useful junk. It provided me with girders and sheets for the roof, and canvas flaps for blacking out my window and door, and fly netting to stretch across all apertures by day. It gave me a steel framework, which, covered with another stretch of tough canvas and mounted on four ammunition boxes, made an

PLATE 5 Fred in his dugout at Alam el Osmaili

excellent bed. Wooden pegs driven in the walls were my wardrobe, an empty beer can with a candle in it was my light, more boxes were my seat and table, and two weights my bookends. I even installed an upcurved metal ledge above the bedhead to prevent sand and beetles from falling in on me during the night.

I spent a considerable time on my home. At best it was nothing more than a hermit's cell – no bigger, and certainly lower, than a small English bathroom. But being sunk so deep, it gave me a feeling of security (Fig. 10). It was a refuge from the ubiquitous and pitiless flies by day: and at night, by means of a careful arrangement of the curtains (blacking out the room but allowing it to be well ventilated) I could write by the light of my candle and smoke in fair comfort. My books were arranged on a shelf at the head of the bed, and before me was hung – another gift from the desert – a small reproduction of Gauguin's *Spirits of the Dead*.

This was my first desert home and I have dear memories of it. I came to the desert with foreboding, and having been used so long to quietness and neatness I anticipated the absence of privacy and the squalor with misgiving. Yet the weeks I spent in my little cell were not unsatisfactory. It was almost a monastic existence. Over and above my operational work,[12] which was light, I was often called upon to spend some of the daylight in manual work. Latrines and pits for refuse had constantly to be dug. Wood had to be brought in daily and on many an afternoon I sweated like a Caliban. Visitors were few. Our only constant caller was the driver of the ration lorry who, every two or three days, brought us hard loaves, tins of meat and vegetables and many unwanted marrows. We lived in almost complete seclusion in a wall-less monastery (Plates 6, 7, 8 and 9). We ate simple food, we drank simple drinks, and spent most of the hours of daylight in some form of labour.

But the evenings I dedicated to study. Through those long autumn evenings, by the light first of a candle and later of a hurricane lamp, I read and wrote. The well-being that came from labour in the sun and

FIGURE 10: 'Home, 606. September 1942.' Fred's pen-and-ink sketch of his dugout at Alam El Osmaili

112 • War's Nomads

Plate 6 'Harry Allen (H. Cookie), 606, September 1942'. The figure on the right is Jack Scott (Cookie)

Plate 7 'Five of us sitting on the roof and in the entrance of my dugout. It looks no great shakes here – but that was before the renovation.' H. Cookie is in front, and the others from the left are: Cpl Pryce, Jack Scott (Cookie), Fred and Jimmy

El Alamein and the Western Desert • 113

Plate 8 Sergeant Clark, Unit 606 (left) and Sergeant Budd, Unit 607 (right), Alam el Osmaili

Plate 9 'Having my hair cut by an Indian,' Alam el Osmaili

air invested me during those evenings, and my pleasures were keen. I remember reading *Romeo and Juliet* there and being moved more poignantly by its beauty than ever before. I remember too how vividly the image of my wife would come to me through the darkness and silence as I wrote; and always, after my reading, it was my habit to throw back the curtains and look before sleeping, for a few moments, at the multitudinous assembly of stars in the unclouded oriental sky.

Black Book: Thursday 10 or Friday 11 September 1942
Snakes alive! Last night while I was on guard, I walked over to the fire, to relieve the monotony of sitting and watching. Halfway across I heard a noise of scampering and hissing, loud enough to make me suspect a large rat or desert dog. I backed and flashed on my torch and in the ring of light saw a snake, the largest I have ever seen wild, although it was no more than 18 inches long. Instinctively I picked up a stone and a luckily accurate shot broke the snake's back. Later I crushed its head with a spade; and left it in a ring of stones, so that I should find it easily in the morning. It was dead enough by morning – an 18 inch-long coil, maybe half an inch in thickness, and light fawn in colour, with darker sandy-coloured spots, and a small head with pinhead jet-black eyes. In a way I regret killing him so brutally and crudely. But he is probably a menace to us, and he and his ilk must go. (Written with a new fountain pen bought from a travelling canteen that has been up in this remote corner of the desert for the last few days.)

I soon began to find that the desert was not without beauty. The Arabs concede little charm to it. They have a legend that tells how Allah first made the mountains, rivers and seas, and then, when the light was failing and it was too dark for him to see clearly what he was doing, he made the sands; and the next morning, he was so ashamed of his handiwork, that he threw stones at it. Had I been compelled to find my living there, I should probably have echoed the feeling that motivated that legend, for the desert is hostile not only to men but to all big creatures. With all its immensity, it can provide only for little things. Lions and gazelles once abounded there, but I saw no wild animal bigger than a hare. I saw only modest creatures that can live on little – lizards, chameleons, ants, scorpions, small snakes, spiders and beetles; and most of the land supports only camel thorn, a dry little shrub whose existence seems a death-in-life. All the year round it seems brittle and leafless. In autumn only, it puts out little red blossoms that make a show for a few days, then quickly fade and shrivel.

Yet this almost inanimate scene can be lovely. In places, the hardness of the land is over-drifted with soft sand and smoothed into gentle contours. In summer, the sky is blue and unclouded; but in autumn and winter, big clouds build themselves up over the horizon, edged and coloured like white roses, and as they pass over the main of the sky, they throw down violet shadows, like the shadows of very still fish on the floor of a pond. Then the hollowed land, all dappled with shadows, shows varied and fair. The nights too are often beautiful and moving. Through the clear dry air, the stars shine brilliantly, seeming to look down with all their eyes; and the stillness is so profound that one can almost feel the darkness falling like leaves to the ground.

Black Book

I am writing this on Sunday 4 October. It is still very hot and the flies are buzzing furiously under my tin roof. A few miles away Stukas have been raiding from beyond no-man's-land. A squadron of friendly fighters is returning eastwards along the coast from their interception. Every now and then comes a detonation from a bomb or a Bofors or blasting, we do not know which. Nor do we greatly care now. These noises are part of our environment, as natural as rain on an English day.

But on one or two occasions we have been scared. Once several Messerschmitts came hunting returning Hurricanes over our site. We knew there were hostile aircraft around us, but did not see them or realize how close they were until two Hurricanes came low and swerving towards us. Immediately there was a pandemonium of firing. Bofors opened up and Lewis guns and machine guns.[13] The noise was so great and so bewilderingly varied that it was impossible to know what was happening. Amid all the din I can remember little accurately except seeing three spurts of white dust where something fell on the rocky ground outside the gharry. Then I flung myself face downward on the floor of the waggon behind the curtain and found Roy and Jack crouching there with me. For a few moments the din went on, and my heart beat as violently and noisily as the gunfire. Then suddenly it was quiet again, and when I looked out, about a mile away were two black ruins with a thin high column of very black smoke coming from each. The two Hurricanes were down and done with for good.

The desert puts on its most glorious beauty at the hour of sunset (Plate 10). Then 'the western conduits run with wine'. The pale clouds catch fire and blaze fiercely while the auriferous sun dispensing colour, seems to shrink from capture. It squeezes itself into strange shapes to keep above the horizon – then falls suddenly and the conflagration of clouds burns itself out to an ashen grey. At moments like these the desert appears very fair, but it can unloose furies, like any other land. On 16–17 October, there blew up the worst sandstorm I have ever experienced. An unnaturally fierce wind rode in from the west, a wind that seemed all the more violent because it followed weeks of still weather. The air was so thick with sand that it grew a deep apricot, and one could see no further than a man in a heavy yellow fog.

Sharp-edged sand grains beat on the sides of the lorry like hail and

PLATE 10 Sunset in the desert, Unit 606, October 1942

stung the face of anyone who ventured out, with a hundred sharp pricks, while the softer dust penetrated the smallest of crevices, choking the mouth and filling the nostrils. Almost all traffic was brought to a standstill, and the trucks that did try to go on through the storm soon lost their way. When I was young, I read that on the approach of a sandstorm, the Arab lies down behind his camel and covers himself till the wind dies. Such a measure would hardly have met this case, for the wind blew without abating for two days and nights. It was only on the morning of 18 October, that we were able to come out into the open without goggles and masks, and wash away all the accumulated grime and dust of forty-eight hours.

A storm like this, however, was rare. The autumn climate in the desert was admirable, and in spite of the melancholy which possessed me when I first came there, I experienced many pleasures in my first desert home. One incident that stands out vividly in my memory took place towards the end of my stay. There came near to our site a regiment of Indian troops.[14] They were very fond of singing and I often listened to them. One evening I stood at the mouth of my dugout listening to them chanting a strange song that seemed to my ears to consist of only one line. Over and over again they would sing that line – then leave off for a few minutes, only to begin again with the same monotonous simple melody. Impatient with their lack of variety, I was about to turn in, when, from the west I heard a most powerful and wonderful voice. I could not see the singer. The sound seemed to come from far away through the darkness – a sustained chant, deep, even-toned, beautifully articulated and carrying powerfully and easily over the sand. I do not think I have ever heard anywhere so impressive a singer. I listened with the delight that always accompanies such unexpected pleasures. Then I remembered that it was the sacred Muslim month of Ramadan and the singer was the *muezzin* calling the faithful to prayer, even on the field of campaign. Presently the invocation ceased, but I heard the singer again at sunrise; and for many sunrises and sunsets after that, I listened to him as the poet to the nightingale.

The journey begins

We spent over two months at Alam el Osmaili (Fig. 6). During these months the Axis forces were still held at the El Alamein line and the Eighth Army prepared for its offensive. We grew used to the daily noises of blasting, ack-ack fire, bombing and dog fights, and accepted the coming and going of aircraft, from both sides, as a townsman accepts the traffic of his town.

> *Black Book: 14 October 1942*
>
> The dogfight drifted towards us from its first skirmishing ground five miles away and out of the melee came two Kittyhawks apparently making for home. Then above them I saw two other planes white and circling.
>
> 'They're Macchi 2025,' said the squadron leader.[15]
>
> The Kittyhawks went past us to the south, low and swinging from side to side. But when they had gone four or five miles they seemed to swerve, and joined battle with the Macchis. Nothing was clearly discernible then until one plane left the melee with a thin column of smoke behind it.
>
> 'Something's hit, sir,' I said.
>
> 'That's a glycol leak,' said the squadron leader.
>
> The handicapped plane dived quickly to make away, but four others dived after it and gave chase, a mile to two behind it.
>
> 'They're Kitties after it,' said the squadron leader, looking through his binoculars.
>
> Then the leading Kitty found a burst of speed – gained rapidly on the injured Macchi[16] which was now trying to make off, flying low but slowly. The Kittyhawk gained air like a greyhound on a lame hare, and when it was no more than a thousand yards away, fired quickly. Then the Macchi turned over like a leaf. In a second it had hit the ground. I saw its nose go into the earth, and a huge sheet of flame rise and envelop it. The next moment there was nothing to be seen but the familiar slender upward-climbing column of black smoke.

On this lovely autumn afternoon a pilot died. I wonder who he was! God heal quickly the grief of whoever will be weeping for him tonight. This was a day of dogfights.

But I have no intention of dealing at length with the military events of this campaign. I have no right to do so, for the grim business of killing and being killed was, in the main, carried on out of our vision. Throughout our journey we were shielded by the heroic Eighth Army, and of the vicissitudes of the fighting, although they decided our movements, and the quality of our living, we were little more than moved and compassionate spectators. Our immunity from serious daily danger was Fortune's gift, and we were grateful for it. It is rather for me to recall those less hazardous and sensational aspects of the desert campaigner's life – his working, eating, sleeping and relaxations, the businesses of his day-to-day life, the beauties and uglinesses of the land he campaigned in, the inconveniences it imposed and the pleasures it afforded (Plate 11).

It is not without misgiving that I write about the liberties and pleasures we enjoyed in the desert, for to many it was the land of long nightmare. I later met two soldiers in Cairo, one of whom told me the moving story of a friend who, thinking in the last retreat from Tobruk that there was no end to the desert, lost heart and took his own life. The second soldier was a

PLATE 11 Fred at Alam el Osmaili wearing his South African bush jacket and boots

sapper whose nerve gave way in the last stages of the advance on Tripoli. After two months of rest in Cairo, he was still ill. He could not exorcise the memory of that day when his lorry had fouled a chain of mines and his friends had been killed. He sat at a little table, opposite me, blinking rapidly: as he talked he kept turning his head away as if he could not look for long at a human face, and putting the palm of his hand against his temple. I did not want him to continue talking about the desert, but he clung to the subject. It was a ghost he could not lay.

After that, I felt that to write about the North African campaign with anything but pity and condemnation of all the forces that had sent us to Libya, was unpardonable. Yet, hoping to commemorate for those soldiers and airmen whose courage and endurance were more than admirable, those scenes over which they campaigned, and those little sights and happenings that relieved the harshness of their life, I have continued.

Our greatest inconvenience in the days of the autumn lull were flies and boredom. I have never seen as many flies as there were at Alamein. We welcomed neighbours – the South African and Indian troops who occasionally camped there, because they shared the flies with us: we regretted their departure less, I think, because we lost their company, than because the fly population, dispersed while they were near, fell back upon us as the only human victims. We learnt to fight them little by little, to use fly traps, the maximum of netting, to spray thoroughly before eating, to hide away every scrap of food and drop of water, and to burn and bury all refuse, and to train the corporal (who could not be trusted in those early days) not to fill the spray with lemon juice. In those days the flies were our worst enemy, our first allies the flit-sprays, and the white wagtails and martins that were arriving from Europe: and we campaigned so well that only one of us caught dysentery, and that he had brought with him from the Delta.

Our establishment soon came to consist of five homes. To keep these adequately lit, we had even to start a candle-making industry, pouring melted fat into verey-light tubes and using tape for the wick. In their dim, smoky dugouts, the men played cards and read from cover to cover the old magazines foraged from the desert. Scavenging like this was one of our means of fighting *le cafard* – desert boredom. The oldest, dirtiest book found there was passed round the whole unit, the smallest piece of equipment was examined, repaired and put to some service.

By the middle of October it grew obvious that the Eighth Army was preparing to attack. The last task of the Indian Regiment, who were our neighbours, was to punch holes in thousands of petrol tins in the shape of a V. They told us these were to go over little lamps to light the path of their night advance. So skilful was the supplying of the forward areas, however, that we had no knowledge of the strength being brought forward to support the advance; but putting our ears to the ground we heard many rumours of the impending offensive, and since we knew that when the army began to advance, it would be our function to follow them, and lend what little aid we could, we began to make preparations for a long journey.

Little by little we laid by a store of provisions, chocolate, milk, sugar, tins of fruit, beer, even spirits and wines. The sergeant installed a big drum on the inside of the gharry and by fitting it with a homemade tap, made a handy extra water cistern. We collected from the desert as many 'jerry cans' as we could find (these were German petrol tins, strong and excellently made) and then we saved water from our daily ration till both cistern and cans were full. After we had laid in a stock of cigarettes and supplemented food reserves with tins of dried fruit and dehydrated potatoes, also – the goddess Hygeia pardon us – salvaged from the desert, we fitted more lights inside the gharry and rehearsed packing till we felt competent to move at a minute's notice.

We had not long to wait. On 6 October, Nature provided us with an unexpected luxury. For many nights we had been given the promise of a storm. Far away to the north, over the distant Mediterranean, we could see big clouds massing, white and grey, and the lightning playing fantastically behind them. At first it was so distant that no sound came from those far flickerings; but after a while, the storm clouds moved in on us and opened over our heads. The desert stood still, then seemed to shiver beneath the unwonted shocks. The thunder filled us with strange emotions. Why did 'the great gods … keep this dreadful pother o'er our heads?' (Shakespeare, *King Lear*, 3, ii). Our first impulse was to run from the unexpected violence, but presently the feeling of primitive alarm passed. Stripping naked, we ran out into the rain, soaped our bodies, and let the shower wash us clean. Then we frisked and jumped into the warm air, letting the water trickle from head to foot.

That deluge did not only give us our best bath for months; aerial reconnaissance the next day disclosed that the enemy's forward landing grounds, particularly El Daba, the Stuka base, were waterlogged by the heavy rains, while, the shower having missed Burg el Arab,[17] our aircraft were still able to take off (Fig. 6). All available British craft were mustered, and made repeated and telling raids on the immobilized German planes and transport.

Finally on the night of 23 October, the army struck. Having been warned to look out for fireworks about half past nine that night, we climbed on the roof of the gharry: and precisely (or so it seemed to us) at 2140 hours, a single white searchlight stood up in the west, white and vertical, and the four hundred and fifty 25-pounders that had been concentrated in the six-mile long northern sector of the front opened up; and with them, the less heavily concentrated artillery on the whole of the forty-mile line.

Has any campaign opened more dramatically? The noise of it rolled in continuously upon us over the dunes, and 'nimble sulphurous flashes' (Shakespeare, *Pericles*, 3, i) raced along the horizon. It was a steady volume of monstrous and portentous sound, broken every now and then by the force of some enormous and extraordinary explosion. And above the ground flashes rose thousands of tracers in wavy hesitant lines, pinpricking the sky with red stars. Then at ten o'clock the barrage paused, and the infantry went in to attack.

The history of the battle is well known now. In nine days the British infantry pierced the Alamein Line and cleared a way for the tanks. In nine hours the tanks broke the best of Rommel's armour at Tel Aqaqqir. When that was accomplished we were ordered to pack and move forward.

We did not know, that early morning when we began loading our tins and pans, that we were about to take part in one of the greatest advances in history. Our main emotions were excitement at the magnificent first success of the attack and at the prospect of seeing new territory, and regret at having to leave our homes. I left my bed, seats, pegs and curtains in my cell. I left too, my Gauguin reproduction and, as an afterthought, I wrote a little note, and stuck it above the picture, addressing it to whoever might come and live there after me: 'I hope you'll like staying here. May you have as much pleasure in this little pit as I have enjoyed.'

I wonder if anyone ever found that note. Probably not, because the desert hides and forgets quickly.

From Alamein to Gambut

We left Alam el Osmaili on the morning of 7 November (Fig. 6). From the first we realized that it was not an ordinary military advance that we were embarking upon. From the periphery of Hitler's Empire we were moving in towards Germany, and beyond Germany lay home. It was possible that we might never return to Egypt, and therefore to us, our advance was a migration. War's nomads, we were moving to new ground, and taking all our possessions with us. When we had first carefully packed our delicate instruments[18] against the jolting which we knew would be inevitable, then stowed away all our stock of equipment and our recent acquisitions, the whole floor of the gharry was raised three feet: and with our piles of bedding and tins, buckets and desert tracks roped to the sides of the waggon, we resembled most of all those migrant families who, in the years of depression, moved from the Bad Lands of America in search of work, and our nickname became *The Grapes of Wrath*.[19]

On the main coast road leading west to Tobruk we found ourselves caught in a great stream of traffic (Fig. 6). No one who saw that stream will easily forget it. It was as if all the traffic in the Middle East had ponded up behind the Alamein Line, and where the Eighth Army had pierced the wall, was pouring through in an inexhaustible flow (Fig. 6). We had to drive very slowly, moving only at the speed of the stream, catching glimpses now and then of the Mediterranean, incomparably blue and still, bandying words in fragmentary conversations with the truck crews, and turning to look at the unvarying desert to the south, as flowerless as the sea and even more impassive. There was a great excitement in the air at the completeness of the first victory, and astonishment at the amount of transport mustered for the advance.

At El Alamein station[20] we caught a quick view of the prisoners of war in their cages (Fig. 6). It was difficult to have any emotion but pity for them. They sat on the ground in dejected groups within the barbed wire compounds, patrolled by a handful of soldiers. No relief at being finished with warfare was visible on their faces. They seemed stunned and overthrown by the violence of the British attack and the sudden reversal of their fortunes. The barrage had battered and dazed them.

Beyond El Alamein the road was littered on both sides with almost unimaginable ruin – tanks, armoured cars, those German infantry carriers which looked as if they had been requisitioned from a fairground, trucks and waggons of every description, shattered gun carriages, old Italian gharries with high cabs and big solid rubber wheels, aircraft old and new, shells and shell cases – all overturned, broken and twisted, as if someone had scooped the derelict steel of an abandoned Rhondda and littered the sand with it (Plates 12 and 13). At one point six OR 42s[21] were lined up by the roadside in trim order, but burnt to skeletons. Around these ruins were scattered a thousand smaller belongings. German newspapers – our first uncensored evidence

PLATE 12 Beyond El Alamein: the debris of war

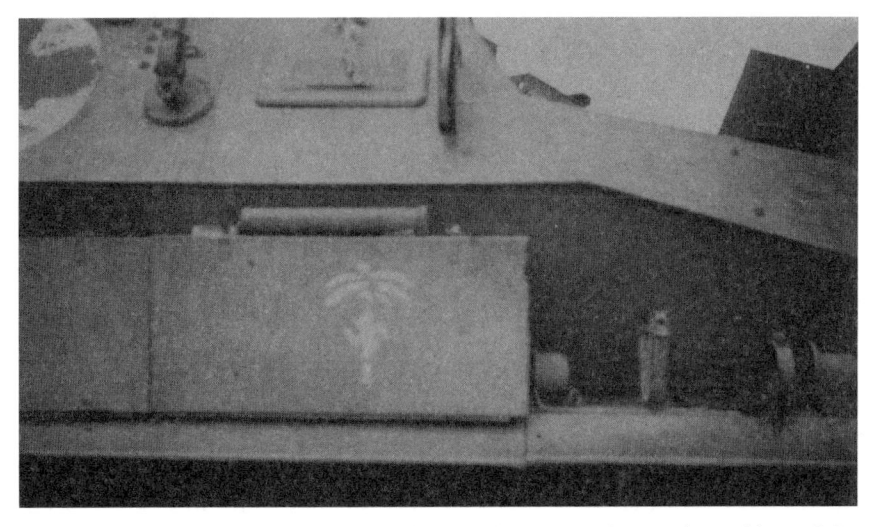

PLATE 13 Abandoned German tank with the palm-tree-and-swastika emblem of the *Afrikakorps*

of their thinkings – were clinging to the thorn bushes: nearby was a dump of abandoned clothing with strange trousers and shirts, boots, packets of coarse Italian cigarettes: and in another place the ground was white with the documents of a ransacked orderly room.

At the end of the first day we slept at El Daba, but by that time, the enemy was in retreat far beyond Fuka (Fig. 6). The next day therefore we continued westward – to Fuka, Galal, Sidi Haneish and on toward Matruh. At Maaten Bagush we came upon trees (Fig. 6), the first I had seen since the Delta, and as we drew near to Matruh, the desert seemed to waken and rise into low hills, reminding me of the hills of Durham and Yorkshire. Just so would those fells have looked if some unkind agency had stripped them of their turf. But of the enemy we saw nothing.

I looked forward to seeing Matruh. Before the war it was a coming seaside resort famous for the coolness and purity of its air. It boasted a hotel with bathrooms. Since the first Italian advance upon Egypt it had been a memorable name. In addition it had a venerable antiquity. In Roman times it possessed a sponge industry, and it was there that Cleopatra, after her inglorious flight from the battle at Actium, waited for the defeated Anthony. Shakespearian editors placed her palace at Alexandria, but it is claimed that it was on the lagoons of Matruh that her barges plied, and the airs that were lovesick of the perfume of her sails were the winds of Matruh.

But an advancing army cannot stay to correct Shakespeare editors. To my disappointment, I saw little of the town and can recall little except the deep ultramarine of the open sea, the pale turquoise of those lagoons that may once have burned under the queen's barges, roofless white houses, overturned wire defences and scattered rags and papers: as if to point my disappointment, the land beyond the town fell to flatness again and presented us a picture so intolerably drab and unrelieved, that it lay like a weight on the mind. A few miles beyond Charing Cross we turned and headed into this dreary wilderness (Fig. 6).

For the next few days, from here to Gambut we had no other road but an improvized desert track: and those few days were our first experience of what the Desert Rat means by the Blue.

Black Book: 10 November

Fourth day of travelling – sand gives way to stony ground as we climb slowly inland – following a battered track and a pipeline to where we are now – a wilderness of rocks – here at last we go operational.[22] But not for long, I think.

It is difficult to picture the discomforts of such a journey. Sometimes we had to make our way over rocky country, hard land filmed over with a thin layer of sand and covered with sharp and chipped rocks and boulders. Over these our heavy waggon bumped and jerked shockingly. Sometimes Roy, who was sitting by me on the rear edge of the water tank, was thrown bodily in the air. I would see him in mid-air flying like an unpractised trapeze artist. Three of the others, Harry, Norman and Cookie lay stretched out in the forward half of the gharry, happily pillowed on folded tents and bedding and old car seats; but the rest of us fared badly. At a bad bump, everything – petrol tins, ladders, bowls and basins rose bodily from the floor of the waggon – and our bodies with them.

Yet the rocky desert was preferable to the sandy desert. There the big wheels of the heavy Crossley revolved deeply into the yielding sand and threw up clouds of pollen-like dust. Big billowing clouds drifted in on us, thickening the sunlight, settling on hands and face, being breathed into nostrils and making grit between the teeth. There was little to do but pull down the flaps, which we had fitted to the back of the gharry, tie a handkerchief around the nose and mouth, and suffer.

If the land was safe we travelled with no more than thirty or forty other gharries: but where there was a possibility of encountering resistance, as in the wide spaces south of Sidi Barrani (Fig. 6), we attached ourselves to bigger and better-armed groups. At one stage we joined an impressive convoy of more than a thousand vehicles of every description. Ten lanes of lorries with more than a hundred vehicles to each lane lined up on an empty plateau and drove off in order.

Life in this convoy was a strange detached experience. The long lanes of marshalled lorries drove from dawn to dusk from nowhere to nowhere, beginning, turning, pausing, slowing and stopping like a regiment of men. Hour after hour nothing was visible but the half-seen lanes of moving traffic, the dry and crushed camel thorn, white with the innumerable shells of the sand snails which had crawled into the twigs and died there, the patterned ruts made by the tyres and an occasional desert hare racing frenziedly to find a way out of this moving terror.

One day followed another without change. Before dawn we struck camp and made breakfast. By the time the bivvies were down and packed away, the tea was ready and the bacon fried. No one washed or shaved. It was said that the wells were poisoned; but had they even been pure, there was no time to find them and draw from them. So great was the haste that washing and shaving was forbidden until the convoy had finished its journey. After a hasty breakfast, eaten standing or sitting on odd tins or boxes, there was time only for a hasty glance at the still forlorn and empty landscape, beautiful in nothing save the fine, coloured sky. Then a thousand engines were started and the convoy moved on again.

Sometimes we drove all day without rest, and there was as little communication between lorry and lorry as there is between ship and ship in an ocean convoy; but more often we halted for tiffin at midday. Then there was always an ecstasy of haste to prepare and consume the maximum amount of food in the allotted time of twenty minutes. As soon as the lorry came to a stop, we jumped down throwing clouds of yellow dust from our clothes as we hit the ground. One drew water from the tank, another filled a cut-down petrol tin with sand, poured in petrol and threw in a match, and a third handed down the hard biscuits and the boxes of bully beef, cheese, margarine, sugar and milk that were always kept handy. If all went well a passable meal could be prepared before the signal to move again was given. The last act was to scramble aboard the moving gharry with one hand, the other clutching the mug of precious undrunk chai.[23]

There was no other halt until the sun was almost down. Just before last light we stopped and dispersed. Sometimes we put up bivvies; sometimes the ground was so stony that we all slept in the open air in a row on a big tarpaulin, like babies in a nursery. It was always a relief to finish the day's travelling, to watch the hundreds of petrol fires flaming and flaring in the falling darkness, to poke the sand beneath the dixie until the flames licked all around it, to eat the hot meat and vegetables tipped from their tins into the pan and warmed through, to sit by the fire till some anonymous voice shouted 'Put them bloody lights out' – to watch them going out like candles, then to look up and see the stars that had been there unnoticed for the last half hour.

But the long evenings were very lonely. If we were fortunate, we tracked down by its sound a wireless set somewhere in the darkness, and listened, sitting around it wrapped in our overcoats; but more often we had nothing to do but to lie between our blankets for warmth, and talk of home and food and water, nostalgic for a place where one need never be hungry, thirsty and dirty. Then Sid and Cookie would joke softly together, the corporal pull the blankets so high over his ginger head that his big boots (he rarely took them off) stuck out at the bottom, and Roy, half asleep, would turn over sighing, 'Oh dear! Oh dear!' By nine we were usually all asleep.

Gambut and Tobruk

Travelling like this we drove through a gap in the big barbed wire barricade which the Italians had built to keep rebel Senussi from escaping into Egypt (Plate 14).

Black Book: 12 November 1942

A long day of travel – from before dawn till almost dark – we reached Sidi Aseiz – a landing ground south of Bardia (Fig. 6). There also we went operational, but only for a few hours. We slept this evening on the tarpaulin again at Sidi Aseiz. On this day crossed border into Libya.

PLATE 14 A view from the tailgate of Unit 606's gharry: the pursuing convoy crosses the wire-line marking 'the entry into Libya, November 1942'

On 13 November we arrived at Gambut (Fig. 6).

Black Book
Water here, as everywhere else, was poisoned.

Gambut consisted of two sets of blockhouses, set on a rocky bluff overlooking a plain and divided by a little defile. There were at least two landing grounds there,[24] one on the bluff and one below it, and both were thick with wreckage. It seemed as if the sand had not had time to overdrift the detritus of one campaign before a new deposit of ruin had been left behind.

It was evident that the Axis forces had retreated quickly and recently from Gambut; what they had been compelled to abandon became our legitimate prize. It was here that we began to furnish our little unit with long-needed conveniences. We found on the landing grounds camp beds, blankets, pillows, maps, tables, chairs, brushes, flit sprays, toolkits, even a big box full of German valves, and a rubber dinghy. Most of these were of great use to us. An extra blanket (although the German blankets were smaller and thinner than ours) was a great comfort when we later came to higher ground: the tables and chairs were the first we had possessed. We had to wait until we came to Castel Benito to find the insecticide to go with the sprays, and Sirte before we could use the dinghy; but most of the treasure trove was immediately useful. Even abandoned enemy ammunition boxes (excellent wooden cases, lined with aluminium or zinc foil, solid and airtight with rubber sealing bands) were taken for food chests. From Gambut to Tunisia the cases that Munich workers had so carefully designed to hold cartridges and patrol lights, served to keep our biscuits, sugar, tea and cheese in good condition.

After collecting as much impedimenta as was useful and interesting, we commandeered one of the blockhouses, swept out a few rooms and installed our new-found beds and chairs. All the rooms were solidly walled with cement floors, and some still had a door. The walls were decorated with drawings of glamour girls (there was one mural of a well-proportioned WAAF wearing only a service hat, and drawn with a realism that would have outraged any Royal Academician) and the spaces that were not filled with sketches were scribbled over. In one room there was a long doggerel poem in praise of the RAF and in another, a flippant and optimistic comment by some British soldier or airman, which read something like this: 'Keep this room clean, Fritz. We'll come back.' This taste for covering blank walls with sketches of seductive ladies was not confined to the British. Rommel's room at El Daba had its murals, and the walls of the barracks at Castel Benito were adorned with sketches of seductive young ladies, African views and nostalgic views of Berlin.

The following morning, having received no orders to move, although it was obvious that the enemy was still in quick retreat, we prepared to enjoy one of the desert's finest luxuries – a hot bath. It was only in smiling times that we could afford to take a bath at all: on a small unit like ours, equipped as we were with only one useless primus stove, fuel even for cooking was always a problem. In our Alamein days we had had to scavenge daily for wood, fetching in and burning old mine boxes, fuse boxes and even camel thorn. But here there was water in plenty and wood everywhere around us. We built big fires, boiled up the water from the pool in the defile in large canisters that lay abandoned on the site, and made baths out of the zinc foil boxes.

You whose hands are rarely soiled and never dirty, who never know what it is to sit down to breakfast without washing, for whom to miss a regular bath is the top and summit of uncleanliness – you who have never been out of hearing of clean running water, will you ever understand the luxury of a desert bath? For a week we had been forbidden to use one drop of water in washing or shaving or cleaning teeth: for a week before that a cold wet cloth over hands and face had been all our ablutions. But here we bathed in hot water, and gallons of it. The pleasure of sousing off a fortnight's dirt from hand, arm, knee, of sluicing the sand from out of the hair and between the toes, and of shaving off the black beard, and feeling chin and jowl smooth again – of putting on clean underwear, stockings and shirts – this was less a simple bath than a purification. When I wash now I often think of that bath of baths – of the vivid pleasure of it that daily use has now unfortunately staled (Plate 15).[25]

After Gambut came Tobruk (Fig. 6) – a name that had come to stand for us as a symbol of first victory, of admirable resistance, of spectacular relief, and lastly, of untimely reversal. To me it was a memorable place, although my experience of it was not crossed with personal memories of victory or hardship. This was my first view of it – a little town taken for good and all, now the shattered ruin of a once trim port. Its environs were littered with wreckage and rubbish. Ransacked and half-burnt equipment stores spread their miscellaneous litter over the ground. The workshops were bombed and roofless. The ground was strewn with fragments of blasted and broken aeroplanes, gliders, motor transport and guns. The harbour was as thick with sunk or listed shipping as a broken well with stones. Yet not even this strewn and spread litter could detract entirely from the beauty of the bay and the little town on the promontory. Distance, hiding its scars, showed it still as a compact glistening little township, looking down on a calm and

EL ALAMEIN AND THE WESTERN DESERT • 133

PLATE 15 AMES Unit 606. Named by Fred as follows: Cpl Jack Pryce, Harry Allen (H. Cookie) back row; Alec, Bob, Fred and Jimmy next-to-back row; Jack Scott (Cookie), Roy, Sarge (Nobby Clark) next-to-front row; Norman and Sid front row. 'Taken at Gambut – one stage of the big offensive.' Fred holds the flit spray, while Jimmy and Sid have rifles. Between Norman's feet is the beautifully made German box for valves labelled *Mechaniker*.

sheltered haven. But perhaps our admiration of it was heightened by the fact that this was the first town of any size that we had seen since Alex. Certainly the long breezy drive down the curling road from the hills was for us a consummation – an advance across the first desert from one land of towns to another.

My recollections of Tobruk come back to me in fragmentary impressions – of Africans of the Pioneer Corps, released after a four-months imprisonment, wobbling on Italian bicycles or trying to walk home, thinking the war was over because they were free again: of frying bacon and tomatoes on the reedy road by the harbour: of the skeletal scaffoldings of Axis observation posts: of a squadron leader[26] stopping to hitch an abandoned caravan to his Jeep and driving off with it: of gliders with broken wings: and of the long slow climbs from the silent town towards Gazala (Fig. 7).

Black Book

At Gazala – where everything was as quiet as a grave – we heard the usual late BBC news. 'Fighting is going on around Gazala.' Yet not a thing disturbed our tarpaulin slumbers – except the usual visitors – mosquitoes.

15 November 1942

Today – put up bivvies etc. at Gazala and watched our Kitties coming in to take over the drome (Table 2).[27] But we learned that we may be pushing on even further before the day is out. Water is short, but adequate. Petrol plentiful – rations rotten. We are living on our emergency stuff. It's cheese, bully, biscuits all day long. Left behind by Sector A – given instructions to move to a new site – packed and crossed the road to come within striking distance for the first time for me of the Med. I slept this night on the ground again in a bivvy and slept well. I hoped we might have stayed for a while at Gazala. The gharry was giving trouble, and we ought to have had mechanics to it. But no such luck.

Gazala is to be remembered for three things. Firstly its mosquitoes, which made life out of cover after sundown a misery. Secondly, it was there that I – novice in Africa – first put foot in the Mediterranean. We were held up for a few days a mile or so from the sea, and nothing would satisfy me but to go and see it at close quarters. Sid, Roy and I walked down to the shore and came to a narrow steep shelving beach, broken into little forelands and masses of seaweed-covered rocks over which apple-green breakers smashed and withdrew furiously. It was an undistinguished corner of the great sea, a strip of whitish sand covered with pumice stone, little ball-like pincushions of brown sea-grass and long strands of diaphanous seaweed. But we have strange ambitions. To visit a place, though the visit brings little insight and little exaltation, is often enough for us. I was content to know that I had at last seen at close quarters the sea of the Phoenicians, the Crusaders and the Corsairs.

Thirdly, we had another pleasant moment there. Walking away one dark night from a group of soldiers to whose wireless set we had been listening, we heard the sound of church bells. It was the bells of England ringing to celebrate 'the end of the beginning' – the victory of Alamein.

Notes

1 Head.
2 The DID was a ration dump.
3 Look.
4 Inserts from the 'Black Book' are used here to amplify Fred's account in his memoir, and are set in a smaller typeface to indicate their source.
5 Lorry.
6 Alam El Osmaili.
7 A rocky watercourse, dry except in the rainy season.
8 Erks were aircraftsmen, though the number in Unit 606 varied from time to time (see Appendix II).
9 To drive the rotation of the antennae of the radar equipment.
10 At Alam Halfa.
11 As explained in the introduction, Unit 606 seems to have followed the same innovation as other North African units with Light Warning Sets. They used the gharry for their radar observations, thus saving on the hour it would have taken them to set up their instruments in a tent.
12 As a radar operator.
13 The Bofors and Lewis guns were to protect the landing grounds and AMES units from German and Italian air attack. Here they were clearly defending the troops at Alam el Osmaili.

14 Part of the British Eighth Army in North Africa.
15 Squadron Leader Young, formerly leader of 213 Squadron, but posted for other duties on 11 October 1942. He led AMES 606 and 607 on the ground for about two weeks after the Eighth Army's breakout from El Alamein, 213 Squadron, ORB, AIR 27/1316, TNA, PRO.
16 The Macchi fighter was manufactured by Macchi Aeronautica.
17 RAF landing grounds clustered around Burg el Arab.
18 Radar equipment.
19 A novel by John Steinbeck.
20 On the railway line leading across Egypt from east to west.
21 OR 42s, enemy field guns.
22 Setting up their radar scanning using 606's lightweight set.
23 Tea.
24 Two main landing grounds and two satellites (Jefford, 2001)
25 Further information about membership of Unit 606 is given in Appendix II.
26 Squadron Leader Young, once more.
27 260 Squadron, 112 Squadron, 250 Squadron and 450 Squadron, all flying Kittyhawks, reached the dromes or landing grounds at Gazala on 15 November, thus marking the end of the El Alamein campaign and the beginning of the Libyan assault.

CHAPTER 5

From the Green Mountain to the Gulf of Sirte

Cyrenaica

The day on which we left Gazala (Fig. 7) the weather broke and we drove along the coast road in heavy rain. Rain in the desert was a luxury and an inconvenience. The desert forces were not equipped to meet wet weather; we had not the clothes or the dwelling places to keep out the rain, or the transport to drive over sodden and boggy ground. This unexpected downpour gave us some uncomfortable moments; but a more important consequence was that it gave the retreating Axis forces breathing space to reassemble: and one commentator has said that this few days' storm preserved Rommel's armies from annihilation.

However, towards the end of the afternoon of that day, we found ourselves entering a more hospitable country. Near a little place called Umm Er Rezan (a few stone houses and a hospital on the top of a climb) grass, green plots and dwarf trees began to appear (Fig. 7). Here was a cluster of short-trunked palms, there a little grove of dwarf thorns with brambly shoots and an undergrowth of wet grass. This was our first 'green belt', and after the hard upthrown glare from the bare sand, the greenness was like balm on the eyes.

Towards evening, after a happy afternoon, we came to the upland village of Maturba (Fig. 7), a cluster of undamaged stone houses by the side of a small single-domed mosque. Below the village and in the valley bottom was a grove of palm trees, screening the square houses and the disused filling station from the road – and even a football pitch complete with goalposts. Best of all to our eyes, between palms and village ran a pipe, flanked by two tall standing Fascist pillars and flowing with fresh greenish water into a big concrete cistern. We lost no time in filling our depleted tanks, cans and bottles.

We camped that night on the high ground above the village, pleased to have the opportunity of resting for a while in this green country.[1] It was more like British scenery than we had seen: it reminded me of Sutherland, as it is inland from Dornoch and Brora.[2] The rolling moorland, bounding and pitching and revealing leagues of distance, was, at close sight, only thinly covered with verdure. Slabs and boulders of grey rock pushed themselves through this thin covering and strewed the near hillsides; and in the shelter of them grew marigolds, big and little, a pale yellow weed-like charlock, lamb's lugs, autumn crocuses flat and starry on the levels of the ground, and best of all, our English lords-and-ladies, Jack-in-the-pulpit – the wild arum. In the distance, boulders, weeds and flowers merged into a duskiness of colouring that gave the impression of uninterrupted heatheriness.

Not even the great cold of these uplands could rob us of a feeling of pleasure at having escaped from the sandy desert. Here we had what we had been longing for for months – coolness, a green landscape, pools of standing water. During our first night we had more water than we desired. The rain came down suddenly, beating with violence on the flimsy bivvies and flowing in streams around and through them. I woke at four o'clock to find little rivers channelling past and underneath me, and the water dripping through the leaky roof of the gharry on to our instruments.

Fortunately, after breakfast, the rain ceased. We had to re-cover the gharry with our useful tarpaulin and look for better quarters. Near us luckily were a few roofless, bomb-blasted Italian aerodrome buildings, with wood enough in them to feed big fires. We managed to dry our blankets, and some of us slept the next night in a native *wogra* – a shocking damp, boggy fold, which we rehabilitated and christened the Charnel House. It was a three-sided stone pen, which we had first to drain and then roof over – a dank vault of a place, smelling of toads and slime – but dry overhead.

> *Black Book: Wednesday 18 November*
> We are still here and operational. It is a blessed rest after our days of hectic travelling. But no complaints. We have travelled 400 miles and more, but have seen less of the war than when we were at PT 97.[3]

A few days later we entered on a period of our journeying of which I do not care to write much. The Crossley, old when we set out, was by this time in serious need of an overhaul, and we had to return to El Adem (Fig. 6) before we found a repair unit capable of dealing with it.[4] No countryside could be barer and more wearying than the land there. After a week of profitless waiting, we took up the chase again, retraced our steps to Maturba, and then began a long drive through the heart of Cyrenaica to Benghasi (Fig. 7).

I shall always think of Monday 30 November as one of the most memorable days in our journey. At first we advanced through Maturba – like moorland, spacious country with vast views and deep wadis filled with white pebbles. On the heights above Maturba village were the ruins of an old Arab stronghold. Farther on, we saw others in better condition, dominating the landscapes like the border castles in England, and in design, not unlike them. But since the highlands of Cyrenaica had never been seriously defended by either side in the desert campaigns, and in the main the landscape hid whatever ruin there was more than the naked sand, it looked a happier country. As we climbed and dropped over a high ridge we came upon a fair land of field, woodland and ploughland – the home of the Cyrenaican colonists. It was uniformly green, with everywhere low bushy coppices of evergreens, thorns and thin-leaved willow-like trees, fine with flowers and musical with birds. Arabs, not the ghostly grey-clad nomads we had seen, went up and down turning over with mule- and camel-drawn ploughs the rich red-brown earth; and the countryside was constellated with the white farmsteads of the Italian colonists.

During our first advance,[5] the colonists had stayed on their farms; during the second,[6] they had crowded into the zone centres; this time they had nearly all been evacuated and we were at liberty to look at their homes. The Italian Government had provided for them a modest but pleasing house. It was neat, appropriate and well-designed. At the front was a shady portico and the main door led from there to a big farm kitchen with wide fireplace and stone floor (Plate 16). This in turn, led on one side into two bedrooms, on another into the sitting room, and on the third into the stockyard, flanked with a big stall which must have served as a byre, stable, sty and roost, all in one. To one side of the building was a capacious underground cistern capable of holding thousands of gallons of water, with inspection covers and a hand pump. With its clear, straight lines and flat roof, its clean whitewash and simple architectural pattern of lines and semicircles, the farmstead looked a compact and efficient little living place.

No one was allowed to forget that fascism had built this house. Fascism had conquered the land, fascism had ploughed and built, fascism had installed the furniture, fascism had transported the settler from Italy to his new home. Each house was marked *Ente Colonizzazione Libya*, followed by the number of the fascist year in which it had been completed. A stone fasces[7] adorned the front wall, a wooden fasces the door of the wardrobe. A saw from the book of Mussolini was stencilled in black on the whitewash, backed up in most cases, with a slogan in bigger letters *Rex, Dux, Credere, Obbedire, Combattere* etc. One abandoned farmstead, which we examined, flaunted this:

        IL DUCE HA SEMPRE RAGIONE
        (The Duce is always right)

in letters worn and fading, as if they were not quite sure now of the truth of their message: and on one of the bigger buildings nearby was this piece of nonsense:

'ACT ALWAYS AS IF THE DUCE HIMSELF WAS WATCHING YOU'

These farmsteads, abandoned, sometimes bullet-marked, and their rooms littered with torn mattresses and the feathers and entrails of immolated chickens and empty bully tins, evoked pity; but the compassion was offset by contempt for the stupidity of those who had provoked the war, who had thought that conceit and bravado were enough to win it and had forgotten how absurd and childish their braggings would look in a day of defeat. In all probability the peasants had not been responsible for these daubed slogans: it looked as if, before Mussolini drove through Cyrenaica to reach Alexandria for the triumphal march, his yes-men had run on before him with tar and brush.

We drove on past these little white villas, with their ploughed and brambly woodlands, until we stopped to camp later in the evening in a little dingle off the road near De Martino (Fig. 7). That evening was full of fine murmurings, and the little notes of birds invisible in the greenery. A still day died lingeringly. Its wraith hung pale apple-green over the western upland. After dinner I climbed in the last light out of

PLATE 16 'Italian colonists' farm near Barce'. The fascist inscription on the facade reads: *Il Duce ha sempre ragione* – 'The Duce is always right'

the dingle and to the summit of a little hill, and looked out over to the west where the pale luminousness gave mystery to the distant ranges and milk-white stars wavered in the darkening sky. There my mind went out with a great longing over the hills and seas, over a continent to where my wife was. I felt as if the distance was annihilated. Just so might I have been looking over the chimneys of my own house over an English moor. I could almost put out my hand and touch my own country. It was a moving moment. A scent came from the bushes and coolness fell from the bright air.

When I found my way back there were glow-worms alight in the bushes, and mushrooms collected and put in water for breakfast. I went to sleep in my bivvy beneath the leaves, grateful for the sight of good country, for water, for peace, and for the visitation of joy that the evening had given.

Some time later, I read how Aeneas in his wanderings had landed on the coast near our camping place, and had spent a forced holiday feasting and hunting the stag over this very country. I re-read in Virgil the story of that holiday, and it seemed that just that pleasure that Virgil had taken in Cyrenaica and had imagined Aeneas enjoying, I too had felt that starry night on the hill near De Martino.

Goodbye to Cyrenaica

The next day there were views more magnificent and arresting than we had hoped for. The road climbed from the little dingle where we had slept for the night (Plate 17), then drawing near to Barce (Fig. 7), fell away, curving through a noble pass. From the head of the pass, driving between craggy boulders and precariously rooted trees flinging out their branches like falling men their arms, we looked down, through a v-shaped frame of hillside, on to a stretching level plain, green with gardens and orchards, and dark-brown with ploughed earth. This was the richest part of Cyrenaica, made fat and fertile by Italian labour.

From the Green Mountain to the Gulf of Sirte • 143

PLATE 17 'Breakfast in the "green belt" near De Martino'

The Tocra pass had been blown, and occasionally JU88s[8] came over to bomb and strafe the waiting traffic: but nothing troubled us and we were soon at Barce. There the natives came running out with eggs, tomatoes, vegetables, chickens and even primus stoves to sell. But we were in a hurry and the eye had to jump from the eggs to pathetic little 'civilian' notices here and there on garden gates, and the foot-high slogans, the *Dux, Rex, Credere, Obbedere, Combattere* daubed everywhere. These catchphrases were growing familiar now, but Barce's special lack of reticence was enough to re-excite disgust. 'Eggis – Eggis – Chai – Eggis', cried the wogs with an egg in one hand and a protesting rooster in the other; but we could not stop.

An opportunity to look more closely at a Cyrenaican zone centre came when we stopped for tiffin near Baracca (Plate 18), a little administrative centre between Barce and Benghasi (Fig. 7). These centres were built to act as focal points for the scattered agricultural settlements – totalitarianism's equivalent of the medieval market town.

PLATE 18 Stopping for tiffin near Baracca: Alec (with mug), Cpl Pryce and Sid

Some of them were admirably designed. At places like Battisti and Olivetti (Fig. 7) all the communal buildings, clubs, shops, school, church, cinema, and the administrative buildings were built together into one imposing and pleasing unit, excellently shaped geometric blocks, clean, white-faced, and with the monotony of straight lines carefully broken by arches and curves. How strongly they were built, I can't say: but they were certainly not entirely jerry-built, and their architecture was graceful. It looked, at quick sight anyhow, as if the Italian colonial administrators had tackled the problem of twentieth century village architecture with enlightenment and freedom from convention.

We looked through one of the administrative buildings at Baracca, a big arcaded building with a clean façade and high airy rooms (Plate 19). The furniture was still there. Apart from one large ornate gilt mirror (with a bullet hole through the middle) it was modern and, if not of the best wood, artistically designed. The floors were laid with good-looking polished stone and the bathroom and lavatories of

From the Green Mountain to the Gulf of Sirte • 145

Plate 19 Baracca: abandoned public building with marble floors. Members of Unit 606 in foreground

white tile. The rooms had not been stingily furnished and any colonial administrator might have been proud of them.

The Italians had had to abandon this equipment. We in turn had to leave it. There was enough furniture to set up more than one ambitious couple: but there it was – useless to conquered and conqueror.

In the afternoon we descended by another fine pass into Tocra (Fig. 7), and after it, the road wandered through well-wooded country to the Mediterranean, visible again. As it unrolled, however, nearer to Benghasi, the land grew level and sandy again. We were re-entering the desert, after a few days' respite. Looking back I saw the Moorish castle which stands at the head of Tocra pass, coloured like clean wood and gleaming in the sun. Quickly it receded, last image of the beautiful and legendary Cyrenaica which we were leaving behind. From Benghasi Corner (Fig. 7) we saw, away over the bay, the mosques and towers and square biscuit-coloured buildings which we had come now to associate with Italian colonial towns, their colour and shape smudged across with the smoke of two tankers burning in the harbour (one was hit by an American bomber on 6 November, and was still burning on 20 November). We stopped for a few minutes, bought tomatoes from the Arab children on the corner, looked at the burnt and broken Bren-carriers in the hedges, and then drove past the ruins of the Agricultural College and south into the desert again. For Benghasi, supposed site of the Garden of the Hesperides, a quick hail, and a quick farewell.

As we sped south, my hopes of seeing the gems of Cyrenaica, Cyrene and Apollonia, grew less and less (Fig. 7). Behind me were the Greek Pentapolis, the basilicas of Cyrene, and the caves and tombs of the early Christians who lived there. But the Axis forces were retreating at record speed. They had withdrawn from Fuka to Mersa Brega, near El Agheila (Fig. 8), about seven hundred miles in eighteen days. Already well behind them, we had no time for sightseeing. Regretting having missed Cyrene, but grateful for what we had seen, we hurried on.

El Agheila

Two days out of Benghasi, along a straight road driven through arid desert and lined with warning signs 'Keep 100 yards interval' – 'You have been warned' – 'Don't be a bloody fool' – 'You will not laugh when Jerry strafes' – we came to Antelat (Fig. 8), another memorable but undistinguished-looking landing ground – a little smoothed out area in a waste of sand. There we stayed long enough to have another luxurious bath, and to see at closer hand some of the natives. Poor wretches, the sport and pity of three great nations, they came to our encampment to beg for biscuits and food. A few were still gay in their dress and cared-for in their appearance, with a few traces of native finery about them, but most were gaunt and ghostly figures, thin and dirty, wrapped for warmth in soiled grey blankets. When they stood up and drew their cloaks around them, close to the neck and over the shoulder, they looked as lean as the stage witches in *Macbeth*.

A few of us went out one day to see their encampment. It was no village but a forlorn collection of drab tents, and as we approached the menfolk came out hastily to bar the way, complaining that for the first time in the war, white soldiers had been molesting their women. It was a puny act of defence, but a show of some kind of honour. Their concern was respected and we withdrew.

A few days later, we assembled with an escort of armoured cars to go forward to the El Agheila positions (Fig. 8), where the Eighth Army was reinforcing to attack Rommel a second time. El Agheila was an ominous name for all Desert Rats. There, both General Wavell and General Auchinleck had been successfully counter-attacked, and the Mersa Brega defences had never been penetrated. We felt that a decisive engagement was to be looked for, and the sight of Agedabia (no pleasant Italian colonial city, but an ugly native town with ugly folk in it, and made even more ugly by bombing and shelling) set the atmosphere for our advance (Fig. 8).

Black Book: Friday 4 December

Off again to the bad lands. There are moments when I feel afraid – I am not afraid to admit it – when I hear we are bound for the bad lands – off right up to the front line – beyond Agedabia.... At times like this, at night, calm, quiet I seem to have conquered fear. I'll experience it again when the bombs begin to fall.

<u>Memo</u> – no fags at all now.

All last night I was sleepless and restless – full of foreboding – yet mindful of Gwen too.... At the end of this day, bedded down, just off the road before El Agheila, dangerously close to enemy lines.

We encamped in a favourable position, in the bottom of a shallow basin, the sides of which shut out all distant views, but gave us a sense of cosiness and security. Not far away from us were fields of sorghum, ploughed and sprouting, and the soil everywhere was fertile and soft. Soil of this texture and depth was always a godsend to us. We could dig ourselves in without over-strenuous labour, and to be dug in did not only mean extra protection, but also additional living space. With the help of a handy *Afrikakorps* shovel (found in an abandoned slit trench) I dug myself a capacious pit and stretched my bivvy over it. Then there was almost room to stand. Certainly there was room to install a camp bed and to have a sand-shelf for books and boxes.

Black Book: Saturday 5 December

Moved nearer the sea and settled down to a second Alamein existence in a strange little place – a saucer-like depression of half greened-over soil. Feeling that I am to stay here a while, I dig my pit.

Sunday wakened early in morning by heavy bombing – JU88s over the road. Two of Bofors crew killed and two injured. During the morning under shell fire. An Italian long-range gun began to shell some of our friends[9] up on the hill and forced them to move – rather unnerving to hear these walloping big bombs bursting every now and then just over the crest of the hill. A miserable frightened sort of day – but shell fire ceased eventually and I spent a fine warm night.

Monday 7 December

In spite of hard work J. Pryce[10] is gone now – I am working one on, two off[11] – had a fairly satisfactory day and in partic had a fine walk during the afternoon....Then a big JU88 came over – all on its own – quite unmolested and we watched it out, out all on its own.

The desert there was like a garden. There was little grass, and the countryside was only lightly filmed over with verdure: but it was abundant with wild flowers, little yellow flowers with unusual petals, stocks, tall tiger lilies that grew to three feet, vivid marigolds and best of all, desert poppies, deep-damask-centred with petals as fine and diaphanous as a wild rose. When we first arrived they were only in bud, but after a week they all began to open and to beautify the scene with their colours and fragrances. As we had by this time no clock or watch that could be relied on (the dust was in them) I conceived the idea of building a sundial. A stick threw the shadow, and cartridges pushed into the soft sand made the figures. It helped the flowers to give us the feeling of having a garden on our doorstep: but it was of little other use.

Our greatest pleasure there was the sea. We knew from the first that it was nearby, and one day I set out to find it. It was a strange walk, over the sandy moorland, across a little plain green with shrubs and weeds, and watched over by a burnt-out Kittyhawk, through a thorny coppice in a gully, where I surprised a flock of sparrows and quail and saw a hare, on to a strange stretch between moorland and water, a ridgy area overdrifted with sand so white that it hurt the eyes, drifted and packed down tight around the roots of bushes till the dying stalks stuck out like thin hair on a bald scalp, and piled in big whalebacked dunes with moulded crests and steep slopes. Near the sea, this moon-white landscape hardened and darkened to redder rock, eroded and laminated in jags and juts, then fell away to the narrow foreshore. This was no pleasure beach. Almost up to the water's edge the sand was overlaid with layers of seaweed, spat up by the little waves, and packed down like hay in a rick.

I was disappointed at first with this spongy fringe of weed, but to my delight, I found beyond it a perfectly sea-worthy sailing boat, without oars, but sound and roomy; and beside it a lifebelt, also in good condition. I stayed just long enough to fix the site in my memory, then hurried back with the good news.

Then began for us a series of happy days. We were well aware of our privations – the poor food, the shortage of water, the absence of news from home – and the greater hardships and daily dangers of the infantry, tank crews, gunners and patrols in front of us, but we were ready to take our fun when it was offered. It was the fortune of our work that at that time there was little to be done, and where there were no weekends or holidays, we took pleasures as they came.

Day after day we walked the four miles over the moors to the beach. Every day the Mediterranean smiled and was beautiful. Beyond the lapping edge of the little waves, it lay warm and still and pure. Our routine was to drag the boat over the weed, put out about fifty yards from the shore, strip and go overboard. No schoolboy ever enjoyed his forbidden dip in the river more than we our daily plunge. To hot bodies the water was cool, to dirty bodies, cleansing. As we walked back with loads of driftwood for the fire on our backs, we felt as fine and hungry as ten men (Plate 20).

We had a second little adventure at El Agheila (Fig. 8). When we were not swimming we explored the unmined countryside. Most of our wanderings were in search of water (we were short at that time and what little we had was almost brackish) and it was this quest that led us one day to two native wells lying in the depressions between the coast and the road. The wells were unfortunately dry, but promised to be interesting. Both had footholds cut in the sides and descent did not appear to be difficult. We decided to go down. We chose first the shallower well. The descent was not quite as simple as it looked for halfway down the walls had collapsed, leaving an awkward gap to manoeuvre past; but by using a length of old telephone wire and leaving one man at the mouth of the hole, we managed to descend in safety.

Plate 20 El Agheila: Corporal Pryce, on the left, and Fred foraging

As soon as we reached the floor of the well, we found that it was more than a simple shaft. Two openings, one in the northern and one in the southern wall, led into caves by narrow low passages. With torches and a hurricane lamp, we investigated, going with caution, because we could not be sure of the floor and were afraid of falling into deeper shafts; but there was no need for great caution. We found that the first short tunnel led into a commodious domed cave, roughly plastered and supported by a stout central stone pillar. The floor was crawling with beetles, there were black scorpions in the corners, and every now and then a bat flew out of the darkness. Neither the bats nor the beetles were pleasant company, but our attention was soon drawn from them. By the light of our lamp, we perceived that the walls of the cave were decorated with an astonishing assortment of pictures. In one place there was a string of unattended camels each chipped out of the plaster; so that it showed up very white against the dull wall. Then came a series of remarkable charcoal sketches. Some were of geometric patterns, the commonest a design of two interlocked triangles, enclosing a sun symbol.

There were line drawings of gazelles, of naked men carrying spears, and one fairly ambitious series of naked men on horseback hunting small deer. Scenting more discoveries, we investigated the second cave, while the air kept good. It was the counterpart of the first – another domed cave showing no signs of recent occupation, and half-filled with sand; and its walls carried similar drawings. There were more camels, more hunting scenes, a problem picture (probably of a woman carrying water with the help of a yoke and surrounded by a halo) and an interesting but confused sketch of a big three-masted sailing boat. The drawings were very unequal in quality. Some were mere scribbles, copies by inferior workmen: but some were characterized by simplicity and vigour. More than that they were provocative. The human sketches were not of Arabs, but of a people who did not dress in full robes, tall, slim naked men resembling black Africans in their carriage and using native spears.

What had these caves been used for? Were they cisterns, dwelling places, or merely refuges in time of raid? Who were the artists – and when did they live? Why did they depict Negroid and not Senussi types? In an attempt to find answers for these questions we descended the second well.

This also turned out to be something more than a well. To the right a tunnel led into a domed cave, but apart from a few rudely chipped figures, it contained nothing new. To the left, another low passage gave access as before to a second cavern, but this time, it in turn, led to a third. Anxious to see everything, we ventured through the second tunnel to find ourselves not in the presence of more carvings, but of bats. There were thousands of them swirling past the unusual light, fluttering in fright up against the roof of the cavern and hanging quivering to the rough wale edges like dirty gloves or pieces of soiled rag. We retired with little ceremony.

This aspect of the day's exploring came to a strange conclusion. Cookie, who had never seen a bat before, and whose only ideas of bats came from Dracula, was half scared, half fascinated by them: and in spite of protests, he fired a few rounds of live ammunition down the shaft. He thought he might stun some of them and be able to examine them at leisure. But the following day when we went down again, not a single bat, dead or alive, was to be seen.

So ended the story of the bats; but the mystery of the cave drawings we have still to solve.

Marble Arch – Soltan

On 13 December, Rommel, in danger of being out-flanked and encircled, withdrew from the El Agheila and Mersa Brega positions, and British troops, for the first time in the campaign, invaded Sirtica. The psychological effect of having broken these defences for the first time was enormous. On 19 December we pulled out of our little valley and prepared with confidence to cross the second great desert.

From the Green Mountain to the Gulf of Sirte • 153

The famous Italian highway ran from Mersa Brega through enervating country; the only relief to the dreary salt lakes, marshes and low bony ridges was occasional glimpses of the ever-blue sea. One day's boring journeying brought us over a weary land to that remarkable monument that had been known to the Eighth Army from the beginning of the campaign by the homely name of Marble Arch (Fig. 8).

Its proper name is Arae Philaenorum, the monument of the Philaeni, and the site on which it stands was marked by other monuments long before General Balbo[12] erected this arrogant arch. It was the burial place of the Philaeni brothers, whose story is a curious one. The legend of their death is this: long ago, the Carthaginians, who ruled from Tunis to Sirte, and the Greeks, who had colonized Cyrenaica down to Agedabia, quarrelled about the ownership of mid-Libya, and the war which broke out was as bitter, and seemed as inconclusive as our desert campaign must have appeared to General Auchinleck's men. Eventually, after a great deal of bloodshed, both parties decided to settle the contest in a curious way.

Two Greek athletes were to set out from Cyrene, the Greek capital, and make for the no-man's-land which ran in those days just where Balbo's arch now stands:[13] and at the same moment two Carthaginians were to leave Tunis. It was to be a walking match and the first pair to arrive were to claim the land for their countrymen. The Philaeni brothers, who walked for the Carthaginians, were the first to arrive, but the Greeks refused to abide by the decision, on the grounds that the Carthaginian brothers had cheated by running. To prove their good faith, the Philaeni brothers volunteered to allow themselves to be buried alive, and the Greeks, to test whether their bluff was being called, called them to abide by their word. They did, and they were buried alive. The Greeks were so impressed by this that they withdrew their objection and the grateful Carthaginians raised an arch to commemorate the honour of their athletes.

I do not know how much of the old structure was left when in the mid-1930s General Balbo conceived the idea of building the new arch and dedicating it to the new fascism. At any rate, only the fascist monument remains now, a high slender erection, threaded through by the Libyan highway, connecting miles of nothingness to more miles of nothingness. The archway is high, a geometric shape of masonry, sloping inward very gently, bearing four cornices at the top, and ending in two triangular ears. On the underside of the arch are bas-reliefs showing the Italians building their famous highway and ploughing up new land for settlers. Two lengthy quotations in Latin are cut on the eastern and western face of the arch and over one of them is a briefer sentence in big well-cut letters. Alme Sol possis nihil Roma visere maius. (Gracious sun, may you never look upon anything greater than the City of Rome). The longer inscriptions say that the Arch portends to show to the whole world the new culture and the new humanity, which are the greatest gifts to mankind of a Rome whose glory and greatness have been restored.

Although the Arch, considered (as it was mainly meant to be) as a piece of publicity, cannot have attracted widespread notice (for Sirtica is too desolate to attract many tourists) it must have impressed those who did pass through it. The land on either side for many miles is so empty of any interest that the most casual traveller must have looked forward to it, as we did, as a break in the visual monotony of the desert. It has a certain elegance, and the view from the unparapeted roof is worthwhile. But it has no strength to its architecture. Compared with the Arch of Marcus Aurelius in Tripoli, or even with the London Marble Arch, its shortcomings are obvious. There is an immature eagerness to gain height and to dominate that robs the structure of solidity and gives an air of flimsiness.

In horizontal niches above the arch are two big male bronze nudes, which must have puzzled many of the Eighth Army soldiers who stopped to look up at the Arch. They are Balbo's bows to the past – the effigies of the Philaeni brothers, whose courageous action prompted this piece of Italian bombast.

Many heroes keep the Philaeni company there now, for in this area the land was treacherously sown with mines of all descriptions. Every step, every turn of the wheel west of El Agheila was a hazard. All along the road the sappers were at work with their detectors, feeling their way like blind men. But they could not detect all the mines, and in the hurry of pursuit, there was always some doubt as to where safe lanes were. One noon, near Nofilia (Fig. 8), one of our airmen, in spite of repeated warnings, cut across a corner at a crossroads. There was a report, and he fell. He had trodden on a small mine that leapt three or four feet into the air and threw pellets outwards in every direction. He was very fortunate, however. Only two of the pellets caught him, one in the shoulder and one in the buttocks, and after a few weeks in a field hospital he recovered.

The crew of one of our sister units had a bad experience.[14] They were landed by aircraft on a landing ground and had to pick their own way through the field to safety. No sooner had they begun to walk than a Bofors unit passed over a mine and all the guncrew was killed. Nevertheless they had to get out of the landing ground to safety. Every step was an adventure but in the end they got to the road without mishap.[15]

We heard many tales of German and Italian cunning. It was said that they laid landmines and booby traps in fruit trees, behind doors and pictures, under the bodies of dead and even wounded soldiers. I cannot speak with any authority about those things, but I do know that the ground all along the line of our advance was as thick with mines as a garden with crocus bulbs.

A few days before Christmas we encamped on the coast near Soltan (Fig. 8). It was considered a dangerous site. Our sergeant, whose weakness was a fondness for exaggerating danger, told us this story:
Meeting an army officer, he asked,
'Just what is there in front of us now sir?'
The officer looked at his watch and said,

'A few minutes ago, there was one patrol between here and the enemy. At the moment there's sweet Fanny Adams.'[16]

But the sergeant had a fondness for shooting a line: no enemy raids came, and the Axis stragglers who were supposed to be working their way along the beaches towards their own lines never showed up. Our greatest anxiety was the presence of mines. It was earnestly dangerous to wander outside the circle of the armoured cars.[17] One had only to watch the sappers at work to know that. A hundred yards away from us, a gang was locating and destroying big Teller mines that had been buried on the road fringes. As each one went off, a monstrous spurt of flame leapt thirty to forty feet in the air with volumed smoke billowing after it; and a noise like a thunderclap made the loose walls of the gharry shake.

However, once more our site was near the sea, and the foreshore still proved a treasure house. Ever since the beginning of our journey we had slept at the best in our little one-man bivvies. We had on board a biggish tent, picked up from heaven knows where, but we had not been able to put it up for lack of poles. However, on the beach at Soltan we found a pile of excellent lengths of wood, all shaped and cut to a uniform size – obviously the jetsam of some wreck. Out of these lengths Bob and Alec, our acknowledged carpenters, cut, sawed and nailed a framework; and two days after our arrival we were able to erect the tent. I think it must have measured about sixteen feet by twelve, and only in the very middle could a man stand up to his full height; but to us it was as roomy as a town hall.

Christmas at Soltan

While we were at Soltan, the enemy was falling back on the defence lines at Buerat (Fig. 8), and relying less on air attack than on mines to hold up the Eighth Army. This was therefore a slack time for us,[18] and we had again a considerable amount of leisure; and we beguiled the time with a new sport. Here the sea was within a few hundred yards and the tracks to it were not mined. The beach was fairly wide, but the water itself was unusually turbulent and dangerous. The bed was strewn with sharp rocks and restless breakers and a heavy back drag made swimming out of the question. However we remembered the German dinghy we had found at Gambut and found we could put it to good use. We waded out with it high above the head, until we were clear of the breakers, then floated it, leapt on board and paddled out. It was surprisingly buoyant. Four of us could find a place for our buttocks on it and ride in on it back to back, with legs dangling over the side (Plate 21). The swell drove it in at first gently, until it was caught by the breakers. Then it rose higher and higher, and sank lower and lower, until the last breaker threw it up, and pitched it down plump, bodies and all, on the beach. Climbing aboard, scrambling for a seat, capsizing, the alarm of rocks below, and the final pitch on the rough sand – these were all part of the fun.

We spent Christmas on this site; in some ways it was the kind of Christmas a dozen castaways might have spent. In the morning we were in the sea with the dinghy; in the afternoon we prepared our

PLATE 21 The German dinghy in the surf at Sirte.

banquet. First we arranged all our available tables (and even made a new one) to make one long banquet board down the middle of the tent; and those who had clean towels went into the depths of their kitbags and spread them for a table cloth. Cookie and Harry built a new oven out of tins and ammunition boxes, while we brought in firewood by relays from the beach. Someone collected flowers and stuck them into empty jars, while I hung the inside of the tent with red berries, the nearest I could find to holly. 'Merry Xmas' was laid out in camel thorn twigs and white shells on smoothed patches of the dunes. The port, the gin, the whisky, the beer, the lime – preserved in a box in the gharry for two months – were brought forth and admired. A fowl of vague kind and condition arrived with the rations, and so did a few mince pies and a slice of cake. The menu was chalked on the side of the gharry, stuffing was made, the 'duck' cleaned and washed, and everything made ready for the great evening meal.

Before we set to, we posed for our photographs, waited for the last watch to be over, and then attacked the finest meal for months. There was duck, pork, vegetables and stuffing, currant dough and cream, Christmas cake, mince pies, biscuits and cheese, beer, oranges and a mug of extra fine Genuine Middle East Golden Brown Brew (as Cookie called his chai). Toasts were proposed – the King, God bless him, the Eighth Army (good old Desert Rats), our wives and sweethearts and mothers in England, 606, the orphans of the desert, the forgotten men – Sgt Clark (cries of Good old Binder,[19] Good old Nobby[20] – Outside with your kitbags). And then we sang. We began with carols, and tackled 'Good King Wenceslas' with myself as the King, and tenor-voiced Nobby as the page – but finding the words of these Christian songs a little unfamiliar, never got to the end. Our will to sing Christmas tunes was there, but memories were weak, and my solo 'Coventry Carol' was appreciated but not enthusiastically received. (A good tune, Fred – a good tune mind – but a bit serious). The sergeant, feeling himself now in voice, broke into,

'If I only had the key of your heart'

and even the unmelodious corporal was prevailed upon to quaver out in the thinnest of voices –

'The sash my fa–ther wore'.

'Do you know?' he said incredulously at the end of it, 'I once sang that in a pub in Ireland – and I got thrown out.' Even Roy chirped out in a bird-like voice, 'By the fireside, we two – just you'. And then Cookie, in the first stage of liquor, 'If I might have a little order, gentlemen, please', began stertorously upon his favourite song,

'You can't put a stop to misfortune
What has to be must be.
I might have been up in the world like you,
And you might have been down like me.'

Soon the war was forgotten; even Christmas was forgotten, in an uproar of maudlin bawling. Jack followed up his melancholy song with the equally dismal, 'I am but a poor blind boy', and finally clung to me weeping and protesting that he'd never had a chance like me, he'd never been educated like me, while the corporal and Roy slept in each other's arms. Cookie was finally put to bed still blubbering and protesting; but this access of tears did not prevent him from rising in the middle of the night and picking the flesh off the duck as clean as a vulture.

So ended our desert Christmas. I had written this poem in October when we were still at Alamein.

> No shepherds watching here by night,
> But sullen armies poised for fight;
> And the artillery's wrathful fire
> Silences the angelic choir.
> Where once the Magi saw a star,
> The heavens now hold a yellow flare,
> And all the parting sky contains
> Is Messerschmidts and Hurricanes.

> Lord, this was once your country. Can
> You not dispense your good again?
> Oh wished-for most, expected least,
> Be born again in the Middle East.

But another Christmas passed without a miracle. Indeed it was a kind of disaster for us. At one magnificent banquet we consumed all our spare rations, and after the feast came the famine. The days after Christmas were dark and hungry, and a mood of deep depression came over us.

I suppose we had reason to be downhearted. The smallness of the unit left us free from the more irksome forms of discipline, but it also left us more isolated than most. We had no spare gharry to fetch for us from ration dumps, from wells and from clothing stores. Ever since we came into the desert we had had to live from hand to mouth, and by the end of the year, we were in poor case. With our own hands and our own scavengings, we had built up some comforts, but there were limits to what could be combed from the desert.

In those days the only good footwear on the unit was several pairs of South African field boots, gifts from an artillery group we had met at Alam el Osmaili (Plate 11). We had only four blankets each. I do not think I could have kept warm through those cold nights if I had not picked up an extra blanket at Gambut; certainly none of us could have kept our beds free from vermin if it had not been for a big tin of anti-louse powder, which Cookie found in a ditch. We received no newspapers. We had no wireless set. Chocolate, sweets, fruit, and all those little extras that a soldier expects to help out his meals with, we rarely saw. All our food came from tins, and night after night, week after week, month after month, M & V[21] was our dinner. We had few books and little light to read by. Tea, sugar and milk were so strictly rationed that for weeks we could not even sweeten the long evenings with a cup of tea. Nearly a thousand miles from Alex (Fig. 5), with Tripoli three hundred miles away to the west, and between us and Tripoli the German and Italian armies, we felt ourselves in

From the Green Mountain to the Gulf of Sirte • 161

civilisation's no-man's-land. Night after night, we had nothing to do but to huddle together in our gharry, in a little space no bigger than, and certainly less comfortable than, a railway compartment, to smoke a few borrowed cigarettes, to discuss endlessly where we could find a little water, where we could beg a tin of milk, where we could borrow a cigarette.

One day we were reduced to cutting down a hard block of ship's tobacco which we found in a drawer, and wrapping the chips in any white paper we could find; and on another occasion, when I found a dead duck lying on a dune, although there was not a shot mark on it, we asked no questions, but ate it.

The miseries must be recorded, but the mind remembers most vividly the pleasures. I recall clearly those sorry hungry nights, but more clearly still my afternoons alone, on the beach of Soltan. It ought to have had sinister associations for me, for shortly before Christmas Day, the sea threw up the body of a dead sailor, bloated and unidentifiable; and he was buried where he was cast up, with only a stick to mark his grave. Yet on that beach I had hours of untroubled pleasure. Over the land the lightly clouded sky would often show a rose red. Far to the south it bloomed with the reflection of the tawny sands that reached down into the heart of the Sahara. But over the sea, the sky was green. At times even the clouds were tinted with green, their whiteness touched to a pale, pure apple green by the upthrown colour of the vivid sea; and beneath this rare sky, the level sea vibrated until it threw up, at its edge, the glorious untameable breakers, battering the beach with their dissolving violence. The land might be harsh and torn with shells and mines and bombs, but the sea could dissolve all disaster into itself. It threw off contamination and perpetually cleansed itself.

Is there an enchantment in the Mediterranean? It has come to be significant for us by a thousand ties. Yet had I never read *Pericles* or the Acts of the Apostles or known where Shelley died, those peaceful afternoons, those walks by the clamorous beach, the crayfish in the pools, the westward and homeward meditations by the rocks, would still have charmed me out of my hunger and melancholy.

Notes

1 According to the 'Black Book', on 16 November Unit 606 'came to our resting place near the drome [at Maturba] and bivvied down for the night'.
2 On the East of Scotland.
3 Peri Track 97, that is the perimeter of airfield or landing ground 97, about 20 miles inland from the Mediterranean between Burg el Arab and Alexandria – probably visited by Fred and other members of 606 during their sojourn at Alam el Osmaili in September–October 1942.
4 The 'Black Book' on Saturday 21 November records: 'Fate settled. We are to go back to Gambut. Roy and Jim left us to go to 607 – poor lads. But we will catch them soon.'
5 Fred is here referring to the British advance from Egypt into Libya in 1941.
6 1942.
7 The *fasces* was a bundle of rods, bound up with an axe in the middle, its blade projecting; hence a symbol of authority adopted by the Italian fascists, led by Mussolini.
8 The JU88 was a high altitude observer plane.
9 The 'friends' were probably another AMES unit, possibly Unit 607.
10 Cpl Pryce.
11 One hour on radar duty, two hours off.
12 Italian governor of Libya.
13 General Balbo's fascist arch was blown up by Col Gadafi in the 1970s, because it was seen as a piece of colonial architecture.
14 An Air Ministry official report recorded: 'as had been foreseen during the preparations for this offensive, it was not always possible for the RDF stations using motor transport to keep up with the speed of the advance. The airborne LWS early warning station was therefore used on 18 December, when it was transported to the Marble Arch landing ground by air. The standard attained by its specially trained RDF crew was excellent – they were able to set up the station and give RDF cover to the landing ground within three-quarters of an hour' (*Radar in Raid Reporting*, 1950, 192). German landmines were no doubt the reason why an AMES 6 series unit was landed.
15 The ORB for 260 Squadron provides interesting complementary details about the difficulty of passing through the minefields. On 19 December a special flying party of forty-eight ground personnel was flown from Belanda [Benghazi] to Marble Arch landing ground in two Lockheed Hudsons and two Bombays. Their purpose was to maintain and refuel the squadron's aircraft until the 'A' party could pass through the minefields of El Agheila and arrive by road. The

arrangements went smoothly, all rations, aviation fuel, bombs and ammunition being supplied by air, AIR 27/1537, TNA, PRO.
16 Nothing at all.
17 Probably provided by the RAF Regiment to supply armed cover for AMES 606 and other radar units in the vicinity.
18 Because there were no incoming German and Italian squadrons, whose detection was the task of Fred's unit, 606.
19 'Binder' – RAF slang for someone who complains excessively.
20 A nickname for anyone called Clark or Clarke. Historically, office clerks and gentry, or 'nobs', wore hats, hence 'nobby'.
21 M & V was short for 'Meat and Vegetables'.

Chapter 6

Out of the Libyan Desert

Privation at Tamet

By New Year's Eve, we were at Tamet, beyond Sirte, at the eastern end of the big salt lakes that stretched west to Misurata and the beginnings of colonized Tripolitania (Fig. 8). Near Sirte, a lonely little town that looked pleasant with its greens and whites, the country was level and misted over with little ragged-petalled flowers that gave off a pleasant scent at evening. Now too, castor oil shrubs with their reddish spiky fruit grew by the roadside. But travelling was tedious and uncomfortable. Almost every bridge and culvert had been blown and every mile brought a difficult up hill and down dale detour round the blown bridge and through the familiar lanes of white ribbon.[1] It was sometimes hazardous to find the safe lane, and on one occasion the huge Crossley sank to the axles in the soft sand. Only the combined use of desert tracks,[2] a digging party and a draught team of three other lorries drew us out of the deep boggy sand.

In the afternoon of New Year's Eve we pitched camp in a stony gully. It was a most forbidding district. Except for a little valley bottom covered with shrubs and flowers it was barren and rocky. Slit trenches could not be dug near the gharry. Two hours work produced only a shallow depression in the rock and two broken precious pick shafts. There was no fuel at hand and no water. Shortly after our arrival there, a dead air-gunner was found nearby and buried in the only place where a grave could be easily dug – the valley bottom less than fifty yards from the mouth of the tent.

The days at Tamet were the most miserable of all our days in North Africa (Fig 8). Normally we had adequate air cover wherever we moved, but here we were undefended for days.[3] Day after day, raiding parties of ME109s came over and swept the landing ground with machine gun fire. At times we would peep out and watch them diving like fishes through the flak; at others we were flat on the ground with faces down while they passed overhead. We heard reports of casualties daily, and during one raid the commander of one of our armoured cars was mortally wounded.[4] Night too brought little respite, except a short interval of peace between sundown and black dark. During those intervals we sat in our hooded camp, devoting the time to one half mug of beer – anticipating it, talking or reading to forget it, deciding when to have it, having it and talking ecstatically about it until the night bombers came. We had managed by this time to dig an efficient slit trench in a stretch of ploughed land nearby: and many a time we had to fall flat, then race across to the trench. But it was bitterly cold there. In the end we would put out our single light and go to bed, opening one eyelid at the distant bumps, two at the closer, and scuttling off at the really close.

This was a wretched, troubled time, and I do not know which was worse – the sudden quick panics of a raid, or the prolonged privations of hunger, thirst and dirt. It seemed that our Christmas banquet had exhausted all our reserves of food. The piled tins of milk, sausage and bacon we had loaded on at El Alamein were used up. We had to depend entirely on our weekly rations – a bad thing, because on active service, supplies are always irregular. At one stage, for four or five days we had no sugar, milk, no bacon, no bread – I do not think we saw one loaf of bread between El Alamein and Tripoli – no sausage, no tomatoes, no cheese, no fruit of any sort, no beans. We had nothing to eat, breakfast, tiffin, dinner, but bully beef, tea without milk and sugar and brewed with brackish water, and marmalade. It was a wretched diet even when supplemented by our dehydrated potatoes. To vary it we took to exchanging surplus tea for margarine and flour from a few soldiers near us, and making pasties. Praise be to those pasties. We whiled away many a tedious hour making flour, cleaning out old derelict mess tins, rendering down margarine and frying (we could do no baking) our sausage-shaped pasties in pools of smoking margarine. The finished articles were a strain on even the soundest digestion – but they were a change from the everyday bully and sodden chips: and what was more, cooking diverted us. In the evenings the tent became a self-contained pastry factory, where, with eyes smarting from the margarine vapour and petrol fumes, we mixed flour, rolled pastry, chopped up bully, and fried and finally devoured the burnt and oil-soaked rolls.

We were hungry. We were exposed to hazard day and night, even from our own primus stove, charged no longer with paraffin, but pure petrol and liable to explode at any moment. We were dirty. We had no more water than the regulation half gallon a day per man, for all purposes: and out of that we could save about half a pint every two or three days for shaving, washing and laundry. Dhobieing[5] was out of the question. Stockings rotted with dirt, and shirts cracked. Our bodies were dirty, our plates were dirty, our utensils dirty, towels dirty, knives, forks and spoons all dirty.

Those were the days of wild daydreaming. While we were sitting together in the vague light Sid would suddenly say, as if he had been thinking of it for hours, 'Just think, Fred, – you go down a street in Blighty. There's pubs to the left, pubs to the right, pubs in front of you and behind you. And inside these pubs there are gallons and gallons of beer – just ready to be pulled. God – all you have to do is to go in – and the girl just pulls like that. And there you have a pint of English beer, with froth at the top.'

And Jack would reply, 'And what about the chocolate, Sid – eh? What about that? You go in, and the chap says, Wot kind would you like? – Wot kind would you like? Stap me. There's stacks of it, Sid – Cadbury's, Motoring Chocolate, Sandwich Block, Milk Tray, all stacked up......'
'And do you remember how you used to hum and ha? My God, I'd give five bob, cash, straight down now, for one sixpenny bar of Cadbury's.'

And one evening we began to talk about water. Most of us had not been in a bath for a year, and the corporal for nearly two years. We began to reckon up how much water an average man used when he took a bath – then how much for his daily washes, how much a water closet used, how much a day's laundry took up, how much for meals and washing up. Why, a man in England might use fifty gallons of water a day. Fifty gallons, and we were allowed half a gallon a day!

We dreamt wildly during the night too, and when we got to comparing our dreams, a curious thing came out. Quite independently, most of us dreamt of coming home, and instead of being welcomed and made much of, we were coldly ignored. Even the conversation in the dreams was alike. 'Yes I'm back from Africa', we would say and the reply, 'Oh, that's very interesting'. And before we could begin to shoot a real line, the conversation was switched to some little gossip about the neighbour, or neighbour's wife.

'I don't think you understand me,' we then said, 'I was at El Alamein when the great breakthrough took place.' But even this was received with the same indifference. 'I was with the Eighth Army', we protested – but no eyebrows were lifted, no eager audience settled to listen to our third-rate exploits. All night long we sat, bewildered, inexplicably ignored and hurt.

What motivated that dream? I think it was a real fear, the deep concern of every man forced to spend years away from his wife, his children, his mother and his father; the fear that time and distance would be too much for even the strongest ties. He feared that he would return, not as a welcomed son, husband or father, but like Ulysses unrecognized, a stranger, out of place in a new order of interests and loyalties that had grown up in his absence.

From the beginning to the end we had little but privation at Tamet. Our days were sometimes cheered by the visit of a mercurial sergeant, who was in charge of our sister station.[6] The prince of scroungers, he had picked up somewhere an abandoned Spa truck, probably contemporary with the Ford T and just as capricious. Happy the moment when 'Fanlight Fannie' was seen approaching with bumps, jerks and snorts over the sand towards 606. If the sergeant did not actually bring much in his pockets, he always had a store of incredible anecdotes, and boundless promises.

But on the whole they were grim days, and they ended as they began. On our very last night, the bombers came while we were trying to play bridge.[7] A bomb fell alarmingly close. We fell flat on the ground, waited and then ran for the trench. Outside the air seemed full of planes. Flares were dropping all around us, and the ground gunners in a ring around us were firing tracers at the little white parachutes. When I come to look back I recall the unusual beauty of the light of the flares, and their pacific downward motion. But I did not stop in my run to make these observations consciously. Streams of bullets came over our heads from all directions, their lines coming closer and closer to the ground as the parachutes dropped; and more curved lines of tracers came from the rear gunners of the invisible German planes. Crouching there, we felt like little animals who had taken shelter in a thicket, but the hunter's lamp was on them and the bead drawn.

Fortunately no one took hurt; and the next morning news came that Rommel had again been outflanked. On the night of 15–16 January he withdrew from the Buerat defences (Fig. 8). Now he was falling back upon Tripoli (Fig. 9), and again we were in pursuit.

Bir Dufan

Of the few days after Tamet, I can remember scarcely anything. For the second time our route took us south, away from the sea, and into the heart of the Blue. Hour after hour we drove through an infinitely dreary landscape without a single landmark to draw our interest. Again the rocky desert pitched us about unmercifully, and the soft desert threw up fine sand into our eyes, nose and mouth. We had only one diversion – to take out a tattered old map of Libya, to reckon from it in what direction we were heading and how far we were from the nearest 'green belt'. The closest cultivated area was Beni Ulid (Fig. 9): the map placed it in a little pool of green colour. So Beni Ulid was our hourly dream. Oh, only to get to Beni Ulid to see grass and trees, to have water and perhaps vegetables! But hour after hour went by and the land was still as dry, sterile and dispiriting as ever.

Near Sedada (Fig. 9), it began at last, to change. We started to drop into deep wadis, to find ourselves surrounded by curious flat-topped hills, hard cores of craggy table-topped rock, falling away at the edges in screes of smaller boulders and sand. Unfortunately the relief was temporary only; beyond Sedada the country levelled out again, and at Bir Dufan (Fig. 9),[8] our next stopping place, we were on the familiar site. It was Burg el Arab, Antelat, Tamet, all over again – an undistinguished level of aridity made into a landing ground and given a name.

Shortly after we had pitched camp, a Senussi came to see us. By this time an Arab had come to be for us a man who probably knew where to find water; and water pure or impure we had to have. He told us there was a well four kilometres away, and immediately we prepared to walk it with him; but he put us off, saying it was too late, and we would be shot at by sentries on the way back. He promised to bring us some water the next day.

We let him go with misgiving. The way of all Arabs was to promise much (*bucra* the whole world; today a little *backsheesh*[9] to be going on with) and to fulfil nothing. However the next morning, to our great surprise, he came back, a little boy with him, and a donkey with two dirty and dinted cans pannier-wise on its back.

The water turned out to be strange-looking stuff, very yellow and clayey, but it made wonderful tea. We showered gifts on the old man, out of pity for him and his son, who was shivering with a bad cold – but more out of gratitude, for water was gold to us. I gave him a white shirt I had picked up at Daba and meant to use for handkerchiefs and bandages, and he draped it tenderly around his little boy. Then we gave him tea, petrol for the sores on his donkeys and camels, and biscuits and marmalade. He was a peaceable old man, very hungry, very solicitous for his son, and grateful. When a second and older son appeared, he ordered him to take back the donkey for more water, and then made himself at home with us. We first feasted him, and then, when he expressed a desire to shave, as Sid was doing, we gave him an old razor, brush and soap, and even an old toothbrush and paste. He was amusingly at ease. That we were strangers did not embarrass him: that we were foreigners did not disconcert him: that we were armed and part of a victorious army did not alarm him. With sangfroid and amusing unconcern he meticulously shaved the little patch of hair above both ears (he would not be persuaded to touch his beard) – then scrubbed and scrubbed with inch after inch of paste at his big blackened teeth. We sat around him, amused at the entertainment, occasionally taunting him with long abusive sentences in English, which, not understood, neither amused nor offended him – and drinking the delicious 'chai'.

A few days later I came across the pool from which the old man had drawn his much-enjoyed water. It was a little sausage-shaped pond under a clump of sturdy gnarled trees. It was filled with mud and old tins, and sheep and goat droppings floated on the surface. It was no more than a foul watering place for animals. Their mouths had slobbered in it, and their soiled feet had paddled in it; this was our delicious 'chai'. This was the finest water we had tasted and drunk since Benghasi. Nevertheless we could not bring ourselves to throw it away: and in the end, puddle or not, we drank it all.

Near the pond I came across a fairly big deserted Arab village. It was apparently recently abandoned, for most of the houses, though unfurnished, were sound. These houses were all made of desert stone, roughly hewn, loosely masoned on the outside but plastered more carefully on the inside. Each separate house consisted of one room only, entered through a very narrow doorway big enough to admit one person only at a time. These doors evidenced the slimness of the

Senussi. Poverty and hard living had kept them all, young and old, very lean. The simpler rooms were in two parts, one half-level with the ground, the other raised a foot or so: the bigger had two daises, leaving a well in the middle. The walls were as thick as a peel tower's, pierced with small circular holes for ventilation and splashed on the inside with a rough pattern in whitewash.

Just inside the entrance (always open for there was no door) was a hollow for a fire and a hook for a lamp: and some of the more ambitiously planned rooms had little stone cupboards in the walls. The floor was of stone, softened over with stamped down earth, and the roof had been made by laying beams of all shapes and thicknesses over the walls, filling in the gaps with smaller boughs, and then bushes and whins, and by covering everything with clay and stones. The houses were all built together haphazardly, crowding up against each other and sometimes walling in a sheep or goat fold. Apparently it is not only lack of living space that makes people build slums. With all the desert to build in, these Senussi had chosen to huddle their houses together as tight as sheep in a threatened flock. With space enough for a mansion each, they preferred to house a family in one room as small as a suburban kitchen.

Out of the desert

When we advanced from Bir Dufan it was with real expectancy (Fig. 9). We knew that little lay now between us and the 'green belt'. Columbus drawing close to the coast of America could hardly have felt greater excitement than we did at the prospect of emerging at last from the howling wilderness. We were bound at last for Beni Ulid, and there we knew was humanity, food, water and shade.

Nevertheless we had still to spend many almost insufferable hours before we came at last to the edge of a valley steep-sided enough to resemble a canyon, with sharp walls that sloped to a flat built-up valley floor. On the edge of the slope were square battlemented buildings, washed over with a dispiriting pink colour. These were the barracks and prisons of the Italian garrison that watched over this outpost of its empire. The floor of the valley and the far slope were close set with native homes, each with its black, narrow slit of a doorway, and all crowded together until the village looked more like a big honeycomb than a human settlement. There were little palm groves, tiny allotments with seedbeds and small plots, small fields divided and sub-divided, water troughs, and pipes gushing with water.

This at last was Beni Ulid (Fig. 9) – the outpost of Tripolitania, won not so long ago by the Italians from a recalcitrant Arab people, and lost by them in a few days. There was not here the verdure we had hoped to find; but there were police courts, a school, road signs, the beginnings of a motor road, and even street lighting. We were in civilization's suburbs. We would soon be in benevolent country again.

About a score or more kilometres along the road, we were granted the vision long awaited. On 20 January 1943 the Eighth Army occupied, and on 21 January we entered the village of Tarhuna, twenty-two miles from Tripoli (Fig.9).

Imagine coming at last out of the dreadful Sirtican Desert; out of the stony places, the dusty tracks, the barren, tawny hills, broken and infructuous, out of a naked flinty land, upon a village conceived by European minds, and built by European hands. Picture a gentle smoothed slope of fertile land, with a metalled road running over it: on each side of the road, grouped with charming irregularity, white and rose-tinted houses, varied in shape and size, but forming together the pleasing pattern of a European village. Imagine the lines and angles and planes of the houses broken, and their tints made more pure, by dark-lined cypresses, and tall tapering poplars. Imagine beyond the purlieus of this little grouping of tinted houses and sombre solid evergreens, orchards of slender-branched olives, gardens of vegetables with beans and peas in flower, and bright red chillies, almond trees in blossom – all an oasis of colour and life. That was how we saw Tarhuna. Who can blame us if we exaggerated the beauty of its position, and heightened to ourselves the colour of its walls and vegetation?

The coming to Tarhuna was perhaps the most exciting of all the events of our long journey ; and it is not difficult to understand the reasons for our pleasure. Now at last, we were on the threshold of humanity's land. Before us were gardens, fruit, shops, roads – and water in abundance. At last we were reprieved from dirty clothes, dirty bodies. We were coming out of the darkness.

We leaguered near a village cistern that night, a few miles beyond Tarhuna. There were Italian colonials to talk with; they spoke quite openly about the mutinousness of the Arabs, who, in the interval between the departure of the Italian and the arrival of the British police, had threatened and looted; and they told us about the famine, the German retreat, the fortifications at Castel Benito (Fig. 9). We drew eighty gallons of water from the cistern, and bathed and supped sumptuously. There were young lettuce and thin spring onions to be had, and with their help our M & V acquired a new flavour. We put up our tents in a big pit, which the Axis soldiers had dug for their gharries. We were relieved and confident.

The Italians were in the main friendly, and their friendliness and readiness to fraternize precluded compassion; but one sight I remember especially. We strolled, rather timorously, into the yard of a big farmhouse. We went hesitantly, not desiring to disturb the privacy of the family. On the steps of the veranda were sitting a youth, an older girl, and behind them, in a rocking chair, was the mother. There was no grown man to be seen. The old woman was knitting, the younger people doing nothing at all. Their silence was so dignified that we hardly dared to approach them; but Jack, the cook, went up to them and said hesitantly, '*Beida? Uova?*' The old woman looked up and said only one word, '*Niente.*' 'Come away, Jack', I said, and we withdrew shamefacedly. *Niente.* Nothing at all. What had that old woman lost, to make her say '*Niente*' so finally and woefully? Who knows?

That night when I lay down to sleep, I could hear somewhere in front of us a dull report – buboom – buboom. It was the noise of two 88mm German guns holding up the spearhead of our advance in the pass between Tarhuna and Castel Benito (Fig. 9). As I fell asleep I could still hear buboom, buboom, buboom. The gunners were still holding the pass. But I woke again for some reason towards early morning, and the guns were silent. The road to Castel Benito was clear.

Castel Benito

The next morning, after a long wait, we began to file slowly through the gorge out of Tarhuna. During the day, word went round that Castel Benito was burning, and when we settled down in the darkness of that evening, we thought we could see the glow of the fires. What a night! Long after darkness had come down, lorry after lorry came rolling out of the gorge, convoy after convoy fanned out and deployed over the plain. It seemed as if all that immense volume of traffic that had poured through the breach at El Alamein, and then dispersed over the Libyan desert, was now reassembling for the entry into Tripoli. Jeep and three-tonner, staff car and 'ops' gharry,[10] gun carriage and supply waggon, all came rumbling out of the defile in endless succession. The big plain, which was the only available leaguering place, was as overcrowded as a slum in half an hour. A quiet corner picked out for safety was invaded by new arrivals even before the tent pegs were driven in; and long after we had gone to bed, the night was loud with the shouting of directions, the clashing of gears, and the churning of big wheels in the soft sand.

We were up again before the stars were out of the sky, and packing hastily to get on to the road before the bulk of the traffic began to move; and of the next hours I can remember scarcely anything. Perhaps we leaguered for another night, perhaps we didn't. Nothing remains in my mind but haste, expectation, trepidation as we swung off the main track through possible mine belts, and a great longing to arrive.

At last, at long last, we were driving along green avenues. It was a gloriously clear morning, all greenness and blueness, with a breeze that made a noise in the leaves of the eucalyptus trees. That little noise was a lovely sound to us. Vivid after the long silence of the treeless desert, it was sounding us into cornfields and orchards again.

Under the peeled eucalyptus trees, and in the groves of olives and lemons, lay the last wreckage of Libya's defenders. At one point near an almond tree in blossom was a shattered medical supply waggon, with phials and bottles and lint and plaster littered in the ditch. At another, someone with a taste for irony had taken a big portrait of Mussolini, and leant it against a tree trunk, so that the grim face of the Duce was looking sternly towards the victorious stream of traffic that was driving upon his prized city. Here the dictator was holding his last Libyan review, and past him came the varied traffic of the conquerors – tank carriers with their crews sitting high, in black berets on the turret; Bren carriers, every rider yellow with dust; soldiers joyriding in captured Volkswagens; carloads of redcaps, stiff and solemn; jeeps with officers with maps on their knees, and gharries of African pioneers wearing overcoats even in this sunshine. Almost every gharry carried the name of some remembered English girl; there were Beryls and Margarets and Gwens by the score. Some flaunted their nicknames, 'The Geordies',[11] 'Brummagem Lads',[12] 'The Rank Outsiders', and some their slogans. One, I remember, displayed a big black painting of a teapot, and round it this gem of desert philosophy – 'When in doubt, brew up'. Down the road they came, nose to tail, all swinging their emblem and tavern sign, the sooty and treasured chai bucket.

Then we were at Castel Benito, parked under the big pylons that belonged to the airport, waiting for the word to jump down and settle in (Fig. 9). It came. On the spot where Mussolini had received the sword of Islam many years ago, General Montgomery received the keys of Tripoli. Rommel was still retreating and Libya was ours at last.

Knowing that we would be given a rest here, we drove the Crossley out into the middle of an olive grove, and commandeered a set of rooms in the Regia Aeronautica[13] buildings. Not one of these blocks had been hit by a bomb. The bombing had been accurately centred on the hangars and the airfield. The fittings were all in disorder, the rooms dirty, and the floor littered with broken wood and paper, glass and documents. But to us, every room was a palace. In half an hour we assembled all our treasure-trove – tables, soft-seated chairs, a kitchen with range and sink, mattresses and beds, bookshelves, suitcases and lamps. We swept the rooms and set up home. Then the Arabs came to the windows, with eggs and vegetables in exchange for tea and biscuits, and we had supper royal in our new establishment. We bathed and changed our clothes, and celebrated the victory with cheap Italian red wine. There was ripe festivity that night, ending, not unexpectedly with Cookie's sporting a black eye acquired in some melee, and meekly receiving another lecture from the puritanical sergeant. But drunk or sober, everyone was filled with a glorious sense of achievement and release.

Yet for the life of me, I could not feel at first the relief I ought to have felt. To begin with, I could not sleep well. I had slept too long on the ground or in the protective hollow of a sagging camp-bed. I even fell out of bed the first night; and every night, as soon as darkness came, I was unusually haunted by a feeling of uneasiness and insecurity. I suppose it was a kind of claustrophobia. After so many months feeding, washing and sleeping in the open, I could not use myself to four walls and a roof. After sunset I was the victim of the most unreasonable fears.

Nevertheless Castel Benito was a beautiful place to us. The hangars on the airfield were only skeletons by the time we got there, with roofs and walls blasted off their bare ribs. The landing ground was littered with abandoned and destroyed aircraft. In one corner the wrecks were piled high. The buildings in the village were deserted, and the school a shambles of maps, inkwells, exercise books, chalk, broken seats and cupboards. But the airfield was green and unploughed.[14] Before the Germans could plough it, the ploughmen who had furrowed such fantastic patterns in the sand at Ghindel and Buerat were dispersed and their ploughs destroyed, and the spring evenings were mellow and peaceful over the broken township. There were orderly olive groves, and fields of young corn coming up, with lines of cypress and eucalyptus along them; the days were steadily fine, and the sun shone brilliantly upon the flowers in the hedges, the almond blossom, and the white of the wellheads. Not even the arrival later of seldom-seen adjutants, discipline corporals and sergeants with their sheets of rules and regulations, could seriously spoil the charm of our stay there.

At Castel Benito I met one evening a group of Italian civilians who had been loosely interned there. They had been evacuated from Benghasi but finally left behind in the hurried evacuation of Tripolitania. Most of them spoke good French and were willing to talk. We said very little about the war. They talked most readily about the archaeological glories of Libya – Cyrene, Leptis Magna and Sabratha; and in turn they asked me about P. G. Wodehouse, Bernard Shaw, Jerome K. Jerome and other English humorists whom they had read and admired. I felt that in our conversations, Mussolini had suffered as great a defeat as at the hands of General Montgomery. The allegiances of these men were not to the much-boasted achievements of fascism, but to the common international achievements of Roman architecture and English literature. The new philosophy of the glorification of war and of race arrogance had left them untouched. I shall always remember those bankers from Benghasi for their learning and their courtesy.

Notes

1 The white ribbon marked the secure track to be followed, as distinct from the dangerous mined areas.
2 Desert tracks were boards, carried on the gharry of Unit 606, which could be placed under the wheels to give them purchase when travelling over soft sand.
3 It is unclear why AMES 606 was left undefended, but new Kittyhawks model III were introduced in December 1942, and it may have been that the rotation of the old and new aircraft affected the cover they could give against air attack.

4　The armoured cars were to protect Unit 606 and its precious radar kit.
5　Washing clothes.
6　Another radar unit, perhaps Unit 607, or a unit of a different series (such as an AMES 500 Unit).
7　From Italy (Sicily) and possibly Greece (Crete) (Fig. 5).
8　260 Squadron's ORB records that their advance party left ahead of AMES 606. 260 Squadron's 'A' party moved on 13 January 'and proceeded to Bir Durfan; this took 6 days. On this occasion 'A' Party followed the army very closely,' 12 January, 1943, AIR 27/ 1537, TNA, PRO.
9　*Backsheesh* means alms or a gift.
10　Ops gharry or radar-carrying gharry.
11　From Newcastle
12　From Birmingham
13　Italian Air Force.
14　Ploughing would have made the airfield beyond the runways unusable as a landing strip.

CHAPTER 7

The Cities and Towns of Tripolitania: Reflections on Libya

Tripoli

At Castel Benito, Homs was behind us, and I knew to my great regret that I had missed Libya's second great sight, the city of Leptis Magna (Fig. 9). Pursuit had hurried me past the remains of both Greek glory in Cyrenaica and Roman glory in Tripolitania. It was for that reason that I looked forward with special anticipation to Tripoli (Fig. 9). Tripoli was one of the great Roman cities in North Africa. Under the strange name of Oea it had attained some consequence, and in the later days of the empire, Septimus Severus, whose statue used to stand in the Piazza near the Castello, had greatly embellished it. It was overrun first by the Berbers and then by the Arabs, became in the Middle Ages a Corsair port, passed eventually under Turkish dominion, and was ruled lackadaisically by the Caramanli Pashas until it was ceded to Italy at the Treaty of Lausanne in 1912. Roman remains, the vestiges of near-eastern picturesqueness, the bold architecture of fascism at its most determined – I hoped to see them all. Besides, having looked so long at a country where Nature only had been at work, I was anxious to see again the handiwork of civilized man.

There was another, more worldly, element in my impatience. While we were near Alamein, we had looked back to Alexandria as the earthly paradise – the town of civilians, lights, cinemas, music, the gastronomic delights of ice cream and chocolate, the human pleasures of clean baths and clean clothes. Once the offensive began, Tripoli became the centre of our hopes and daydreams. It shone in our imaginations as the second Alex, the home of all luxuries.

Our doubts as to Tripoli's fitness to play the part of another Alexandria to hungry and thirsty campaigners were first awakened by the Italian civilians at Castel Benito. When I told them how much we were looking forward to ice cream and iced beer and fresh fruit, they laughed and said, 'So are we, Monsieur! We too have forgotten what those things taste like. But you will find nothing at Tripoli. It is *une ville morte.*'

So indeed it looked when we first visited it – a sad, frightened, dead town. There were very few Italians on the streets, and no shops were open. It was a town of shocked and mistrustful citizens still unsure as to how the British were going to treat them. Within a few days however they gathered confidence. When they realized that the Tommies were not the vicious decadent Anglo-Saxon looters that fascist propaganda had made them out to be, but honest folk, prepared to pay for everything they had, they began to take down the shutters and open the doors, and stocks of souvenirs and clothing, hidden away for weeks, were brought out for sale. Before this happened and shopping began in earnest, I had time to look round the city and see it as it was in the first few days of occupation.

Like all eastern cities where Europeans rule, it consisted of two parts – the old and the new. In Tripoli those two parts were clearly separate, and the point of division was the Moorish Castello. The Castello stood in the heart of the city, and was almost the midpoint of the large arc formed by the harbour. The harbour itself was small, protected by two moles, which almost closed it in, and halcyon in its calmness. A great number of ships lay burnt, broken and listed there. One most forlorn wreck was the burnt skeleton of a big green and white troopship, which lay across the mouth of the bay; but the arc of blue water was bounded by a fine almost unspoilt promenade, the Lungomare Conte Volpi, an elegant drive balustraded, and planted with little greens and dwarf palms, and spoilt only by the rows of rather ugly iron flagpoles set all along its length. Near the castle, a broad flight of steps ran up from the water's edge to the promenade, flanked by two tall shapely but fragile pillars, one carrying a statue of the wolf suckling Romulus and Remus, and the other a three-masted schooner, the emblem of Tripoli. It was just behind those pillars that the big, solid Moorish castle rose – with its back towards the old city and its face turned towards the new city – and beneath it a statue of Mussolini, mercifully hidden from ironic eyes by walls of sandbags.

The old city behind it was a maze of small alleys, wide enough only for wheelbarrows, arched over for most of their length with trellis work carrying old vine stems, and housing diminutive shops with diminutive windows, diminutive counters and diminutive stocks, so dark inside that a candle was necessary even at midday. From these ways led even smaller alleys and wynds with mysterious house fronts, doors bolted and shut, leading to sordid penthouses where silversmiths worked, to broader rooms hung with carpets and smelling exotically of strong perfumes, to mosques with thick pillars and carved arches. Here were grimy artisans, notably industrious, forging with heaps of charcoal and cinders at their side, or hammering away at knick-knacks; there, wealthier citizens in black silk galabeyas and gold-coloured headdresses. Occasionally a reverend and patriarchal Senussi sat drinking coffee from a tiny cup in the open street, while past him wandered poor Italians, Jews, Berbers, Palestinians and Africans. Everywhere there was a fascinating play of light and shadow in the alleyways, glimpses of mystery, of past riches and hidden magnificence.

But if there was age and charm of age in the old town, it was modern, industrial, mass-producing Italy that filled the shops. These shops, most of them the size of a good English cupboard, were laid out hugger-mugger with cheap laces, garish silks, inferior soaps, razors and blades, poor postcards and tawdry little handkerchiefs with *Ricorda da Libya* stamped carelessly on them. Foolish to look for treasures of eastern craftsmanship. The Tripoli Arab was the Cairo Arab all over again, with the same eye for profit. The silversmiths, for example, lost no time in bringing their wares up to date. The ring that had been begun for an *Afrikakorps* panzer soldier ended on the finger of a kilted Scot.

The new town was not as well planned as it might have been. The unity, which was the excellence of the finer zone centres, was not so well sustained here. Nevertheless the streets were wide and spacious, leading away from the Castello in bold straight lines. Most of the buildings were good in design, modern and coloured a glistening white. The severity of their rectangularity was in places relieved by ornamental balconies in filigree ironwork, painted a pleasant green for easy contrast; and on the outskirts of the town masses of bougainvillea made the whiteness of the walls whiter still. Had the general architectural style (which enabled modern buildings like the tall Hotel Waddan to harmonize with older structures like the Castello) been consistently employed, Tripoli would have been a real triumph; but here and there the Italian decorators had unhappily varied the pure white of their best buildings with a dull dispiriting pink, and abandoned the simplicity of their best architectural form for the neo-orientalism of the Grand Hotel and the baroque of the Cathedral. In spite of these mistakes, Tripoli must have had in the days of peace the virtues of cleanliness and elegance. Most of its buildings are worthy civic architecture, and it impressed as a whiter and brighter city than Cairo.

When we came to it, however, it was broken, hungry and poor. Soldiers and airmen were forbidden to buy essential foods from civilians; but the ban was unnecessary. There was virtually no food for sale. Natives hawked a few bitter oranges, slabs of sticky almond toffee, sweetbreads of strange make, and villainous ice cream; and in the bazaars we could buy a few nuts. But the people were gravely short of cereals, and over the disorganized city hung the other threat of typhus. Soon the old city was out of bounds.

For most of the men who saw it in those days, Tripoli was a great disappointment. The last and most prized city of the Italian empire, where there was to be feasting and carousing, turned out to be a hungry and fever-stricken city where it was easier to buy a ring for a quarter pound of tea than a pound note, and a packet of biscuits was more welcome to a shopkeeper than a shilling.

Before we left Tripoli I saw one of the relics of the Roman city, the arch of Marcus Aurelius, a seventeen hundred year old monument, which the Italians found buried but still standing when they occupied Tripoli. This arch does not aspire to the soaring ambitiousness of the fascist propaganda monuments. It is only about twenty-five feet high and eight feet of that is below the level of the square in which it stands. Arab builders consciously or unconsciously did their best to hide or overshadow it; even now it stands in unimposing surroundings. The Italians however restored it, cleaned it, and tidied the adjacent pathways; so that even against its rather untidy background it stands out as a solid and impressive structure, preaching the same moral – the solidity and durability of old Roman building seen against the chancy fragility of the more arrogant fascist erections.

West of Tripoli

While we were resting at Castel Benito, the indefatigable Eighth Army was driving the Axis out of the last corners of Tripolitania; and after a while, we moved forward to rejoin them. It was a glorious sunny morning when we pulled out of our olive grove and drove through Tripoli's suburbs, with Alec and myself riding on the high roof of the gharry to lift trailing telephone wires over the aerial.[1] We passed through the oasis of Sansur, drove through a magnificent palm grove at Zavia and past the tiny Italian railway with its comical stations, and came towards the end of the first day to the village of Sorman (Fig. 9).

Near Sorman we saw our first troglodyte dwellings. Just off the main road, and within a few yards of the traffic, was a shallow pit with an uneven mouth. The floor of the pit, which was about fifteen feet below the surface of the road, was littered with fodder, wet and decaying, and from it opened four or five rude caves, some with a door, others with a clumsy ill-fitting framework of boards to keep out rain and cold. None of the caves had windows or chimneys, but they were inhabited. Outside one opening, an old man sat in the sun, cross-legged like a tailor. He seemed blind and infirm. The flies settled on his head and face, but he made no effort to drive them off. He sat with his head down, feeling for his skin under his rags, and scratching. In the well space with him were a cow and a donkey, both eating the wet and stinking fodder, and the ground everywhere was dotted with dung. Presently an old woman came out of the darkness of one of the caves and climbed slowly out of the pit. She was old and hideous. Her clothes were filthy rags. When she saw us she pulled the hem of her garment across her face and looked past it with one eye. I caught a glimpse of her face before she hid it. It was scabbed and mottled blue with some dreadful disease.

I do not think I have ever seen human beings so wretched. How could humanity, and humanity under the protection of a modern power, live so vilely? Age and infirmity, dirt and disease, vermin and darkness – even animals lived cleaner than this. Here humanity drew near to the reptile in the cave. Pity was swamped by nausea. Fortunately the events of the next few days helped me to forget this dreadful sight. We drove on from there, and before darkness came, put up our tent on the outskirts of an oasis a mile or two away.

There we leaguered for a while in an admirable place. The homes of the villagers, whose neighbours we became, were primitive, loosely-built huts of dry palm branches, put up without skill or care, and incapable of holding out the weather. But the villagers themselves were clean, diligent and friendly. Their wells were carefully built and rigged, and the small cultivated patches near the houses planned and orderly. Their bigger fields were hedged with dykes of soil piled high and flattened into the shape of a thick wall. They had pride in their agriculture, and any children who wantonly damaged these walls were strictly taken to task. We pitched our tent under the palms, and their clustered trunks gave us shade and shelter, a sense of security and cosiness. Water was plentiful and good, and the natives, in addition to being unusually industrious, turned out to be less servile, more frank, less greedy and more amusing than we had met before.

As soon as we had settled, the boys came running to see who we were and what we had (for every unit was to them a body of potential tradesmen). When they found we had tea to spare, they ran off excitedly, and man and boy came in procession to offer us eggs, carrots, and dried dates in barter. The conversation that invariably followed the arrival of the egg-bringers was no masterpiece of colloquial Arabic. It was conducted in a working vocabulary of far less than a dozen words – *quoiz* and *mushquoiz* – good and no good; *shufti*, show; *bucra*, tomorrow; a few numerals, and of course, *backsheesh*. But accompanied by a versatile display of miming, these few words were adequate. Initial generosity, patent fair play, astonishment at dissatisfaction, indignation and final softening on our part – dismay, protest and supplication on theirs, culminating in the final magnanimity of the *backsheesh* – that was the routine comedy of the transaction, richly enjoyed by both sides.

Biscuits were a welcome *backsheesh*, because there was at that time a great grain shortage. Probably cereals had been scarce for some time, for although the grown men were lean but strong and muscular, the children were all undernourished and undersized. They had an insatiable appetite for our hard service biscuits, and were always grateful for them. And not only were they permanently hungry; they were all badly clothed and shod. During our stay at Sorman it rained frequently and heavily, and a cold wind blew. Although all seemed pleased with the rain, and told us that it was good for the crops, the children fared badly. The ground was constantly damp under their bare feet, and they must have slept wet. Most of them had a cold and some of them coughed shockingly. Yet they were gay and grateful youngsters. We brought them around our fire and fed them. There they chatted and laughed, trotting out the few Italian words they had picked up in the fascist schools, and learning English words and names. Few would eat our English dinner but biscuits they never tired of, and any scrap of clothing was a welcome gift. Most of us had bush jackets given us by the South Africans,[2] and these made long and absurd but warm overcoats for the boys. After they had been given clothing they ran off home and some brought their fathers, who thanked us not with words but with their eyes.

But the most grateful of all the natives of Sorman was a disreputable unsavoury old beggar who haunted our campsite. He came every day, but had nothing to sell or to exchange. He was ugly and dirty, and, like most human beings, we preferred to give to those who were pleasant and gay rather than the unpleasant and ugly. On the morning of our departure, however, we could not help feeling sorry for him. It was a very damp day. A light drizzling rain was falling and the air was chilly.

He had nothing to protect him from the weather but a ragged undergarment and an even more ragged blanket cloak pulled around his head and shoulders. He stood fearfully a few yards from us, pointing to his bare legs and crying '*Saggar, saggar!*' (cold, cold). It seemed a shame to leave him cold and bare. Two of us gave him a shilling each, and told him as best we could to go to the Suq and buy himself cloth. He was transformed with delight, less at having received alms than at having been at last noticed and considered. He grinned and nodded, crying '*Quoiz, quoiz!*' hopping now on one foot and then on the other. As he went off, he kept looking back, still dancing for pleasure and crying '*Enta quoiz – enta quoizqateer*'. He vanished into the palm grove still hopping in his strange way.

Our stay at Sorman was a happy one. These Senussi were nearer to us in spirit than any other natives we had met. One handsome young man named Miub came to be a great friend. He was a lightish-skinned boy who dressed well in white pantaloons, embroidered waistcoat and black velvet cloak hemmed with scarlet. He brought us eggs and dates, showed us which wells were good, and took us one day to the Suq. He was a good boy, a beggar of course, but a beggar who enjoyed the fun and was not greatly concerned with what he got out of it. At Sorman we found lemons and desert sandals, and it was during my stay there that I saw what was to me the finest of all the desert sights, the old theatre at Sabratha.

Sabratha

When I was at Sorman, I recalled my conversation with the Italian refugees at Castel Benito, and wondered if I were yet within easy distance of the Roman theatre at Sabratha (Fig. 9); and when Miub told me that the ruins were only a few kilometres away, I made up my mind to see them, by hook or by crook. One afternoon therefore, feeling sure that we were not likely to move at short notice, I begged Roy to take my watch, and set out.

Many months had gone by since I first sat, lonely and friendless by the side of Mussolini's North African road. I had learnt since then that it was easier to travel there than anywhere else in the world, for the Eighth Army drivers would take any of their comrades anywhere, at any inconvenience. Within half an hour of leaving camp, I was put down in the middle of Sabratha village.

There still stood, undamaged, a big clean signpost pointing the way to the *Scavi di Sabratha*; and from it led a fine metalled road lined with decorative poplars and pointing towards a high building in fawn-coloured stone. There were mines on either side of the avenue and booby traps in the houses. But my concern was not to dawdle and explore side tracks, but to reach the ruins as quickly as possible. I felt on that glorious Tripolitanian afternoon the awakening of an almost forgotten excitement. The day was cloudless and quiet; the slender cypresses moved their topmost branches lightly back and forward; hard heels rang pleasantly on the unaccustomed metal of the highway. In just such a pleasure of anticipation I had walked, in the days before the war, over the Northumbrian moors to see Borcovicus, or over the Surrey ploughland to see the mosaics at Bignor. To be drawing near again to antique beauty and all its surprises of art and poetry was to revive an old thrill.

At the end of the avenue, passing through a gate upon which some Eighth Army signwriter had generously painted 'Ancient ruins – do not damage' and leaving a big cream-coloured house on my left, I came at last upon the ruins. Here had stood one of the great cities of Roman Tripolitania; and here fascist Italy, with a care and devotion that it denied to human beings, had worked to restore ancient glory, and linked hands with a culture it envied but could not equal.

My first emotion was pleasurable bewilderment. Where to turn among such profusion of ruins? To the right and left of the excavated street where I stood were mosaic floors, some in sober blacks and greys, others gayer with buttercup yellow and willow-herb red, and almost pattern complete. In corners the broken pieces of even more floors were piled in treasure heaps, with fragments of figured pottery and lamps and vessels. Here columns, broken half way up, stood firm and vertical; there others, broken into drums and cylinders, lay across marbled floors. No two marbles seemed alike – they were milk-white and sheened, porphyry, a misted green veined with jade, blood red, gazelle brown. Near the forum, floors of more marble lay almost intact, and fragments of panelling stood upright, still flush with the solid stone, and hinting at rooms once cool and delightfully coloured in the African sun. Wells, conduits, baths, chambers, steps and stairs, Corinthian capitals, fragments of statuary, arms, fingers, and feet in alabaster, beautifully incised inscriptions provoking with incomplete statements. The wealth of the city seemed inexhaustible, ample evidence of a civic grandeur that was the pride of the old world. In the spacious forum, in the noble basilica, wealth had joined hands with art and with piety to build beautifully.

From the town led a paved roadway, its banks overhung with flowers and shrubs, and its flagstones clean and worn. This must have been the processional way, the road for priests and garlanded oxen from the town to the gem of all its buildings – the theatre.

Seen from the town, the theatre raises a high semicircle of superimposed arches, rising above the landscape and showing against the sea. From inside the semicircle, it can be seen that the diameter is a towering stage set, three flights of stone and marble columns and architraves rising above one another, and looking down upon a stage so spacious that the actors must have been dwarfed against this background of grandeur and elegance. Beyond the stage is a sunken orchestra, faced by a dropwall adorned with bas-reliefs, showing the chorus in their masks and cothurni, and the players resting in their dressing room, and backed by a dividing wall which curls in a semicircle around the priests' seats, and ends in two carved dolphins. Behind this low wall the broad sets rise in concentric circles, tier after tier until from the topmost ring, the spectator can command a view not only of the vast stage, but of the fields beyond, and through the marble columns of the stage scene, the blue and sparkling Mediterranean.

The theatre does not impress by its size; its virtues are rather the lightness and elegance of its architecture, the charm of its colouring, and the felicity of its situation. Here, on the edge of a great alien continent, with its back towards the forbidding desert, and its face to the memorable Mediterranean and Rome and Europe, with the elements of land, sea and sky as the silent ever-present actors – here surely was a place to build a theatre, and here a fitting background against which to play out dramas of the destiny of man.

There was more beauty to see at Sabratha. The museum was a worthy building, and its gardens were tastefully set out with walks and alleys, adorned with tablets and statuary. The floor of the main room in the museum was an immense mosaic of the Tree of Life, taken from a hall in the old town. I learnt more there about the history of Sabratha, that the town and the theatre had probably been built in the second century AD when the Caesars had all the resources of the known world to draw upon and build with, that Professor Giacomo Guidi had spent years in excavation and reconstruction; that the Italians had, as recently as 1937, given a performance of *Oedipus Rex* there, that the stone setting was eighty feet high, and that the building could hold about ten thousand.

But the pleasure I took in this information was trivial compared with the first impact of the beauty and purity of the building upon my mind. To me, coming out of the desert, with months behind me in which my only link with the culture of yesterday had been an old Shakespeare and an older *Golden Treasury*,[3] the sight of Sabratha was a major aesthetic experience. Europe, all that civic grace and architectural glory wedded to literary vision that Europe had stood for and might still stand for, rose up and welcomed me in the shape of that old theatre. It pointed the way west and north to Sophocles, Dante, Shakespeare, Paris, the medieval cathedrals…… My excitement was touched by a more poignant homesickness for Europe than I had felt for many weeks.

The end of Libya

The charm of Sabratha led us to expect finer country in the last western corner of Tripolitania, but we found that Libya was to end for us as it had begun – in wilderness. Between Sabratha and Zouara the country was level, neglected and wretchedly waterlogged by the recent rains (Fig. 9). The harbour of Zouara Marina was colourful with its native boats at anchor, but the town itself was a shabby little place with few traces of European colonization. It consisted of a few streets of huddled native shops with dark interiors, leading to an untidy and muddy market place. However, strangely enough, Zouara was a place where one could still buy. There we bought German razor blades, soap, peanuts, walnuts, an odd camera film and even a drink; and there was in the market place a Palestinian barber. To have a haircut by a professional barber who possessed shears was in itself a luxury.

This was the first pair of shears I had seen for over a thousand miles. Since El Alamein we had taken turns at cutting each other's hair with a broken comb and a pair of scissors from the first-aid box. It was a sad commentary on the state of things in Tripolitania at that time that the barber would not take my lire but asked me, aside, if I could bring him a packet of biscuits.

However, we saw little of the town, for typhus broke out there too, and we were confined for the remainder of our stay to our own campsite. That was far less of a hardship than it had been, for little by little we had perfected comforts and conveniences for ourselves. Completely patched and mended, our tent was now a fairly snug little home. Almost all had camp beds, and the tent was lit by a cable running from the gharry. There was even a press switch so that I, who was usually last to sleep, could turn off the light without getting out of bed. We had learnt cunning methods of folding the blankets so that there was most warmth in them. Best of all we had acquired a radio (though I hesitate to tell from where). Rewired and adjusted, it brought us the news faithfully every six o'clock in the evening; and it had long become a ritual for us to assemble and listen in closely to see how the war, in which we were taking a part, was going. Food was fairly plentiful after the fall of Tripoli, and eggs for service biscuits seemed a legitimate exchange. We had schooled ourselves to win water and fuel from every available source, and I had learnt to pick up useful reading matter from every dune, palm clump and abandoned campsite. The little scraps of information went into my notebook; notes on Gauguin, Renoir, Toulouse Lautrec (scavenged from the abandoned reading matter of four nations) I still value.

Then too, from bickering and squabbling in the early days, the ten of us had come to value each other more and more. The rather humourless sergeant, Sergeant Clark, whose infirmity it was to call everything by its official RAF vocabulary title (so that topees became Wolseleys, and pay books, part two's), was nevertheless a good workman and a devoted NCO. The corporal, Corporal Pryce, had a knack of doing even the simplest operation wrongly, but we could not have done without the humour he provided. Roy Hazlewood, who every night went to bed and cried out in his sleep, 'Oh dear! Oh dear!' was the kindest hearted of companions. Each man had his talent and his virtue and both came more and more into play each day. Sid Rapperport was a jester, Alec Young and Bob Holden the technicians, Norman Taylor the official photographer, Harry Allen (H. Cookie) and Jack Scott (Cookie)[4] loyal cooks and handymen. We had learnt to pull together; and though we were often weary, this solidarity and the sense that we were working together in a winning battle buoyed us up.

We hoped that from Zouara for the rest of the campaign we would be allowed to keep to the coast road. But by this time it was obvious that Rommel was going to stand on the Mareth Line and our forces would have to be deployed along a fairly wide front (Fig. 9). We drove inland again to El Assa, of which I remember little except that it was another windy, dusty, sorry place that drove us back upon our old privations of hunger and thirst. We were not sorry when after a few days we packed again, drove without fuss over the western boundary of Libya, saw a little white hut flying the tricolor[5] and knew that we were in Tunisia.

Reflections on Libya

We crossed the eastern boundary of Libya on 12 November 1942 and entered Tunisia on 23 February 1943. Little more than three months spent in any country is not an excellent qualification for generalizing about it, but it was long enough for us to form firm opinions.

This part of the North African littoral was once a fertile land. The Greeks colonized Cyrenaica and the Romans, Tripolitania (Fig. 5). Cyrenaica, under Greek control, supported five towns, and Tripolitania three fine cities, Sabratha, Oea (Tripoli) and Leptis Magna (Homs)(Fig. 9). However centuries of Berber and Arab neglect wasted the land, and let the sand come in from the desert almost to the sea's edge. When the

Italians took Libya over from the Turks in 1912, it must have appeared to the first colonists a grim and unprofitable land.

However unprepossessing it was, the Italians meant to occupy it and to use it, and many years were spent in quelling the refractory Senussi and building up an adequate garrison organization. It seems, however, that it was only with the advent of fascism that colonization began in earnest. Libya therefore had for us the interest of being one of the world's youngest colonies, one of the most recent examples of what an industrial European nation could and could not achieve in modern colonization. It was a working model of the impact of Europe's newest political system upon a backward land and a backward people.

The Italians accomplished much. They built a continuous metalled road from border to border – not the magnificent highway it was boasted to be (although we saw it when the traffic of three years of war had passed over it and repairs had been cut to a minimum) – but in comparison, for instance, with East African roads,[6] a creditable achievement. Along this road, they built commodious rest houses about fifty or sixty kilometres apart. They extended other good roads with good hotels south into the desert. The Libyan railways were poor, and covered little of the colony: but the Libyan towns were fairly well built. Benghasi, Derna, Tobruk and Bardia (Figs. 6 and 7) were the equivalent of the Greek Cyrenaican ports; Homs and Misurata took the place of Leptis Magna (Fig. 9); and Tripoli was converted from a rather squalid oriental settlement into a well-designed modern town with twentieth-century architecture and twentieth-century amenities.

Most important of all, the Italians reclaimed wasted acres of the world's land. In an earnest attempt to revive the fertility of Libya, they planted eucalyptus and wattle to fix the drifting sand, and sank thousands of wells. The water that lay in hidden reservoirs below the Sahara sand was not always drinkable, but it made plants grow. Where a generation before there was nothing but camel thorn, Italian colonists grew olives, vines, cereals and oranges.

Upon this reclaimed land, the Italian government planned to settle about twenty thousand colonists every year. They gave the colonists every incentive to migrate. Before their arrival, the land was tractor-ploughed, and the limits of each farm were drawn. A farmhouse was built and equipped with furniture, outhouses and a water cistern. The fact that these houses were of a standard type, did not prevent them from being attractive and adequate homes. When the colonists arrived, they found a ready-made farm awaiting nothing but their labour. Each settlement had cost the government £1,500, two-thirds of which the settler was expected to refund within twenty years.

I do not know whether they found any difficulty in repaying the loan; but apparently the settlers were on the whole contented. They had been chosen for their poverty, industry, large families and sound political views. Life was hard enough, but living was cheap. It was lonely, but the zone centre was there to provide a little amusement and communal pleasure. Castel Benito, for instance, had shops, a theatre-cum-cinema, and a good little school. I was able to see at first hand how well-fitted and equipped the school was. There were flush lavatories, white hand-basins, new wall maps, good infant school apparatus, good text books, well printed, designed and coloured. Of course everything had a strong fascist bias. Even the children's exercise books had their covers plastered with photographs of the Duce, of naval reviews, bombers over Spain, and elementary lessons in flying; and there was too much of the *Bimbi, amate Benito Mussolini*. But these did not detract from the technical excellence of the equipment.

On the whole the colonists were contented and hardworking, and each pioneer looked forward to a day when he could hand over to his son a freehold farm in a flourishing condition. The Italians not only added to the wealth of the world by putting back into cultivation land that Africa had lost, they also beautified the reclaimed land. Some of the more ambitious estates were admirably laid out, and the very disposition of houses and orchards gave the wilderness a grace it had not possessed for seventeen centuries. The builders of the newer zone centres were pioneers in architecture; compared with villages like Battisti and Olivetti (Fig. 7), the smaller towns of Kenya, for example, are badly planned and inadequate. In addition, although they may have had ulterior motives in this, they reclaimed from oblivion less tangible wealths – the buried architectural wealth of Greece and Rome. Though Sabratha and Leptis Magna may have been excavated (Fig. 9), partly to attract tourists, partly to remind the peaceable Italian peasants from home of the power and dominance of the old Caesars, the excavations and reconstructions were nevertheless done with great skill and reverence for past beauty. No one can scorn labour in such causes.

The Italians accomplished much in a short time; but their achievements were costly, and perhaps the biggest price they had to pay was the forfeiting of the allegiance of the Arabs. The conquest of Libya began in massacre and bloodshed, and colonization continued on a basis of cruel disregard of the right of the native. The slogan of the colonial administration was – 'For the white settlers, the fertile land; for the Arabs, the desert.' Always mistrusted, the Italians inspired in the Arab a resentment he did not easily forget. The Libyan native is, on the whole, a treacherous man, and the conventional greeting with which he met the British advancing troops – '*Inglesi quoiz – Italiano mushquoiz*', had no doubt been reversed every time he found himself on a different side of the battlefield. But even discounting this hypocrisy we know that the settlers at villages like Tarhuna (Fig. 9) found themselves faced in defeat, not with looting Tommies but insurgent Arabs.

In his treatment of the Libyan native, it seems that the Italian failed, and his failure is probably an indication of what would have followed upon the acquisition of colonies by fascist Germany. But when the fate of Libya is finally settled, Italy's achievements must not be forgotten. If her ill-fated but courageous attempt to make the desert blossom again is allowed to lapse, and the wilderness to creep again over a colonized land, the world will be poorer in a commodity it cannot afford to lose – fertile and habitable land.

Notes

1. The aerial for the radar was located on the roof of the gharry (see Plate 4).
2. Troops met at Alam el Osmaili.
3. Presumably the collected works of Shakespeare and Palgrave's *Golden Treasury*.
4. This, plus Fred Grice, was the core crew that took part in the whole trip from El Alamein to Tunisia.
5. The French flag.
6. The first draft of 'Erk in the Desert' was written at RAF Eastleigh in Kenya, East Africa in 1943.

Chapter 8

Tunisian Finale

Into Tunisia

At first Tunisia was indistinguishable from Libya. The roads were as bad, the countryside as dreary. We drove on with the same apathy, until we came to the Seven Sweepers' Bridge (Fig. 9), scene of a recent heroic action. Not long before, a patrol had crossed the marshes there to find itself cut off from its supplies by a sudden rain. However, although under constant fire from artillery and aircraft, the Eighth Army Engineers, with wood requisitioned from as far back as Tripoli, bridged the marsh with this primitive causeway and relieved their comrades. And someone with taste had chosen for it a name as poetical and musical as the action was heroic.

At Ben Gardane more than the language of the streets and signposts reminded us that we were now in French territory. The settlements in Tripolitania were predominantly Italian but here it seemed that the Arabs had been more welcome in French towns. Medenine (Fig. 9), to which we eventually came, seemed to carry a far higher proportion of native houses than an Italian village like Sabratha.

Medenine was not a beautiful town. Its core was of European houses, originally white and ornamented with wrought balconies and windows, but now wrecked by bombardment. The bulk of it, however, was primitive native architecture. The commonest building was an agglomeration of small barrel-vaulted houses, stuck together like loaves in a big bakery, desert-coloured, dark and with narrow doors. The native *Kasr* or stronghold was an extraordinary structure of scores of such hovels, glued together until they looked like a big man-made honeycomb; and each room was about the size of a coke oven. Beyond the town the land went levelly away to the north to a flat coast line, and to the Isle of Djerba (Fig. 9), legendary island of the Lotos Eaters; but before it rose the Mareth Hills, a 2000 feet high barrier of unfamiliar mountain. These were the hills that the French had fortified in days when young fascists went about clamouring for Nice, Tunis and Corsica; and there Rommel was waiting.

We camped on a site above and to the south of the town, in full view of the hills, and fortunately near a big gravity tank which controlled Medenine's water supply. Water to us was as an orchard to a boy. By day we climbed to the top of the tank, drew gallons and gallons of liquid gold, and lowered it to the ground with cable. Even after we had been warned off, we climbed the tank in the dark, and kept our containers full to capacity.

In spite of the water our stay at Medenine was not comfortable. Having entrenched themselves, the enemy began to hit back. We were raided continuously for days by fighter bombers, withdrew again and again from long range artillery fire, and finally settled down to endure as best we could. The climax to the excitement came on Saturday 6 March. We were awakened early in the morning by the noise of an artillery duel. By breakfast the news was through that the German tanks were coming out of the hills to attack, and we were ordered to get out of the way of the battle. That was an extraordinary day. After a perilous journey through the shelled town, we pulled up about eleven miles behind the battlefield, and waited. To know there was a battle raging, to hear the duellings, to see the outfliers of the battle coming over our heads, the formations of Junkers 88s and Focke Wolfs, and the counter-attacking Kitties and Spitfires,[1] all on their way to bomb and strafe someone else – to be almost a spectator at the struggle, within gunshot yet able to sit on the sand and talk with the reservists by their guns, this was a remarkable experience. I talked the afternoon away with a young New Zealander, a reserve anti-tank gunner who was waiting to see his first action. He had not been so long from home that his heart was still with his farm and his sheep. As he talked about the home he had just left, I hoped that he would not be needed that day.

He was not needed. Towards four o'clock the battle died down. The best of the Axis tanks had been superbly held by our anti-tank gunners. Before evening, Rommel, who had told his men that morning that if they did not smash the Eighth Army with this attack, their days in Africa were numbered, accepted defeat, and retired to the hills. He had excused his long retreat by pleading shortage of petrol. But even with his new supplies he was a beaten general.

I cannot leave Medenine without mentioning a heroic padre whom I never saw. Shortly after the occupation of the town, he commandeered a house, turned one of the rooms into a reading and writing room, and equipped another with a billiard table he acquired from somewhere. This house was the Desert Rats' Club, but more than the Seventh Armoured Division (the true Desert Rats) were allowed to use it. There we could buy stamps, a few NAAFI goods and even chai and sandwiches. The club was little more than ten miles from the enemy lines, and came under bombardment day after day; but as far as I know there was always chai there – for those who dared go for it. All honour to the unknown padre who so coolly kept this club open while the town day after day was an open target for that dreadful artillery.

Beyond Mareth

Undeterred by the abortive German assault on 6 March, the Eighth Army continued to prepare for its next offensive. While the bulk of the British forces were to make a frontal assault on the hill positions, the New Zealanders were briefed to proceed south, penetrate the Mareth Hills and outflank the enemy; and we were ordered to accompany them.

Exactly one week after the 'bloody nose' battle, we packed and drove southwards toward Foum Tataouine (Fig. 9). At the end of the first day we halted and pitched camp about one mile north of the town.

We were fortunate in our site here, for we pulled off the road onto a soft-soiled plain, behind which rose the first Mareth range. Here we had moved away from the enemy and were out of reach of their artillery. The land was fairer and less devastated than around Medenine, and there was still a civil population in the town.

No sooner had we pitched camp than we were invaded by a crowd of Arabs selling eggs, bread and vegetables – but not for money. Money had ceased to be a currency from the time we had moved out of range of Alexandria. In Tripolitania the wealthiest were those who had stocks not of cash, but tea; in Tunisia the desideratum was tobacco. The Tunisian Arabs were so hungry for tobacco that they would buy eagerly at three times the price charged by the NAAFI. Any man who had cigarettes to sell could make 200 per cent profit on each packet. There must be many ways of making a fortune in this world, but I commend to any enterprising and ambitious would-be millionaire the sale of tea in Libya and tobacco in Tunisia. Certainly ours was a brisk market. The natives swarmed around the back of the gharry, and clambered up the tailboard, waving their bank notes, thrusting eggs, loaves, carrots, photographs and leather purses upon us, crying in chorus, '*Sigara, Sigara!*' They had to be pushed forcibly away, and did not disperse until we strode among them shouting, '*Le marché est fini – absolument fini!*'

We stayed long enough on this site to replenish our store of eggs (which we carried packed in a wooden box full of sand), and to climb to the French-built casemate[2] above the town. This was one of the strongholds which formed part of the Mareth defences, but it had been abandoned by Rommel, who preferred to keep his artillery mobile. It was a romantic eyrie, a twentieth century bandit's lair. A steep road curled around a conical hill 1500 feet high, until it stopped at the gateway of a dun-coloured fort, built so cunningly on the bare rock that it seemed to grow out of it. In the body of the fort were rooms for a small garrison, an open cistern for collecting water, guardrooms, and a cylindrical look-out; and from the blockhouse a vertical iron ladder led down a narrow pit by three or four dark flights to a network of underground caverns and galleries, like a little coal mine. In these galleries there were more cisterns, store rooms, stables, ammunition dumps and cupboards; and each gallery ended in a machine-gun nest, heavily concreted, fitted with thick steel floors and provided with ammunition chutes. With these nests commanding all the roads and approaches, the fort might have held out for months in the days when war was less fluid and swift. It could be held by an invisible force; the gunners could fire, retire and be relieved by rested troops without once exposing themselves, and only the most accurate and heavy bombardment could have broken the strength of the casemate. But the Germans had chosen not to occupy it. In desert warfare artillery must be more mobile than the French had imagined. Romantic and lonely, it looked out over the gullied ranges where Rommel was making his most desperate stand.

The day after the visit to the fort, we moved further south as if making for Borj le Boeuf (Fig. 9); but before reaching it, we were assembled and given orders to file singly through the hills in a north-westerly direction, towards Jebel Nefusa. This was one of the most mysterious of our journeys. Every so often a single gharry was dispatched over the sand and through the pass, with instructions not to exceed ten miles an hour. The tell-tale dust trails were to be kept down to a minimum. At this wearying speed we drove for hours and hours, slowing to a snail's pace whenever a wind blew up a dust trail that might have given away our position and direction to high-flying recce planes. Hour after hour we bumped along over the plain, then up and through the rocky pass, until towards evening we came to our objective. Beyond the pass were the New Zealand forces, already arrived and settled in, and so excellently dispersed and camouflaged that to estimate their strength must have been a puzzle, and to hope to destroy them by bombing, a despair. They were leaguering, scattered over the broad valleys like a herd, the epitome of discretion, discipline and strength.

As if realizing the futility of attempting to harm this force, no enemy bombers came; and on the evening of 19 March, the army began to assemble to go into battle. This was a memorable sight. As the afternoon faded, the scattered forces began to congregate. First came the tanks, filing over the crests of the hills, and lining up in long columns as if for a race. They came in a great concourse, with their noses down, breaking the camel thorn beneath them, over the ridges and down the winding tracks. Then the Bren-gun carriers, the supply gharries, the 25-pounders, the ammo trucks that had drawn together on the distant hill slopes where they looked like herds of strange animals, began to move in and take up their place behind the tanks. Before six every waggon was in place; and exactly at six a thousand engines were started and the whole formidable convoy began to move. They drove past us like a review, Shermans and Crusaders with their commanders in earphones and the familiar black berets, Bofors carriers and heavy ack-ack, two-tonner, six-tonner, six-pounder and twenty-five-pounder, and last of all the ambulances. And as if not to be outdone, the western sky behind the hills staged its own pageantry. A falling sun kindled the tumbled clouds till they burnt fire red and there was splendour over the purpled landscape.

'Cheerio!' the men shouted as we ran down to them to shake hands and give them cigarettes, 'Cheerio – we'll get the bastards' scalps, if they don't get ours!'
'Cheerio!' we shouted back. 'We'll be with you *baden!*'
But I, for one, did not follow. The next day, before we could get away, I was recalled to Cairo. While the battle was being fought, I was on my way back.

Goodbye to the desert

From Medenine to Castel Benito I saw the desert as I had not seen it before (Fig. 9). Flying low, I could look down and see all the colour which the desert showed only to the sun and the flyer – the light fawn of the sand, the grey and brown of the clumps of scrub, the pale mauve of drying salt-pans glistening like frost in the sunlight, the pale green mist of young corn and the more brilliant buttercup yellow of the desert weeds, the white of Italian villages against the sombre-hued poplars and cypresses. But from Castel Benito to Cairo, we climbed high. From 5000 feet, only the major markings of the desert were visible, the branched figurings of the wadis, as if water had been spilt there, and had dried dark brown, and the unfinished fields of the ploughed land, dark against the paleness of the sand. There was one moment of extreme beauty when, as the sun lowered, it threw its beams almost horizontally, and caught the ears of standing corn, making them pollen-coloured in the gathering darkness.

But all the signs of the great battles seemed to have gone. The littered wreckage, the vast dumps of abandoned material, the fortifications in the wadis, the once-famous battle lines and tracks had faded like ghosts. The desert had already begun to smooth them out.

I knew that, just as the sand was smudging out all the visible signs of that three-year-long struggle, so too time would blur for me the memory of those days. Not long after the end of the campaign, I met an officer who had been in the desert with Wavell and Auchinleck, and up to Benghasi in the last offensive. We began talking about the places we knew.
'Do you remember,' he said, 'that landing ground inland from Derna? Oh that was a bloody cold place if ever there was one. It was – what did they call the damned place? Damn me, I've forgotten it already.'

Only a few months after leaving the desert, he was forgetting it. So that I should not forget, and perhaps to help others not to forget, I have written this account.

The desert was a grim place, but I said goodbye to it with mixed feelings. Nowhere had I felt so godforsaken, nowhere nearer to Lear's poor un-accommodated man, nowhere less at the mercy of a stony-hearted Nature that gave no comforts. Yet some good came out of it. In that land where Nature stinted almost everything, we went close to the mentality of a poor un-provided people, who have little to rejoice in but their own effort. We were like the Aran islanders, for whom a board, a piece of rope, a stick were so irreplaceable that they assumed a value denied them in a world of plenty: and against this background of poverty and privation, pleasures won added poignancy. Over and above these, out of the abounding health that sun and air and labour bequeathed us, there often rose a power of mystical exaltation in the presence of the great expanses of land and sky.

In these last few lines, let me pay out my tributes. First, to our faithful old gharry; it was almost obsolete when it was first brought out from Cairo. On our very first journey, the petrol feedpipe broke,[3] and continued to break for the next five months. The engine often refused to start, yet it never failed to get under way in the end. The roof leaked until we nailed an old tarpaulin over it. The rocky desert shook all the screws in the framework loose, but we re-screwed them to the framework and it held together. It sank up to the axles in marsh, but it was always pulled out. There was water in the sump and the air pump would not work. Yet it carried nine men to Mareth, and eight on from there to Tunis, and was in at the death.[4]

Secondly, here is a record of the names of the men who made up the unit, who bickered and quarrelled like any other body of men but who shared possessions of pocket and mind, and played their part, although a very minor part in the defeat of the Germans: Sergeant Clark from Tynemouth, Corporal Pryce from Wrexham, Bob Holden from Leeds (killed in action, autumn 1943), Alec Young from Glasgow, Norman Taylor from Walsall, Roy Hazlewood from Burton, Jack Scott from Blackburn, Harry Allen from Nottingham, and Sid Rapperport from Cambridge (see Appendix II).

Lastly, all honour to the Eighth Army and the rest of the Navy and Air Force men who fought in this campaign. Their heroism protected us every day; they were the best of companions, and it was through their valour that the three-year Libyan nightmare ended in victory and jubilation.

Notes

1 Hurricanes were in the process of being replaced by Spitfires in North Africa early in 1943.
2 A fortification in which guns are mounted.
3 The feedpipe from the petrol tank to the engine.
4 The Germans hung on in Tunisia until May 1943.

Epilogue

Ironically, Fred's departure from the desert coincided with that of the defeated Field Marshal Rommel, though unlike Rommel, Fred still had many years ahead of him. His re-call to Cairo, where he was offered a commission, and subsequent deployment to Eastleigh in Kenya, where he became a Flight Lieutenant and Education Officer until the end of the war, in many ways marked the beginning of the rest of his life. Thanks to Fred's substantial experience of adult education in Africa he was ideally suited, after demobilization in 1946, to join the English Department of the newly-founded Teacher Training College in Worcester. He remained in Worcester until his death; surprisingly, given his deep attachment to the landscapes of the north of England, Worcester rather than Durham, became his home.

As the *Highland Monarch* was pulling away from the dock in Avonmouth in 1942, Fred wrote prophetically, 'many a good man and boy will not come back from this voyage – *or if he does, never the same fellow*'. He could not have known that the same words would apply equally to the wives and sweethearts left behind. Gwen, so ardently missed and idealized in Fred's verse, had a very different war from his. She struggled with a sharp drop in income (for a long time Fred's teacher's salary was reduced to that of an aircraftsman), danger from frequent nightly air-raids, the loneliness of bringing up a young child on her own and finally ill-health caused by malnutrition. Once Fred was demobilized, Gwen was determined to put the war and the North East behind her.

While many of Fred's later wartime experiences in Africa are recorded in his journals, they are sporadic and never quite equal the excitement and camaraderie of life in Unit 606. This intense period, living and working in close proximity with a disparate group of men, must have been the nearest Fred ever came as an adult to experiencing once again the warmth, closeness and shared endeavour of the colliery in which he grew up. The sense of belonging to that impoverished but tight-knit community was something he missed for the rest of his life. Fred had enjoyed many aspects of the military campaign in the desert. Despite the plain diet of M & V, he was, for those months on the move, uncharacteristically free from digestive problems. Sleeping close to nature, under the stars or in a tent, was always his idea of bliss. As a family we camped for many years in the most rudimentary of tents and with the minimum of equipment, apart from Fred's trusty RAF billy-can and folding canvas washstand!

Gillian Clarke

Appendix I

Frederick Grice's Major Publications

Folk Tales of the North Country, London: Nelson, 1944.
Folk Tales of the West Midlands, London: Nelson, 1952.
Folk Tales of Lancashire, London: Nelson, 1953.
Aidan and the Strollers, London: Jonathan Cape, 1960.
The Bonny Pit Laddie, London: OUP, 1960.
The Moving Finger, London: OUP, 1962.
Rebels and Fugitives, London: Batsford, 1963.
A Severnside Story, London: OUP, 1964.
Dildrum King of the Cats, London: OUP, 1967.
The Luckless Apple, London: OUP, 1966.
The Oak and the Ash, London: OUP, 1968.
The Courage of Andy Robson, London: OUP, 1969
The Black Hand Gang, London: OUP, 1971.
Young Tom Sawbones, London: OUP, 1972.
Nine Days' Wonder, London: OUP, 1976.
Johnny Head-in-Air, Oxford: OUP, 1978.
Francis Kilvert and his World, Horsham: Caliban Books, 1982.
Water Break its Neck, Oxford: OUP, 1986.

Appendix II

Members of Unit 606 as recorded in the Photographs (Plates 3 and 15)

Flight Sergeant Nobby Clark, Tynemouth
Corporal Jack Pryce, Wrexham
Harry Allen (H. Cookie), Nottingham
Fred Grice, Durham
*Roy Hazlewood, Burton
Robert (Bob) Holden, Leeds, killed 1943
Sid Rapperport, Cambridge
Jack Scott (Cookie), Blackburn
Norman Taylor, Walsall
Alec Young, Glasgow

*Roy and Jimmy (who appears in the photographs, but not in Fred's listing at the end of the book) left Unit 606 to joint Unit 607 before El Adem, but Roy returned to Unit 606 by Christmas 1942.

Associates of Unit 606:
Sergeant Budd was in charge of Unit 607, but appears in some photographs.
Squadron Leader M. H. Young was in charge of 606 and 607 and perhaps more units on the ground for a short time in October-November 1942.

Index

Numbers in italics denote pages with illustrations

606 Unit, AMES Type 6 mobile radar unit, 2, 5, 9, 10–12, 16, 20, 22, 24–7, 29–32, 32 n8
 at Alam el Osmaili Egypt 16, 20, 32 n8, 106–14, *107*, 162 n3, 163 n17, n18
 Fred's posting to 5, 20, 103–6
 in Tunisia *xviii*, 30, 197–202
 journey through Egypt *xv*, 123–9
  to Gambut 123–9, *125*, 162 n4
 journey through Libya *xv–xviii*, 129–96
 Cyrenaica *xvi*, 137–46
 personnel
  Allen, Harry (H. Cookie) *112*, 127, *133*, 158, 192, 204, 210
  Clark, Nobby, Flight Sgt *113*, *133*, 158, 163 n20, 191, 204, 210
  Grice, Fred *see* Grice, Fred
  Hazlewood, Roy 116, 127, 129, *133*, 134–5, 159, 162 n4, 192, 204, 210
  Holden, Robert (Bob) *133*, 156, 192, 204, 210
  'Jimmy' *112*, *133*, 162 n4, 210
  Pryce, Jack, Corporal *112*, *133*, *144*, 148, *150*, 159, 162 n10, 191–2, 204, 210
  Rapperport, Sid 13, *133*, 134, *144*, 166, 170, 192, 204, 210
  Scott, Jack (Cookie) *112*, 116, 127, 129, *133*, 152, 159, 160, 166, 173, 176, 192, 204, 210
  Taylor, Norman 127, *133*, 192, 204, 210
  Young, M. H., Squadron Leader 9–10, 31–2, 136 n15, n26, 210
  Young, Alec *133*, *144*, 156, 192, 204, 210
 see also Air Ministry Experimental Station (AMES) Units
Afrikakorps 1, 20, 21, 23, *125*, 148, 182 *see also* Axis forces
Air Ministry Experimental Station (AMES) Units 9–12, 24–32, 32 n8, 104, 162 n14
 607 Unit 10, 26, 31–2, 32 n8, 162 n4, n9, 178 n6

 Sergeant Budd *113*, 210
 77n (Isle of Man) 14–16, *15*
 Light Warning Set (LWS)/Units 2, 26–7, 29, 32 n13, 135 n11, 136 n22
Alam el Osmaili, Egypt 16, 20, 32 n8, 106–14, 107, 162
 description of 105–9, 114–15, 116, *116*, 120–1
 Fred's dugout 109–14, *110–12*
Alexandria, Egypt 20, 23, 24, 25, 102, 103, 104, 126, 133, 141, 160, 162 n3, 180
Allen, Harry (H. Cookie) *112*, 127, *133*, 158, 192, 204, 210
Auchinleck, Claude John Eyre, General 23, 147, 203
Axis forces 21, 23–4, 25, 28, 29, 102, 118, 130, 146, 173, 183, 199 *see also* Afrikakorps

Baracca, Libya 143–5, *144–5*
Barce, Libya *141*, 142–4
bath/bathing 65, 80, 122, 131–2, 148, 167, 173, 176, 180
Benghasi, Libya 26, 139, 143, 145–6, 170, 177, 193, 203
Beni Ulid, Libya 169, 171–2
Bir Dufan, Libya 168–71
 encounter with old man 169–70, 178 n8
'Black Book' 8–9, 13, 17, 18, 31, 87, 104, 108–9, 114, 115–16, 118–19, 127, 129–30, 134, 139, 147, 148, 162 n1, 162 n4
Bletchley Park, Ultra decrypts 20, 21–2, 24, 25
Burg el Arab, Egypt 24, 28, 103, 104, 122, 162 n3, 169

Cairo, Egypt *xiii*, 16, 18, 27, 103, 105, 119, 182
 description of 89–91, 97–8, 202, 203, 204, 206
 visit to pyramids 91–3
Cape Town, S. Africa *xi*, *xii*, 17–18, 19
 description and living conditions 78–82

212 • INDEX

card and other games 38–9, 47, 48–9, 59–60, 121, 168
Castel Benito, Libya 131, 173–7, 179, 183, 194, 203
   accommodation 176
   description of 176–7
   encounter with Italian bankers 177, 180
cave drawings, El Agheila 151–2

Clark Nobby, Flight Sgt *113*, *133*, 158, 163 n20, 191, 204, 210
Clarke, Gillian *see* Grice, Gillian
class distinction 16–18, 50–1
Crossley waggon 10, 29, 31, 105, 139, 164, 176 *see also* gharry

Desert Rats (Seventh Armoured Division) 126, 147, 158, 199
DID (rations dump) 103, 104, 108
dreams/daydreams 47, 51, 94–5, 166–7, 169, 180

Eastleigh, Kenya, Education Corps, 6, 13, 22
   Fred's posting to 22, 206
Eighth Army 1, 20–4, 29–30, 103, 118, 119, 121, 124, 147, 154, 158, 167, 172, 183, 187, 197, 199, 205, *see also* El Alamein campaign *and* Western Desert War
El Agheila, Libya 22, 24, 28, 146–52, 162 n15
   cave drawings 151–2
   description of 147–9
   exploring cisterns and caves at 150–2
   swimming and foraging expeditions 149–50, *150*
El Alamein campaign, Egypt 1, 16, 20–1, 22, 23–24, 25, 28, 29, 32, 102–23, 165, 174, 191
   dogfights 118
   sounds of battle 115–16, 122–3
Embarkation Personnel Centre (W. Kirby) 36–44
   description of and living conditions 36–9
'erk' (aircraftsman) 1, 18, 20, 22, 106, *107*, 125 n8
'Erk in the Desert' 2, 5, 8–9, 12, 13–14, 20–32, 102–205

fascism/fascist propaganda 140–1, 154, 177, 180
food/meals/provisioning 30, 45, 56, 57, 58, 59, 67–8, 72–4, 84, 85, 94, 103, 106, 108–9, 121, 128, 129, 132, 134, 138, 146, 149, 160, 161, 165–6, 169, 170, 173, 176, 182–3, 191
   officers' 50, 67–8, 72–4
Freetown, S. Africa *xi*, 17–18, 65, 70

Gambut, Egypt 129–32, 157
   description of 131–2
Gazala, Libya 134–5, 137
gharry (truck) 12, 25, 31, 103, 105, 106, 107, *107*, 108, 122, 123, 124, 128, *130*, 134, 135 n11, 138, 158, 160, 161, 173, 175, 177 n2, n10, 201, 204 *see also* Crossley waggon
Grice, Erica 6
Grice, Fred *15*, *110*, *112*, *113*, *119*, *133*, *150*
   books
      as biographer 7–8, 209
      for adults 1, 209
      for children 6–8, 209
      literary award 7
   education and civilian career 5–8
   Erica (daughter) 6
   father 5, 6, 17
   Gillian (daughter) 5, 86, 95, 96, 99 n4
   Gwen (wife) 5, 12, 17, 40, 47, 51–53, 61, 68–9, 85–87, 94–7, 147
      evacuated to Makendon 85–7, 95–7, 99 n4
      hardship of wartime life 17, 206
      sells house 99, 100 n14
   grammar school teaching 1–2, 5, 16, 17
      A. J. Dawson School, Wingate 4, 14, 54 n8, 99 n5
   journals 1–2, 6, 7, 8–9, 12–13, 206
      'Black Book' 8–9, 13, 17, 18, 30, 87, 104, 108–9, 114, 115–16, 118–19, 129–30, 134, 139, 147, 148, 162 n1, 162 n4
      'On Draft' 2, 3, 5, 8–9, 12, 14–20
   posting
      back to Cairo after Tripoli 22, 202–3
      to 606 Unit 5, 20, 103–6
      to Eastleigh, Kenya 22, 206
   RAF/radar training and career development 14–17, 77 n1
   Worcester, Teacher/Emergency Training College 6, 13, 206
Grice, Gillian 5, 86, 95, 96, 99 n4
Grice, Gwen 5, 12, 17, 40, 47, 51–3, 61, 68–9, 85–7, 94–7, 147
   evacuated to Makendon 85–7, 95–7, 99 n4

Index • 213

hardship of wartime life 17, 206
   sells house 99, 100 n14

Harding, Ivor 83, 88–89
Hazlewood, Roy 116, 127, 129, *133*, 134–5, 159, 162 n4, 192, 204, 210
Heliopolis and Almaza, Egypt 89–90, 93–4
Highland Monarch (troopship code number J10, 62A in Winston Special Convoy WS 19) *x*, 17–18, 46, 54 n5, n6, 82, 87, 206 *see also* troopship (*Highland Monarch*)
Holden, Robert (Bob) *133*, 156, 192, 204, 210
Homs, Libya *see* Leptis Magna
Hurricane (fighter) 9–10, 30, 108, 115–6, 205 n1

Il Duce see Mussolini
Indian troops 117, 120, 121
Italian
   African highway 153, 154, 187, 193
   air force 2, 100 n10, 135 n13, 138–9, 163 n18, 178 n13
   army/garrison 20, 22–3, 148, 160, 172, 193
   colony and colonists in Libya 25, 80, 129, 140–2, *141*, 145–6, 147, 173, 180, 182–3, 193–6, 203
   equipment, abandoned 124–5, *125*, 144–5

'Jimmy' *112*, *133*, 162 n4, 210

Kabrit, Egypt *xi*, 88–9, 100 n9
kit/kitbag 26–7, 29, 36, 37, 40, 43, 44–5, 55, 64, 65, 71–2, 79, 104, 106, 107, 158
Kittyhawk ('Kitty') 5, 30, 118, 134, 136 n27, 149, 177 n3, 198

landing grounds 2–4, 11–12, 22–5, 27, 29, 130, 135 n13, 136 n27, 146, 155, 169, 176
landmine/minefield 29, 108, 120, 155, 156–7, 161, 162 n14, n15, 174, 177 n1, 187
landscape, description of
   Alam el Osmaili 114–15, 116, *116*
   Bir Dufan 170–1
   Beni Ulid 172
   El Agheila 147–9
   Gazala 135
   Mareth 200–1
   Matruh 126
   Maturba 138–40
   on flight to Cairo 203

Soltan 161
Tarhuna 172–3
Leptis Magna (Homs), Libya 24, 177, 179, 192, 193, 195
Libyan history 192–5
Light Warning Set (LWS)/Units 2, 26–7, 29, 32 n13, 135 n11, 136 n22

Marble Arch (Arae Philaenorum), Libya 152–4, 162 n13
   landing ground 29, 162 n14, n15
   legend of the Philaeni brothers 153–4
Mareth offensive, Tunisia 22, 30, 192, 199–202, 204
Matruh, Egypt 21, 126
Maturba, Libya 137–8, 162 n1
Medenine, Tunisia 22, 197–9
   air-raids over 198–9, 200, 203
Mersa Brega, Libya 146, 152, 153
mine *see* landmine/minefield
Misurata, Libya 164, 193
Mobile Radio Unit (MRU) 25–6, 28–9
Montgomery, Bernard Law, General 16, 20–2, 23, 28, 175, 177
Mussolini, Benito (*Il Duce*) 141, 162 n7 175, 177, 181, 187, 194

New Amsterdam, troopship 19, 80
New Zealand forces in Tunisia 22, 30, 199, 201

Operation Torch 21–2, 31
Operations Record Book (ORB)
   213 Squadron 9–12, 33 n14
   260 Squadron 11–12, 162 n15, 178 n8
   AMES Units 10–12, 30, 31, 32 n8

padre 18, 46, 58, 65, 76, 199
parade 38, 39, 43–4, 45, 79, 82
poems (of Fred Grice)
   'Before sleep' 63–4
   'Education' 19
   'Fear' 39
   'Little white seagull with the black back ...' 50
   'No shepherds watching here by night ...' 159–60
   'When I come home' 41–2
   'When many years after this ...' 47–8
Pryce, Jack, Corporal *112*, *133*, *144*, 148, *150*, 159, 162 n10, 191–2, 204, 210

Radar (Radio Detection and Finding (RDF))
crew and stations 25–32, 162 n14
  Light Warning Set (LWS)/Units 2, 26–7, 29, 32 n13, 135 n11, 136 n22
  see also 606 Unit *and* Air Ministry Experimental Station (AMES) Units
Rapperport, Sid 13, *133*, 134, *144*, 166, 170, 192, 204, 210
Rommel, Erwin, Field Marshal 1, 20–1, 22–3, 28, 30, 31, 102, 123, 137, 147, 152, 168, 175, 192, 198, 199, 206
Royal Air Force (RAF) 1, 2, 5, 9, 14, 16–17, 24–5, 27, 29–30, 32 n13, 67, 100 n9, n14, 103, 131, 163 n17, n19, 191, 207
  landing grounds 2–4, 11–12, 22–5, 27, 29, 130, 135 n13, 136 n27, 146, 155, 169, 176

Sabratha, Libya 177, 187–90, 192, 195, 197
sanitary and washing/bathing arrangements/conditions 37, 46, 80, 82, 83, 109, 111, 144–5, 146, 166, 170, 194
  bath/bathing 65, 80, 122, 131–2, 148, 167, 173, 176, 180
Scott, Jack (Cookie) *112*, 116, 127, 129, *133*, 152, 159, 160, 166, 173, 176, 192, 204, 210
Senussi 129, 152, 169, 171, 181, 185–7, 193
ship's convoy x, 17, 54 n5
Sidi Barrakat, Egypt (RAF Station) 103, 104
Sirte/Gulf of Sirte, Libya *xvii*, 22, 131, 137, *157*, 164, 183
Soltan, Libya 155–62, *157*
  Christmas dinner at 157–60
Sorman, Libya 183–7
  troglodyte dwellings at 184
  encounters with local people 185–7
Spitfire 30, 198, 205 n1
Suez Canal *xi*, 16, 19, 20, 25–6
  description of area 87–8

Tamet, Libya 164–8, 169
  German attacks on 165–6
Tarhuna, Libya 172–4, 195
  encounter with Italian family 173
Taylor, Norman 127, *133*, 192, 204, 210
Tobruk, Libya 23, 26, 102, 119, 124, 193
  description of 132–4

Tocra/Tocra Pass, Libya 143, 145–6
transit camp
  Burg el Arab 104, 105
  Retreat, nr Cape Town 82–5
Tripoli, Libya 21, 22, 24, 30, 120, 160, 165, 168, 193
  decription of 180–3
  fall of 174–7
  history 179–80
troopship (*Highland Monarch*)
  boat drill 58, 66–7
  Brains Trust 18, 76–7
  concerts 55, 61, 65
  description and living conditions 44–6, 79
  lectures on board 76–7
  meals and washing up 56, 57, 58, 59, 67–8, 72, 73–4
  mess deck 55–6, 74, 79, 82
  officers and their behaviour 18, 45, 50–51, 63, 67–8, 72–4
  sleeping arrangements 46, 62–3, 71, 72–3, 82
  voyage to Cairo via Suez *x*, *xi*, 87–9,
  voyage to Freetown *x*, *xi*, 17–19, 43–77
  'X' (unpleasant companion) 56–7
troopship (*New Amsterdam*) 19, 80

water, drinking/fresh 44, 72, 73, 75, 77 n4, 104, 120, 128, 130, 132, 138, 142, 151, 161, 165, 169–71, 172, 173, 185, 191, 193, 198
  cisterns 90, 121, 138, 140, 150–2, 173, 185, 194, 198, 201
  shortage of 18, 121, 134, 149, 150, 164, 166
weather 55, 60–1, 63, 70–2, 78, 81, 84–85, 137–8, 165, 175, 185–6, 187
  storm 116–17, 121–2
Western Desert War *xiv–xviii*, 1, 2, 12, 14, 20–32, 102–32
Worcester, Teacher/Emergency Training College 6, 13, 206

Young, M. H., Squadron Leader 9–10, 31–2, 136 n15, n26, 210
Young, Alec *133*, *144*, 156, 192, 204, 210

Zouara, Libya 190–2